ADVANCING
VOCABULARY
SKILLS *SECOND EDITION*

ADVANCING
VOCABULARY
SKILLS *SECOND EDITION*

DONALD J. GOODMAN
MUSKEGON COMMUNITY COLLEGE

SHERRIE L. NIST
UNIVERSITY OF GEORGIA

CAROLE MOHR

TOWNSEND PRESS Marlton, NJ 08053

Books in the Townsend Press Vocabulary Series:

GROUNDWORK FOR A BETTER VOCABULARY, 2/e
BUILDING VOCABULARY SKILLS, 2/e
IMPROVING VOCABULARY SKILLS, 2/e
ADVANCING VOCABULARY SKILLS, 2/e
BUILDING VOCABULARY SKILLS, SHORT VERSION, 2/e
IMPROVING VOCABULARY SKILLS, SHORT VERSION, 2/e
ADVANCING VOCABULARY SKILLS, SHORT VERSION, 2/e

Books in the Townsend Press Reading Series:

GROUNDWORK FOR COLLEGE READING, 2/e
KEYS TO BETTER COLLEGE READING
TEN STEPS TO BUILDING COLLEGE READING SKILLS, FORM A, 2/e
TEN STEPS TO BUILDING COLLEGE READING SKILLS, FORM B, 2/e
TEN STEPS TO IMPROVING COLLEGE READING SKILLS, 2/e
IMPROVING READING COMPREHENSION SKILLS
TEN STEPS TO ADVANCING COLLEGE READING SKILLS, 2/e

Supplements Available for Most Books:

Instructor's Edition
Instructor's Manual, Test Bank, and Computer Guide
Set of Computer Disks (IBM or Macintosh)

Copyright © 1997 by Townsend Press, Inc.
Printed in the United States of America
ISBN 0-944210-36-8
9 8 7 6 5 4 3

Send book orders to:

Townsend Press
1038 Industrial Drive
West Berlin, New Jersey 08091

For even faster service, call us at our toll-free number:

1-800-772-6410

Or FAX your request to:

1-609-753-0649

ISBN 0-944210-36-8

Contents

Note: Twenty-six of the chapters present ten words apiece. The other four chapters each cover ten word parts and are so marked. For ease of reference, the title of the selection that closes each chapter is included.

UNIT FOUR

UNIT FIVE

APPENDIXES

Preface

The problem is all too familiar: *students just don't know enough words*. Reading, writing, and content teachers agree that many students' vocabularies are inadequate for the demands of courses. Weak vocabularies limit students' understanding of what they read and the clarity and depth of what they write.

The purpose of *Advancing Vocabulary Skills* and the other books in the Townsend Press vocabulary series is to provide a solid, workable solution to the vocabulary problem. In the course of 30 chapters, *Advancing Vocabulary Skills* teaches 260 important words and 40 common word parts. Here are the book's distinctive features:

1 **An intensive words-in-context approach.** Studies show that students learn words best by reading them repeatedly in different contexts, not through rote memorization. The book gives students an intensive in-context experience by presenting each word in six different contexts. Each chapter takes students through a productive sequence of steps:

- Students infer the meaning of each word by considering two sentences in which it appears and then choosing from multiple-choice options.
- On the basis of their inferences, students identify each word's meaning in a matching test. They are then in a solid position to deepen their knowledge of a word.
- Finally, they strengthen their understanding of a word by applying it three times: in two sentence practices and in a selection practice.

Each encounter with a word brings it closer to becoming part of the student's permanent word bank.

2 **Abundant practice.** Along with extensive practice in each chapter, there are a crossword puzzle and a set of unit tests at the end of every six-chapter unit. The puzzle and tests reinforce students' knowledge of the words in each chapter. In addition, most chapters reuse several words from earlier chapters (such repeated words are marked with small circles), allowing for more reinforcement. Last, there are supplementary tests in the *Test Bank* and the computer disks that accompany the book. All this practice means that students learn in the surest possible way: by working closely and repeatedly with each word.

3 **Controlled feedback.** The opening activity in each chapter gives students three multiple-choice options to help them decide on the meaning of a given word. The multiple-choice options also help students to complete the matching test that is the second activity of each chapter. A limited answer key at the back of the book then provides answers for the third activity in the chapter. All these features enable students to take an active role in their own learning.

4 **Focus on essential words.** A good deal of time and research went into selecting the 260 words and 40 word parts featured in the book. Word frequency lists were consulted, along with lists in a wide range of vocabulary books. In addition, the authors and editors each prepared their own lists. A computer was used to help in the consolidation of the many word lists. A long process of group discussion then led to final decisions about the words and word parts that would be most helpful for students on a basic reading level.

5 **Appealing content.** Dull practice materials work against learning. On the other hand, meaningful, lively, and at times even funny sentences and selections can spark students' attention and thus enhance their grasp of the material. For this reason, a great deal of effort was put into creating sentences and selections with both widespread appeal and solid context support. We have tried throughout to make the practice materials truly enjoyable for teachers and students alike. Look, for example, at the selection on page 11 that closes the first chapter of this book.

6 **Clear format.** The book has been designed so that the format itself contributes to the learning process. Each chapter consists of two two-page spreads. In the first two-page spread (the first such spread is on pages 8–9), students can easily refer to all ten words in context while working on the matching test, which provides a clear meaning for each word. In the second two-page spread, students can refer to a box that shows all ten words while they work through the fill-in activities on these pages.

7 **Supplementary materials.**

a A convenient *Instructor's Edition* is available at no charge to instructors using the book. It is identical to the student book except that it contains answers to all of the activities and tests.

b A combined *Instructor's Manual and Test Bank* is also offered at no charge to instructors who have adopted the book. This booklet contains a general vocabulary placement test as well as a pretest and a posttest for the book and for each of the five units in the text. It also includes teaching guidelines, suggested syllabi, an answer key, and an additional mastery test for each chapter.

c A *comprehensive series of computer disks* also accompanies the book. Free to adopters of 200 or more copies, these disks provide up to four tests for each vocabulary chapter in the book. The disks include a number of user- and instructor-friendly features: brief explanations of answers, a sound option, frequent mention of the user's first name, a running score at the bottom of the screen, a record-keeping file, and (in the case of the Macintosh disks) actual pronunciation of each word.

Probably in no other area of reading instruction is the computer more useful than in reinforcing vocabulary. This vocabulary program takes full advantage of the computer's unique capabilities and motivational appeal. Here's how the program works:

- Students are tested on the ten words in a chapter, with each word in a sentence context different from any in the book itself.

- After students answer each question, they receive immediate feedback: The computer tells if a student is right or wrong and why, frequently using the student's first name and providing a running score.

- When the test is over, the computer supplies a test score and—this especially is what is unique about this program—a chance to retest on the specific words the student got wrong. For example, if a student misses four items on a test, the retest provides four different sentences that test just those four words. Students then receive a score for this special retest. What is so valuable about this, of course, is that the computer gives students added practice in the words they most need to review.

- In addition, the computer offers a second, more challenging test in which students must identify the meanings of the chapter words without the benefit of context. This test is a final check that students have really learned the words. And, again, there is the option of a retest, tailor-made to recheck only those words missed on the first definition test.

By the end of this program, students' knowledge of each word in the chapter will have been carefully reinforced. And this reinforcement will be the more effective for having occurred in an electronic medium that especially engages today's students.

To obtain a copy of any of the above materials, instructors may write to the Reading Editor, Townsend Press, Pavilions at Greentree—408, Marlton, NJ 08053. Alternatively, instructors may call our toll-free number: 1-800-772-6410.

8 **Realistic pricing.** As with the first edition, the goal has been to offer the highest possible quality at the best possible price. While *Advancing Vocabulary Skills* is comprehensive enough to serve as a primary text, its modest price also makes it an inexpensive supplement.

9 **One in a sequence of books.** The most basic book in the Townsend Press vocabulary series is *Groundwork for a Better Vocabulary*. It is followed by the three main books in the series: *Building Vocabulary Skills* (also a basic text), *Improving Vocabulary Skills* (an intermediate text), and *Advancing Vocabulary Skills* (a more advanced text). There are also short versions of these three books. Suggested grade levels for the books are included in the *Instructor's Manual*. Together, the books can help create a vocabulary foundation that will make any student a better reader, writer, and thinker.

NOTES ON THE SECOND EDITION

A number of changes have been made to the book.

- Instead of an opening preview, each chapter now begins with a new format that uses a multiple-choice question to get students interacting immediately with each word. Teachers' and students' responses to this change have been extremely favorable.

- For ease of grading, including the use of Scantron machines, answer spaces can now be marked either with the letter or number of the word or with the word itself.

- The print in the book has been enlarged, a pronunciation key now appears on the inside front cover, a crossword puzzle has been added as a unit review, and the introduction to the book has been expanded. In addition, hundreds of changes have been made throughout the book to make each practice item work as clearly and effectively as possible.

- Thanks to feedback from reviewers and users, many of the words in each chapter are now repeated in context in later chapters (and marked with small circles). Such repetition provides students with even more review and reinforcement.

ACKNOWLEDGMENTS

We are grateful for the enthusiastic comments provided by users of the Townsend Press vocabulary books over the life of the first edition. Particular thanks go to the following reviewers for their many helpful suggestions: Barbara Brennan Culhane, Nassau Community College; Carol Dietrick, Miami-Dade Community College; Larry Falxa, Ventura College; Jacquelin Hanselman, Hillsborough Community College; Shiela P. Kerr, Florida Community College at Jacksonville; John M. Kopec, Boston University; Belinda E. Smith, Wake Technical Community College; Daniel Snook, Montcalm Community College; and William Walcott, Montgomery College. We appreciate as well the help of Eliza Comodromos and Paul Langan; the extensive editing work of Susan Gamer; and the design, editing, and proofreading skills of the multi-talented Janet M. Goldstein. Finally, we dedicate this book to the memory of our computer programmer, Terry Hutchison.

Donald J. Goodman   *Sherrie L. Nist*   *Carole Mohr*

Introduction

WHY VOCABULARY DEVELOPMENT COUNTS

You have probably often heard it said, "Building vocabulary is important." Maybe you've politely nodded in agreement and then forgotten the matter. But it would be fair for you to ask, "*Why* is vocabulary development important? Provide some evidence." Here are four compelling kinds of evidence.

1 Common sense tells you what many research studies have shown as well: vocabulary is a basic part of reading comprehension. Simply put, if you don't know enough words, you are going to have trouble understanding what you read. An occasional word may not stop you, but if there are too many words you don't know, comprehension will suffer. The content of textbooks is often challenging enough; you don't want to work as well on understanding the words that express that content.

2 Vocabulary is a major part of almost every standardized test, including reading achievement tests, college entrance exams, and armed forces and vocational placement tests. Test developers know that vocabulary is a key measure of both one's learning and one's ability to learn. It is for this reason that they include a separate vocabulary section as well as a reading comprehension section. The more words you know, then, the better you are likely to do on such important tests.

3 Studies have indicated that students with strong vocabularies are more successful in school. And one widely known study found that a good vocabulary, more than any other factor, was common to people enjoying successful careers in life. Words are in fact the tools not just of better reading, but of better writing, speaking, listening, and thinking as well. The more words you have at your command, the more effective your communication can be, and the more influence you can have on the people around you.

4 In today's world, a good vocabulary counts more than ever. Far fewer people work on farms or in factories. Far more are in jobs that provide services or process information. More than ever, words are the tools of our trade: words we use in reading, writing, listening, and speaking. Furthermore, experts say that workers of tomorrow will be called on to change jobs and learn new skills at an ever-increasing pace. The keys to survival and success will be the abilities to communicate skillfully and to learn quickly. A solid vocabulary is essential for both of these skills.

Clearly, the evidence is overwhelming that building vocabulary is crucial. The question then becomes, "What is the best way of going about it?"

WORDS IN CONTEXT: THE KEY TO VOCABULARY DEVELOPMENT

Memorizing lists of words is a traditional method of vocabulary development. However, a person is likely to forget such memorized lists quickly. Studies show that to master a word (or a word part), you must see and use it in various contexts. By working actively and repeatedly with a word, you greatly increase the chance of really learning it.

The following activity will make clear how this book is organized and how it uses a words-in-context approach. Answer the questions or fill in the missing words in the spaces provided.

Inside Front Cover and Contents

Turn to the inside front cover.

- The inside front cover provides a _____ that will help you pronounce all the vocabulary words in the book.

Now turn to the table of contents on pages v–vi.

- How many chapters are in the book? _____

- Most chapters present vocabulary words. How many chapters present word parts? _____

- Three short sections follow the last chapter. The first of these sections provides a limited answer key, the second gives helpful information on using _____, and the third is an index of the 260 words and 40 word parts in the book.

Vocabulary Chapters

Turn to Chapter 1 on pages 8–11. This chapter, like all the others, consists of five parts:

- The *first part* of the chapter, on pages 8–9, is titled _____.

The left-hand column lists the ten words. Under each **boldfaced** word is its _____ (in parentheses). For example, the pronunciation of *detriment* is _____. For a guide to pronunciation, see the inside front cover as well as "Dictionary Use" on page 179.

Below the pronunciation guide for each word is its part of speech. The part of speech shown for *detriment* is _____. The vocabulary words in this book are mostly nouns, adjectives, and verbs. **Nouns** are words used to name something—a person, place, thing, or idea. Familiar nouns include *boyfriend, city, hat,* and *truth.* **Adjectives** are words that describe nouns, as in the following word pairs: *former* boyfriend, *large* city, *red* hat, *whole* truth. All of the **verbs** in this book express an action of some sort. They tell what someone or something is doing. Common verbs include *sing, separate, support,* and *imagine.*

To the right of each word are two sentences that will help you understand its meaning. In each sentence, the **context**—the words surrounding the boldfaced word—provides clues you can use to figure out the definition. There are four common types of context clues: examples, synonyms, antonyms, and the general sense of the sentence. Each is briefly described below.

> *1 Examples*

A sentence may include examples that reveal what an unfamiliar word means. For instance, take a look at the following sentence from Chapter 1 for the word *scrupulous:*

> The judge was **scrupulous** about never accepting a bribe or allowing a personal threat to influence his decisions.

The sentence provides two examples of what makes the judge scrupulous. The first is that he never accepted a bribe. The second is that the judge did not allow personal threats to influence his decisions. What do these two examples have in common? The answer to that question will tell you what *scrupulous* means. Look at the answer choices below, and in the answer space provided, write the letter of the one you feel is correct.

___ *Scrupulous* means   a. ethical.   b. economical.   c. unjust.

Both of the examples given in the sentences about the judge tell us that he is honest, or ethical. So if you wrote *a*, you chose the correct answer.

2 *Synonyms*

Synonyms are words that mean the same or almost the same as another word. For example, the words *joyful, happy*, and *delighted* are synonyms—they all mean about the same thing. Synonyms serve as context clues by providing the meaning of an unknown word that is nearby. The sentence below from Chapter 2 provides a synonym clue for *collaborate*.

When Sarah and I were asked to **collaborate** on an article for the school newspaper, we found it difficult to work together.

Instead of using *collaborate* twice, the author used a synonym in the second part of the sentence. Find that synonym, and then choose the letter of the correct answer from the choices below.

___ *Collaborate* means   a. to compete.   b. to stop work.   c. to team up.

The author uses two terms to express what Sarah and the speaker had to do: *collaborate* and *work together*. Therefore, *collaborate* must be another way of saying *work together*. (The author could have written, "Sarah and I were asked to *work together*.") Since *work together* can also mean *team up*, the correct answer is *c*.

3 *Antonyms*

Antonyms are words with opposite meanings. For example, *help* and *harm* are antonyms, as are *work* and *rest*. Antonyms serve as context clues by providing the opposite meaning of an unknown word. For instance, the sentence below from Chapter 1 provides an antonym clue for the word *gregarious*.

My **gregarious** brother loves parties, but my sister is shy and prefers to be alone.

The author is contrasting the brother's and sister's different personalities, so we can assume that *gregarious* and *shy* have opposite, or contrasting, meanings. Using that contrast as a clue, write the letter of the answer that you think best defines *gregarious*.

___ *Gregarious* means   a. attractive.   b. outgoing.   c. humorous.

The correct answer is *b*. Because *gregarious* is the opposite of *shy*, it must mean "outgoing."

4 *General Sense of the Sentence*

Even when there is no example, synonym, or antonym clue in a sentence, you can still deduce the meaning of an unfamiliar word. For example, look at the sentence from Chapter 1 for the word *detriment*.

Smoking is a **detriment** to your health. It's estimated that each cigarette you smoke will shorten your life by one and a half minutes.

After studying the context carefully, you should be able to figure out the connection between smoking and health. That will be the meaning of *detriment*. Write the letter of your choice.

___ *Detriment* means   a. an aid.   b. a discovery.   c. a disadvantage.

Since the sentence says that each cigarette will shorten the smoker's life by one and a half minutes, it is logical to conclude that smoking has a bad effect on health. Thus answer *c* is correct.

By looking closely at the pair of sentences provided for each word, as well as the answer choices, you should be able to decide on the meaning of a word. As you figure out each meaning, you are working actively with the word. You are creating the groundwork you need to understand and to remember the word. *Getting involved with the word and developing a feel for it, based upon its use in context, is the key to word mastery.*

It is with good reason, then, that the directions at the top of page 8 tell you to use the context to figure out each word's _____. Doing so deepens your sense of the word and prepares you for the next activity.

- The *second part* of the chapter, on page 9, is titled _____.

According to research, it is not enough to see a word in context. At a certain point, it is helpful as well to see the meaning of a word. The matching test provides that meaning, but it also makes you look for and think about that meaning. In other words, it continues the active learning that is your surest route to learning and remembering a word.

Note the caution that follows the test. Do not proceed any further until you are sure that you know the correct meaning of each word as used in context.

Keep in mind that a word may have more than one meaning. In fact, some words have quite a few meanings. (If you doubt it, try looking up in a dictionary, for example, the word *make* or *draw*.) In this book, you will focus on one common meaning for each vocabulary word. However, many of the words have additional meanings. For example, in Chapter 13, you will learn that *inclusive* means "including much or everything," as in the sentence "The newspaper's coverage of the trial was inclusive." If you then look up *inclusive* in the dictionary, you will discover that it has another meaning—"including the stated limits," as in "The weekend auto show takes place from Friday through Monday inclusive." After you learn one common meaning of a word, you will find yourself gradually learning its other meanings in the course of your school and personal reading.

- The *third part* of the chapter, on page 10, is titled _____.

Here are ten sentences that give you an opportunity to apply your understanding of the ten words. After inserting the words, check your answers in the limited key at the back of the book. Be sure to use the answer key as a learning tool only. Doing so will help you to master the words and to prepare for the last two activities and the unit tests, for which answers are not provided.

- The *fourth and fifth parts* of the chapter, on pages 10–11, are titled _____ and _____.

Each practice tests you on all ten words, giving you two more chances to deepen your mastery. In the fifth part, you have the context of an entire passage in which you can practice applying the words.

At the bottom of the last page of this chapter is a box where you can enter your score for the final two checks. These scores should also be entered into the vocabulary performance chart located on the inside back page of the book. To get your score, take 10% off for each item wrong. For example, 0 wrong = 100%, 1 wrong = 90%, 2 wrong = 80%, 3 wrong = 70%, 4 wrong = 60%, and so on.

Word Parts Chapters

Word parts are building blocks used in many English words. Learning word parts can help you to spell and pronounce words, unlock the meanings of unfamiliar words, and remember new words.

This book covers forty word parts—prefixes, suffixes, and roots. **Prefixes** are word parts that are put at the beginning of words. When written separately, a prefix is followed by a hyphen to show that something follows it. For example, the prefix *extra* is written like this: *extra-*. One common meaning of *extra-* is "beyond," as in the words *extracurricular* and *extrasensory*.

Suffixes are word parts that are added to the end of words. To show that something always comes before a suffix, a hyphen is placed at the beginning. For instance, the suffix *cide* is written like this: *-cide*. A common meaning of *-cide* is "killing," as in the words *homicide* and *genocide*.

Finally, **roots** are word parts that carry the basic meaning of a word. Roots cannot be used alone. To make a complete word, a root must be combined with at least one other word part. Roots are written without hyphens. One common root is *dorm*, which means "sleep," as in the words *dormant* and *dormitory*.

Each of the four chapters on word parts follows the same sequence as the chapters on vocabulary do. Keep the following guidelines in mind as well. To find the meaning of a word part, you should do two things.

1 First decide on the meaning of each **boldfaced** word in "Ten Word Parts in Context." If you don't know a meaning, use context clues to find it. For example, consider the two sentences and the answer options for the word part *ante-* or *anti-* in Chapter 6. Write the letter of your choice.

> Before you enter Mel's living room, you pass through a small **anteroom**, where guests can leave their coats.

> A clever saying warns us not to **anticipate** trouble before it happens: "Worrying casts tomorrow's clouds over today's sunshine."

> ___ The word part *ante-* or *anti-* means   a. after.   b. free.   c. before.

You can conclude that if the anteroom is before the living room, *anteroom* means "room before." You can also determine that *anticipate* means "to think about beforehand."

2 Then decide on the meaning each pair of boldfaced words has in common. This will also be the meaning of the word part they share. In the case of the two sentences above, both words include the idea of something coming before something else. Thus *ante-* or *anti-* must mean _____.

You now know, in a nutshell, how to proceed with the words in each chapter. Make sure that you do each page very carefully. *Remember that as you work through the activities, you are learning the words.*

How many times in all will you use each word? If you look, you'll see that each chapter gives you the opportunity to work with each word six times. Each "impression" adds to the likelihood that the word will become part of your active vocabulary. You will have further opportunities to use the word in the crossword puzzle and unit tests that end each unit and on the computer disks that are available with the book.

In addition, many of the words are repeated in context in later chapters of the book. Such repeated words are marked with small circles (°). For example, which words from Chapter 1 are repeated in the Final Check on page 15 of Chapter 2?

_____   _____

A FINAL THOUGHT

The facts are in. A strong vocabulary is a source of power. Words can make you a better reader, writer, speaker, thinker, and learner. They can dramatically increase your chances of success in school and in your job.

But words will not come automatically. They must be learned in a program of regular study. If you commit yourself to learning words, and if you work actively and honestly with the chapters in this book, you will not only enrich your vocabulary—you will enrich your life as well.

Unit One

Chapter 1

detriment	optimum
dexterous	ostentatious
discretion	scrupulous
facetious	sensory
gregarious	vicarious

Chapter 2

collaborate	rudimentary
despondent	scoff
instigate	squelch
resilient	venerate
retrospect	zealot

Chapter 3

ambiguous	juxtapose
dissident	lethargy
embellish	sporadic
inadvertent	squander
inane	subsidize

Chapter 4

berate	maudlin
estrange	regress
euphoric	relinquish
impetuous	ubiquitous
infallible	zenith

Chapter 5

charlatan	hoist
corroborate	illicit
disseminate	irrevocable
diverge	precipitate
dormant	proliferation

Chapter 6

ante-, anti-	extra-
chron, chrono-	ject
-cide	liber, liver
de-	vit, viv
dorm	voc, vok

CHAPTER 1

detriment	optimum
dexterous	ostentatious
discretion	scrupulous
facetious	sensory
gregarious	vicarious

Ten Words in Context

In the space provided, write the letter of the meaning closest to that of each **boldfaced** word. Use the context of the sentences to help you figure out each word's meaning.

1 detriment
(dĕ′trə-mənt)
-noun

- Loni's purple hair may be a **detriment** when she goes for a job interview.
- Smoking is a **detriment** to your health. It's estimated that each cigarette you smoke will shorten your life by one and a half minutes.

___ *Detriment* means   a. an aid.   b. a discovery.   c. a disadvantage.

2 dexterous
(dĕks′tər-əs)
-adjective

- The juggler was so **dexterous** that he managed to keep five balls in motion at once.
- Although he has arthritis in his hands, Phil is very **dexterous**. For example, he builds detailed model airplanes.

___ *Dexterous* means   a. skilled.   b. educated.   c. awkward.

3 discretion
(dĭ-skrĕsh′ən)
-noun

- Ali wasn't using much **discretion** when he passed a police car at eighty miles an hour.
- Small children haven't yet developed **discretion**. They ask embarrassing questions like "When will you be dead, Grandpa?"

___ *Discretion* means   a. skill.   b. good sense.   c. courage.

4 facetious
(fə-sē′shəs)
-adjective

- Professor Segura has a **facetious** sign on his office door: "I'd like to help you out. Which way did you come in?"
- My boss always says, "You don't have to be crazy to work here, but it helps." I hope she's just being **facetious**.

___ *Facetious* means   a. serious.   b. dishonest.   c. funny.

5 gregarious
(grĭ-gâr′ē-əs)
-adjective

- Melissa is so **gregarious** that she wants to be with other people even when she's studying.
- My **gregarious** brother loves parties, but my sister is shy and prefers to be alone.

___ *Gregarious* means   a. attractive.   b. outgoing.   c. humorous.

6 optimum
(ŏp′tə-məm)
-adjective

- The road was so icy that the **optimum** driving speed was only about ten miles an hour.
- For the weary traveler, **optimum** hotel accommodations include a quiet room, a comfortable bed, and efficient room service.

___ *Optimum* means   a. ideal.   b. hopeful.   c. questionable.

7 **ostentatious**
(ŏs′tən-tā′shəs)
-*adjective*

- My show-off aunt has some **ostentatious** jewelry, such as a gold bracelet that's so heavy she can hardly lift her arm.
- To impress customers, the manager's office is **ostentatious**, with fancy furniture and a thick rug. The rest of the department looks cheap and shabby.

__ *Ostentatious* means   a. humble.   b. showy.   c. clean.

8 **scrupulous**
(skro͞o′pyə-ləs)
-*adjective*

- The judge was **scrupulous** about never accepting a bribe or allowing a personal threat to influence his decisions.
- The senator promised to run a **scrupulous** campaign, but her ads were filled with lies about her opponent's personal life.

__ *Scrupulous* means   a. ethical.   b. economical.   c. unjust.

9 **sensory**
(sĕn′sə-rē)
-*adjective*

- Since our **sensory** experiences are interrelated, what we taste is greatly influenced by what we smell.
- A person in a flotation tank has almost no **sensory** stimulation. The tank is dark and soundproof, and the person floats in water at body temperature, unable to see or hear and scarcely able to feel anything.

__ *Sensory* means   a. of the senses.   b. social.   c. intellectual.

10 **vicarious**
(vī-kâr′ē-əs)
-*adjective*

- I don't like to take risks myself, but I love the **vicarious** thrill of watching death-defying adventures in a movie.
- If you can't afford to travel, reading guidebooks can give you a **vicarious** experience of traveling in foreign countries.

__ *Vicarious* means   a. thorough.   b. indirect.   c. skillful.

Matching Words with Definitions

Following are definitions of the ten words. Clearly write or print each word next to its definition. The sentences above and on the previous page will help you decide on the meaning of each word.

1. _____ Humorous; playfully joking
2. _____ Meant to impress others; flashy
3. _____ Best possible; most favorable; most desirable
4. _____ Something that causes damage, harm, or loss
5. _____ Experienced through the imagination; not experienced directly
6. _____ Skillful in using the hands or body
7. _____ Careful about moral standards; conscientious
8. _____ Sociable; enjoying and seeking the company of others
9. _____ Good judgment or tact in actions or speaking
10. _____ Having to do with seeing, hearing, feeling, tasting, or smelling

CAUTION: Do not go any further until you are sure the above answers are correct. Then you can use the definitions to help you in the following practices. Your goal is eventually to know the words well enough so that you don't need to check the definitions at all.

➤ *Sentence Check 1*

Using the answer line provided, complete each item below with the correct word from the box. Use each word once.

a. **detriment**	b. **dexterous**	c. **discretion**	d. **facetious**	e. **gregarious**
f. **optimum**	g. **ostentatious**	h. **scrupulous**	i. **sensory**	j. **vicarious**

_____ 1. Any employee who wants to use ___ would simply ignore a piece of spinach on the boss's front tooth.

_____ 2. A weak voice is a serious ___ to a stage actor's or actress's career.

_____ 3. Playing with blocks and puzzles makes children more ___ with their hands.

_____ 4. My roommate used to be ___, but since he was mugged, he's begun to avoid people.

_____ 5. Lonnie is so ___ about filling out his tax return that he even reported the $12.50 he was paid for jury duty.

_____ 6. Jasmine wants to practice her vocabulary skills, so she's not just being ___ when she uses long words.

_____ 7. Do you think a spectator sport gives the fans ___ triumphs and defeats, or real ones?

_____ 8. The ___ order in which to answer test questions is from easiest to most difficult, so that you can give the answers you know before time runs out.

_____ 9. Wandering through the bee-filled fields of red and yellow flowers was an amazing ___ experience, one that appealed to the eyes, ears, and nose.

_____ 10. The performer Oscar Levant had a tendency to cause disasters. He once made the ___ comment, "In my hands, Jell-O is a deadly weapon."

NOTE: Now check your answers to these questions by turning to page 175. Going over the answers carefully will help you prepare for the next two practices, for which answers are not given.

➤ *Sentence Check 2*

Using the answer lines provided, complete each item below with **two** words from the box. Use each word once.

_____
_____ 1–2. "You have to use ___ in choosing your friends," my father said. "If your associates are dishonest, people will think that you yourself may not be ___."

_____
_____ 3–4. Seth is being ___ when he says he's as ___ a dancer as Fred Astaire. That's his way of making fun of his own clumsiness.

_____
_____ 5–6. When you take vitamins, be sure to take only the recommended dose. Anything more than this ___ amount can be a dangerous ___ to your health.

_____   7–8. My neighbors give a lot of parties, but not because they're ___. They

_____   just want to impress the guests with their ___ home and furnishings.

_____   9–10. Our cousin in Nigeria writes great letters, filled with ___ details that

_____   give us a(n) ___ acquaintance with the sights and sounds of an African

village.

➤ _Final Check:_ Apartment Problems

Here is a final opportunity for you to strengthen your knowledge of the ten words. First read the following
selection carefully. Then fill in each blank with a word from the box at the top of the previous page.
(Context clues will help you figure out which word goes in which blank.) Use each word once.

Although I'm ordinarily a(n) (1)_____ person, I'm tempted to move
into a cave, far from other people—and landlords. Okay, I admit that I didn't use enough
(2)_____ in choosing apartments to rent. But does every one of them have
to be a (3)_____ to my health, mental stability, and checkbook?

When I moved into my first apartment, I discovered that the previous tenant had already
subleased the place to a very large family—of cockroaches. Although I kept trying, I was never
(4)_____ enough to swat any of them; they were able to dodge all my
blows. In time, they became so bold that they paraded across the kitchen floor in the daytime in
a(n) (5)_____ manner meant to impress upon me how useless it was to try
to stop them. As soon as I could, I moved out.

My second apartment was a(n) (6)_____ nightmare—the filth was
hard on the eyes and the nose. The place even assaulted the ears, as the walls were as thin as
cardboard. My neighbors played music until all hours. Since I was too poor to buy a stereo, I
became a dedicated listener. I even attended some of the neighbors' parties, in a(n)
(7)_____ way—with my ear to the wall. When my landlord found out, he tried
to charge me seven dollars a day for entertainment, and he wasn't being (8)_____
—he meant it. I moved again, hoping to find a decent, (9)_____ landlord.

I rented my last apartment because it was supposedly located in an area of
(10)_____ safety, considering the rent I can afford. A week after I moved in,
I came home to find the locks broken and my belongings all over the floor. On the dresser was an
angry note: "What gives you the right to live in such a nice neighborhood and not have anything
worth stealing?"

Maybe I should have stayed with the cockroaches. At least they were honest.

| _Scores_ | Sentence Check 2 _____% | Final Check _____% |

Enter your scores above and in the vocabulary performance chart on the inside back cover of the book.

collaborate	rudimentary
despondent	scoff
instigate	squelch
resilient	venerate
retrospect	zealot

Ten Words in Context

In the space provided, write the letter of the meaning closest to that of each **boldfaced** word. Use the context of the sentences to help you figure out each word's meaning.

1 collaborate
(kə-lăb′ə-rāt)
-verb

- When Sarah and I were asked to **collaborate** on an article for the school newspaper, we found it difficult to work together.
- Several writers and editors have **collaborated** in preparing this vocabulary text, sharing their knowledge and skills.

__ *Collaborate* means   a. to compete.   b. to stop work.   c. to team up.

2 despondent
(dĭ-spŏn′dənt)
-adjective

- Devon becomes **despondent** too easily. If he gets even one bad grade, he loses all hope of succeeding in school.
- For months after his wife died, Mr. Craig was **despondent**. He even considered suicide.

__ *Despondent* means   a. ill.   b. depressed.   c. angry.

3 instigate
(ĭn′stə-gāt′)
-verb

- The rock group's violent performance **instigated** a riot in the audience.
- An English captain named Robert Jenkins **instigated** a war in 1738 by displaying his pickled ear, which he said had been cut off by a Spanish patrol. The horrified British declared war on Spain—the "War of Jenkins's Ear."

__ *Instigate* means   a. to prevent.   b. to predict.   c. to cause.

4 resilient
(rĭ-zĭl′yənt)
-adjective

- Children can be amazingly **resilient**. Having faced sad and frightening experiences, they often bounce back to their normal cheerful selves.
- Plant life is **resilient**. For example, within a few weeks after the Mount St. Helens volcano erupted, flowers were growing in the ashes.

__ *Resilient* means   a. widespread.   b. slow to recover.   c. quick to recover.

5 retrospect
(rĕ′trə-spĕkt′)
-noun

- After hobbling around on her broken foot for a week before seeing a doctor, Mae then needed surgery. In **retrospect**, it's clear she should have gotten help sooner.
- When I took Professor Klein's writing course, I thought she was too demanding. In **retrospect**, though, I realize that she taught me more than anyone else.

__ *In retrospect* means   a. looking back.   b. looking for excuses.   c. looking ahead.

6 rudimentary
(rōō′də-mĕn′tər-ē)
-adjective

- A grammar book usually starts with **rudimentary** skills, such as identifying nouns and verbs.
- I'm so used to adding and subtracting on a calculator that I've probably forgotten how to do those **rudimentary** mathematical calculations on my own.

__ *Rudimentary* means   a. basic.   b. intermediate.   c. advanced.

7 scoff
(skŏf)
-*verb*

• Bystanders **scoffed** at the street musician playing a tune on a row of tin cans, but he seemed unaware that people were making fun of him.

• Tony **scoffed** at reports that a hurricane was coming until he saw the winds knocking down trees and overturning cars.

___ *Scoff at* means   a. to ridicule.   b. to watch.   c. to take seriously.

8 squelch
(skwĕlch)
-*verb*

• My history instructor shot me a dirty look during his lecture when I couldn't quite manage to **squelch** a burp.

• Decades of communism in Eastern Europe didn't **squelch** the desire for freedom. As soon as they could, the people in these countries began to form democracies.

___ *Squelch* means   a. to encourage.   b. to hold back.   c. to release.

9 venerate
(vĕn′ər-āt′)
-*verb*

• The Tlingit Indians **venerate** the wolf and the raven, and their totem poles illustrate stories in praise of these animals.

• The guests at our dean's retirement banquet made it clear that they **venerated** her; when she entered the room, everyone rose.

___ *Venerate* means   a. to pity.   b. to honor.   c. to remember.

10 zealot
(zĕl′ət)
-*noun*

• Annie, a **zealot** about health, runs a hundred miles a week and never lets a grain of sugar touch her lips.

• The Crusaders were Christian **zealots** during the Middle Ages who left their homes and families and went off to try to capture the Holy Land.

___ *Zealot* means   a. an extremist.   b. an observer.   c. a doubter.

Matching Words with Definitions

Following are definitions of the ten words. Clearly write or print each word next to its definition. The sentences above and on the previous page will help you decide on the meaning of each word.

1. _____   To bring about by moving others to action; stir up

2. _____   Fundamental; necessary to learn first

3. _____   Able to recover quickly from harm, illness, or misfortune

4. _____   To work together on a project; cooperate in an effort

5. _____   A person totally devoted to a purpose or cause

6. _____   To silence or suppress; crush

7. _____   To respect deeply; revere

8. _____   Downhearted; hopeless; overwhelmed with sadness

9. _____   Reviewing the past; considering past events

10. _____   To make fun of; mock; refuse to take seriously

CAUTION: Do not go any further until you are sure the above answers are correct. Then you can use the definitions to help you in the following practices. Your goal is eventually to know the words well enough so that you don't need to check the definitions at all.

➤ *Sentence Check 1*

Using the answer line provided, complete each item below with the correct word from the box. Use each word once.

a. **collaborate**	b. **despondent**	c. **instigate**	d. **resilient**	e. **retrospect**
f. **rudimentary**	g. **scoff**	h. **squelch**	i. **venerate**	j. **zealot**

_____ 1. My ability to speak Spanish is ___, but I can at least manage to ask directions or order a meal.

_____ 2. Jaime was ___ over the death of his dog, his companion for fourteen years.

_____ 3. The gang leader wasn't present at the robbery himself, but he was the one who had ___(e)d it.

_____ 4. Dawn is a ___ about banning nuclear weapons. She has walked for miles in protest marches and stood in the rain for hours during demonstrations.

_____ 5. Mother Teresa, who devoted her life to helping the poor, is ___(e)d by some people as a twentieth-century saint.

_____ 6. The Cord, in the 1920s, was the first car with front-wheel drive, but in those days most people considered the idea ridiculous and ___(e)d at it.

_____ 7. Marie and Pierre Curie ___(e)d on important scientific experiments involving radioactivity.

_____ 8. Kim's parents nagged her so hard about practicing the piano that they finally ___(e)d any interest she might have had in music.

_____ 9. Since I'd like to be a photographer, I can see, in ___, that I would have gained valuable experience if I'd taken pictures for the college newspaper.

_____ 10. Athletes need to be ___. After a defeat, an individual or a team must be able to come back and fight for victory the next time.

NOTE: Now check your answers to these questions by turning to page 175. Going over the answers carefully will help you prepare for the next two practices, for which answers are not given.

➤ *Sentence Check 2*

Using the answer lines provided, complete each item below with **two** words from the box. Use each word once.

_____ 1–2. Even though their knowledge of carpentry was only ____, the boys
_____   ___(e)d on building a treasure chest.

_____ 3–4. "Everyone gets ___(e)d at now and then," Lynn said. "You just have to
_____   be ___ enough to bounce back after a facetious° remark."

_____ 5–6. Many people who ___(e)d Dr. Martin Luther King, Jr., were ___ when
_____   he was killed, but then courageously vowed to carry on his work.

_____   7–8. At the time of the American Revolution, many people viewed those
_____   who ____(e)d the rebellion as troublemakers. In ___, however, we view
                                  them as heroes.

_____   9–10. Being illiterate until the age of 20 didn't ___ George Washington
_____   Carver's spirit. He went on to become a great botanist—and a ___
                                  about using peanuts, from which he made such products as ink,
                                  shampoo, and linoleum.

➤ *Final Check:* Hardly a Loser

Here is a final opportunity for you to strengthen your knowledge of the ten words. First read the following selection carefully. Then fill in each blank with a word from the box at the top of the previous page. (Context clues will help you figure out which word goes in which blank.) Use each word once.

Tom seemed to be a loser born into a long line of losers. His great-grandfather, condemned to death during the Revolutionary War for siding with the British, had fled to Canada. Tom's father, wanted for arrest after he helped (1)_____ a plot to overthrow the Canadian government, had fled back to the United States.

Tom never received even the most (2)_____ formal education. During his mere three months of schooling, he stayed at the bottom of his class. The teacher (3)_____(e)d at him, telling him that he was hopelessly stupid.

Tom's first job, selling papers and candy on a train, ended when he accidentally set the baggage car on fire. His second, as a telegraph operator, ended when he was caught sleeping on the job. At 22, he was jobless, penniless, and sleeping in a cellar. Obviously, Tom's youth had not provided the optimum° foundation for success.

Tom, however, didn't allow his situation to be a detriment° or to (4)_____ his hopes. Instead of becoming (5)_____, he was (6)_____ enough to recover from his misfortunes and find another job. He managed, in fact, to save enough money to open a workshop, where he (7)_____(e)d with an electrical engineer in designing and then selling machines. A (8)_____ when it came to solving mechanical puzzles, Tom worked nearly nonstop, sleeping only about four hours each night.

By the time he was in his 80s, Tom was credited with over a thousand inventions, including the phonograph, light bulb, and motion picture camera. He was also very famous—so much so that he was (9)_____(e)d nationwide as the greatest living American.

In (10)_____, Thomas Alva Edison wasn't such a loser after all.

| *Scores* | Sentence Check 2 _____% | Final Check _____% |

Enter your scores above and in the vocabulary performance chart on the inside back cover of the book.

ambiguous	juxtapose
dissident	lethargy
embellish	sporadic
inadvertent	squander
inane	subsidize

Ten Words in Context

In the space provided, write the letter of the meaning closest to that of each **boldfaced** word. Use the context of the sentences to help you figure out each word's meaning.

1 **ambiguous**
(ăm-bĭg′yoo-əs)
-*adjective*
- The portrait known as the "Mona Lisa" is famous for the woman's **ambiguous** expression. Is she smiling or not?
- Lee left an **ambiguous** message on my answering machine: "Meet me at twelve o'clock." I couldn't tell whether he meant noon or midnight.

__ *Ambiguous* means   a. unclear.   b. unintentional.   c. unpleasant.

2 **dissident**
(dĭs′ə-dənt)
-*noun*
- Some **dissidents** in the Catholic church favor female priests, marriage for priests, and birth control.
- In a dictatorship, **dissidents** are not tolerated. People who speak out against the goverment may be imprisoned or even executed.

__ *Dissident* means   a. a rebel.   b. a dishonest person.   c. a foolish person.

3 **embellish**
(ĕm-bĕl′ĭsh)
-*verb*
- Lauren **embellished** the door of her locker with postcards from her friends and photos of her cats.
- The cover of the biology textbook was **embellished** with a pattern of colorful seashells.

__ *Embellish* means   a. to hide.   b. to decorate.   c. to damage.

4 **inadvertent**
(ĭn-ăd-vûr′t'nt)
-*adjective*
- Alexander Fleming's discovery of penicillin was **inadvertent**. He forgot to cover a dish of bacteria, and some mold got into it. The next day, Fleming found that the mold had killed the bacteria.
- The final draft of Nancy's paper was shorter than the previous version, but this was **inadvertent**. She had accidentally deleted an entire page without realizing it.

__ *Inadvertent* means   a. not required.   b. not finished.   c. not intended.

5 **inane**
(ĭn-ān′)
-*adjective*
- The conversation at the party was **inane**, consisting mainly of foolish comments about whose clothes were the most "awesome."
- Television programming is often so **inane** that TV has been described as "bubble gum for the mind."

__ *Inane* means   a. silly.   b. interesting.   c. shocking.

6 **juxtapose**
(jŭks′tə-pōz′)
-*verb*
- The photograph dramatically **juxtaposed** white birch trees and a dark gray sky.
- Dottie spread her new dress out on her bed and then **juxtaposed** it with all her scarves and jackets to see which combination would look best.

__ *Juxtapose* means   a. to cover up.   b. to put side by side.   c. to replace.

7 lethargy
(lĕth′ər-jē)
-noun

- Although Wendy seemed to recover from the flu, one symptom persisted—**lethargy**. She felt exhausted for weeks.
- With the hot weather, **lethargy** descended upon the class. The students had trouble staying awake, and even the instructor gazed dreamily out the window.

___ *Lethargy* means   a. inactivity.   b. hopelessness.   c. foolishness.

8 sporadic
(spə-răd′ĭk)
-adjective

- It rained continuously until noon. After that, there were only **sporadic** showers.
- Dave makes **sporadic** attempts to give up smoking, but his occasional efforts have been halfhearted.

___ *Sporadic* means   a. steady.   b. irregular.   c. long.

9 squander
(skwŏn′dər)
-verb

- I thought my little sister would **squander** her entire allowance on M&Ms, but instead of wasting her money, she put it in her piggy bank.
- Vince **squanders** both his time and his money playing game after game in video arcades.

___ *Squander* means   a. to earn.   b. to count.   c. to spend carelessly.

10 subsidize
(sŭb′sə-dīz)
-verb

- During college, many students are **subsidized** by their parents, while others rely on grants or loans.
- Public television is **subsidized** by various grants and by individual and community donations.

___ *Subsidize* means   a. to pay for.   b. to advertise.   c. to criticize.

Matching Words with Definitions

Following are definitions of the ten words. Clearly write or print each word next to its definition. The sentences above and on the previous page will help you decide on the meaning of each word.

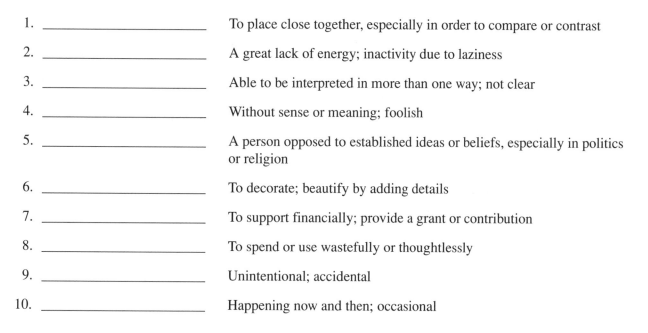

1. _____   To place close together, especially in order to compare or contrast

2. _____   A great lack of energy; inactivity due to laziness

3. _____   Able to be interpreted in more than one way; not clear

4. _____   Without sense or meaning; foolish

5. _____   A person opposed to established ideas or beliefs, especially in politics or religion

6. _____   To decorate; beautify by adding details

7. _____   To support financially; provide a grant or contribution

8. _____   To spend or use wastefully or thoughtlessly

9. _____   Unintentional; accidental

10. _____   Happening now and then; occasional

CAUTION: Do not go any further until you are sure the above answers are correct. Then you can use the definitions to help you in the following practices. Your goal is eventually to know the words well enough so that you don't need to check the definitions at all.

➤ *Sentence Check 1*

Using the answer line provided, complete each item below with the correct word from the box. Use each word once.

a. **ambiguous**	b. **dissident**	c. **embellish**	d. **inadvertent**	e. **inane**
f. **juxtapose**	g. **lethargy**	h. **sporadic**	i. **squander**	j. **subsidize**

_____ 1. Instead of refreshing me, an afternoon nap only deepens my ___; I wake up even sleepier than I was before.

_____ 2. I get news of Darren only now and then, in ___ letters from him or his mother.

_____ 3. A research grant will ___ Belinda's study of common fears among the elderly.

_____ 4. My recent trip to Newark was ___. I got on the wrong train.

_____ 5. Tracy has learned the hard way not to ___ her affection on men who aren't worth her respect.

_____ 6. My little brother has ___(e)d his bedroom ceiling with stars arranged like several of the constellations.

_____ 7. In plays and movies, good and evil characters are often ___(e)d. This contrast makes the good ones seem even better and the bad ones seem even worse.

_____ 8. When student ___s led a protest against China's communist leaders in 1989, some students were killed by government troops.

_____ 9. Checking a job applicant's references, the personnel manager was puzzled by one ___ comment: "You will be lucky if you can get her to work for you."

_____10. Steve Martin was poking fun at ___ ideas for products when he said, "I got a fur sink, an electric dog polisher, a gasoline-powered turtleneck sweater—and, of course, I bought some dumb stuff too."

NOTE: Now check your answers to these questions by turning to page 175. Going over the answers carefully will help you prepare for the next two practices, for which answers are not given.

➤ *Sentence Check 2*

Using the answer lines provided, complete each item below with **two** words from the box. Use each word once.

_____ 1–2. "Spring fever" isn't really a detriment° to health, but it often includes
_____   ___: people just want to sleep. Also, attention to work is interrupted off and on by a ___ need to daydream.

_____ 3–4. On the cover of the news magazine, two pictures were ___(e)d: those of
_____   a young ___ and the elderly ruler he was opposing.

_____   5–6. Local businesses ___(e)d our club's Christmas party for the homeless,
_____   so we were able to afford a special meal as well as decorations to ___
                                  the room.

_____   7–8. Why do you want to ___ your money on tickets for that silly movie
_____   when all the critics agree that it's ___?

_____   9–10. This week's episode of one television serial had a(n) ___ ending: we
_____   don't know whether one of the characters survives his heart attack or
                                   dies. In retrospect°, I don't think this was ___. I believe the producers
                                   want to keep us guessing so we'll tune in again next week.

➤ *Final Check:* Grandfather at the Art Museum

Here is a final opportunity for you to strengthen your knowledge of the ten words. First read the following
selection carefully. Then fill in each blank with a word from the box at the top of the previous page.
(Context clues will help you figure out which word goes in which blank.) Use each word once.

Last Saturday, my grandfather and I spent some time in the modern section of an art museum.
Our visit was completely (1)_____. We'd come to see a show of nature
photographs and wandered into the wrong room. Instead of leaving, Grandfather just stood there,
staring at the paintings. His idea of worthwhile art is the soft-focus photography on greeting cards,
and here was an exhibit of angry paintings by political (2)_____s.

In one painting, an empty plate and a plate piled high with food had been
(3)_____(e)d on a table; the tablecloth that was an American flag. Around
this painting was a golden frame that had been (4)_____(e)d with tiny
plastic models of hot dogs, apple pies, and other typical American foods. There was nothing
(5)_____ about the message—it was crystal-clear. The artist was saying that
some people in this country don't have enough to eat. After a few moments of stunned silence, my
grandfather jolted the sleepy-looking guard out of his (6)_____ by shouting,
"Garbage! What is this garbage?"

When we learned from the guard that two major corporations had collaborated° to
(7)_____ this exhibit, Grandfather was outraged. "How dare they
(8)_____ their money on this unpatriotic trash while people are starving?"
I tried to explain that the painting itself was a protest against starvation, but Grandfather just
scoffed° at me. "Don't be _____," he said. "Let's get out of here." So we did.

On the way home, Grandfather stared out the car window. He was silent except for
(10)_____ sputterings of "Garbage!" and "Incredible!"

Scores	Sentence Check 2 _____%	Final Check _____%

Enter your scores above and in the vocabulary performance chart on the inside back cover of the book.

CHAPTER

4

berate	maudlin
estrange	regress
euphoric	relinquish
impetuous	ubiquitous
infallible	zenith

Ten Words in Context

In the space provided, write the letter of the meaning closest to that of each **boldfaced** word. Use the context of the sentences to help you figure out each word's meaning.

1 **berate**
(bē-rāt′)
-*verb*

• Nick's mother often **berates** him. And when she isn't angrily finding fault with him, she ignores him.

• Goldie can accept reasonable criticism, but she was upset when her boss **berated** her loudly in front of everyone else in the office.

__ *Berate* means   a. to disappoint.   b. to neglect.   c. to scold.

2 **estrange**
(ĕ-strānj′)
-*verb*

• My cousin's recent moodiness has **estranged** some of his old friends.

• After his divorce, Shawn didn't want to **estrange** his children, so he called and visited them often.

__ *Estrange* means   a. to frighten.   b. to drive away.   c. to dislike.

3 **euphoric**
(yōō-fôr′ĭk)
-*adjective*

• I was **euphoric** when I received my grades. To my amazement and joy, they were all A's and B's.

• Joanne is **euphoric** this morning, and it's easy to see why she's in such high spirits. She's just gotten the lead role in the campus production of *Hello, Dolly.*

__ *Euphoric* means   a. very happy.   b. boastful.   c. sentimental.

4 **impetuous**
(ĭm-pĕch′ōō-əs)
-*adjective*

• Whenever I make an **impetuous** purchase, I end up being dissatisfied: the shoes aren't comfortable, the shirt is the wrong color, the jacket costs too much. From now on, I intend to think more carefully before I buy.

• Children tend to be **impetuous** and often don't think about the consequences of their actions. For instance, they'll throw snowballs at passing cars without worrying about causing an accident.

__ *Impetuous* means   a. impulsive.   b. considerate.   c. imaginative.

5 **infallible**
(ĭn-făl′ə-bəl)
-*adjective*

• Computers aren't **infallible**. If you put the wrong data into a computer, you'll get wrong answers.

• A sign over my sister's desk reads, "I'm **infallible**. I never make misteaks."

__ *Infallible* means   a. perfect.   b. imperfect.   c. everywhere.

6 **maudlin**
(môd′lĭn)
-*adjective*

• The verses in greeting cards are often far too sentimental. I prefer humor to such **maudlin** messages.

• The authors of **maudlin** soap operas must feel that they haven't done their job unless viewers are crying by the end of each show.

__ *Maudlin* means   a. short.   b. comical.   c. overly emotional.

20

7 **regress**
(rē-grĕs′)
-*verb*

- When his baby sister was born, seven-year-old Jeremy **regressed** for a while and began sucking his thumb again.
- Adolescents under stress sometimes **regress** to childish ways: dependency, temper tantrums, and silliness.

__ *Regress* means   a. to go backward.   b. to reach a high point.   c. to act hastily.

8 **relinquish**
(rĭ-lĭng′kwĭsh)
-*verb*

- No beer is allowed in the "family area" of the stadium, so fans must **relinquish** their six-packs at the gate before they take their seats.
- Donna had to **relinquish** her share in the beach house because she couldn't afford it anymore.

__ *Relinquish* means   a. to buy.   b. to yield.   c. to enjoy.

9 **ubiquitous**
(yōō-bĭk′wə-təs)
-*adjective*

- Mites are **ubiquitous**. They live on top of Mt. Everest, in the depths of the ocean, at the South Pole, and even around the roots of your hairs.
- We postponed our plan to drive home on Sunday because a dense fog was **ubiquitous**. It covered the entire island.

__ *Ubiquitous* means   a. scarce.   b. newly discovered.   c. found everywhere.

10 **zenith**
(zē′nĭth)
-*noun*

- Florence reached the **zenith** of her career when she became president of Ace Products.
- At age 50, my uncle is afraid that he has already passed the **zenith** of his life; but at age 52, my father thinks the best is yet to come.

__ *Zenith* means   a. an end.   b. an earlier condition.   c. the highest point.

Matching Words with Definitions

Following are definitions of the ten words. Clearly write or print each word next to its definition. The sentences above and on the previous page will help you decide on the meaning of each word.

1. _____   To surrender (something); give (something) up

2. _____   Done or acting in a hurry, with little thought; impulsive

3. _____   Tearfully sentimental; overemotional

4. _____   To criticize or scold harshly

5. _____   Existing or seeming to exist everywhere at the same time

6. _____   The highest point or condition; peak

7. _____   To make unsympathetic or unfriendly; alienate

8. _____   Not capable of error or failure; unable to make a mistake

9. _____   Overjoyed; having an intense feeling of well-being

10. _____   To return to an earlier, generally worse, condition or behavior

CAUTION: Do not go any further until you are sure the above answers are correct. Then you can use the definitions to help you in the following practices. Your goal is eventually to know the words well enough so that you don't need to check the definitions at all.

➤ *Sentence Check 1*

Using the answer line provided, complete each item below with the correct word from the box. Use each word once.

a. berate	b. estrange	c. euphoric	d. impetuous	e. infallible
f. maudlin	g. regress	h. relinquish	i. ubiquitous	j. zenith

_____   1. People in bombed-out, war-torn cities sometimes ___ to more primitive ways of life.

_____   2. To many people, Mozart's works represent the ___ of eighteenth-century music.

_____   3. Mei Lin was ___ when the college that was her first choice accepted her.

_____   4. When Dad lost his job, he had to ___ his identification card, his employee parking permit, and the key to his desk.

_____   5. Rosina used to be friendly, but since her promotion, she has become so cold that she has ___(e)d former coworkers.

_____   6. "I don't expect you to be ___," our boss said, "but I don't want you to make the same mistakes over and over."

_____   7. "I know I was late," Liz said, "but you could have pointed it out quietly. You didn't have to ___ me."

_____   8. In our neighborhood, litter is ___—the sidewalks are ankle-deep in trash. We need a cleanup campaign.

_____   9. Uncle Antonio becomes ___ when he talks about his dear old mother in Italy. And tears also come to the eyes of all who listen.

_____   10. Joyce isn't usually ___, but last week she had a sudden urge to try out her nephew's skateboard. Everyone in the office has already signed the cast on her broken wrist.

NOTE: Now check your answers to these questions by turning to page 175. Going over the answers carefully will help you prepare for the next two practices, for which answers are not given.

➤ *Sentence Check 2*

Using the answer lines provided, complete each item below with **two** words from the box. Use each word once.

_____
_____   1–2. If people were ___, we could ___ our erasers, our correction tape or fluid, and the "delete" key.

_____
_____   3–4. I'm trying to be less ___, but I still sometimes act on impulse. Later, in retrospect°, I always ___ myself for not using better judgment.

_____
_____   5–6. Since my father died, reminders of him seem ___. I know I'm being ___, but everywhere I look I see something that makes me cry.

_____ 7–8. Patrick ___(e)d his wife when he wasted their money on gambling and

_____   ostentatious° clothes. Since their separation, their young daughter has

                               ___(e)d to infantile behavior.

_____ 9–10. Our neighborhood basketball team reached its ___ when it won the

_____   citywide championship. The local businesses that had subsidized° the

                               team were delighted, and the players themselves were ___.

➤ *Final Check:* My Brother's Mental Illness

Here is a final opportunity for you to strengthen your knowledge of the ten words. First read the following selection carefully. Then fill in each blank with a word from the box at the top of the previous page. (Context clues will help you figure out which word goes in which blank.) Use each word once.

My brother Gary is mentally ill. At first my parents thought it was their fault, but now we know that his illness has much more to do with his body chemistry than with anything they did.

Gary's illness involves extreme mood swings. For weeks, he'll be (1)_____, feeling that the world is great and that he's at the (2)_____ of life. He may even view himself as (3)_____ and get angry if anyone even suggests he has made a mistake. Sometimes, too, he becomes a(n) (4)_____ shopper, spending thousands of dollars on whatever appeals to him. When we ask him to (5)_____ the expensive things he's bought so that we can return them, he refuses, saying he wants to "live like a king." At such times, Gary has to go to the hospital.

Gary's "highs," however, are nothing compared with his "lows." At first, he is simply (6)_____. He may sit in the living room all evening, talking and crying about his former girlfriends, our dead grandmother, or childhood hurts. Misfortune and horror, he says, are (7)_____ in his life—there's nowhere he can go to avoid them. Within days, he is very despondent° and so overcome with lethargy° that he can't even get out of bed. Shutting out everyone around him, he (8)_____s his family and friends. Then he (9)_____(e)s himself for all the faults he feels he has. Finally, he tries to kill himself. Again, he must go to the hospital.

When Gary takes his medicine, he does very well. He is charming, bright, and full of life. But when he feels good, he soon stops taking his medicine and begins to (10)_____. Then we know he is headed for another severe mood swing.

I love my brother dearly, but living with him is like living on a roller coaster. For all of our sakes, I wish we could help him more.

Scores   Sentence Check 2 _____%   Final Check _____%

Enter your scores above and in the vocabulary performance chart on the inside back cover of the book.

CHAPTER

5

charlatan	hoist
corroborate	illicit
disseminate	irrevocable
diverge	precipitate
dormant	proliferation

Ten Words in Context

In the space provided, write the letter of the meaning closest to that of each **boldfaced** word. Use the context of the sentences to help you figure out each word's meaning.

1 **charlatan**
(shär′lə-tən)
-*noun*

- My grandmother once bought a "magnetic box" from a **charlatan** who assured her that it would cure her arthritis. Of course, the box was worthless.
- In the days of the Wild West, **charlatans** sold "snake oil" as a remedy for everything from baldness to insanity.

___ *Charlatan* means   a. an investor.   b. an expert.   c. a con artist.

2 **corroborate**
(kə-rŏb′ə-rāt′)
-*verb*

- You claim you were at a soccer game when the crime was committed. Can anyone **corroborate** your story?
- Sid says he saw a flying saucer in the park, but no one else in the area has come forward to **corroborate** his account.

___ *Corroborate* means   a. to question.   b. to confirm.   c. to understand.

3 **disseminate**
(dĭs-sĕm′ə-nāt′)
-*verb*

- Campaign workers went all over the city to **disseminate** pamphlets and flyers about their candidate.
- What would be the best way to **disseminate** information about the next school board meeting? It's important for all parents to attend.

___ *Disseminate* means   a. to spread.   b. to conceal.   c. to improve.

4 **diverge**
(dī-vûrj′)
-*verb*

- The brothers' paths **diverged** greatly. One became a famous lawyer, and the other ended up in jail for armed robbery.
- In a well-known poem, Robert Frost uses a branching path as a symbol of life's decisions: "Two roads **diverged** in a wood, and I—I took the one less traveled by."

___ *Diverge* means   a. to go in different directions.   b. to come together.   c. to disappear.

5 **dormant**
(dôr′mənt)
-*adjective*

- Many insects lay eggs that remain **dormant** all winter and do not hatch until spring, in the warmer weather.
- A visit to Puerto Rico reawakened Anita's **dormant** interest in Spanish, the language of her childhood.

___ *Dormant* means   a. not active.   b. irreversible.   c. growing.

6 **hoist**
(hoist)
-*verb*

- Let's go over to the construction site and watch the crane **hoist** the beams into place for the new skyscraper.
- So far, attempts to **hoist** the wreckage of the jetliner from the ocean floor have been unsuccessful.

___ *Hoist* means   a. to follow.   b. to display.   c. to raise.

7 illicit
(ĭl-lĭs′ĭt)
-adjective

- Gene was introduced to **illicit** activities at a young age, when he was hired as a lookout by a drug dealer.
- Ted's business is **illicit**: he drives an unlicensed passenger van along a route that's supposed to be used only by city buses.

___ *Illicit* means   a. fake.   b. unlawful.   c. unprofitable.

8 irrevocable
(ĭr-rĕv′ə-kə-bəl)
-adjective

- Patty would like to break off her engagement to Steven, but she feels that her promise to marry him is **irrevocable**.
- Giving a child up for adoption has become a subject of debate. Should the mother be allowed to change her mind, or should her decision be **irrevocable**?

___ *Irrevocable* means   a. not reversible.   b. mistaken.   c. not certain.

9 precipitate
(prē-sĭp′ə-tāt′)
-verb

- Mark's search for a larger house was **precipitated** by his marriage to a woman with four children.
- The discovery that Elliot had been setting fires **precipitated** his parents' decision to consult a child psychologist.

___ *Precipitate* means   a. to bring on.   b. to prevent.   c. to permit.

10 proliferation
(prō-lĭf′ər-ā′shən)
-noun

- Hana's doctors hope that chemotherapy will halt the **proliferation** of cancer cells in her body.
- The **proliferation** of dandelions in my yard is too much for me to handle. They're growing faster than I can destroy them.

___ *Proliferation* means   a. damage.   b. a shortage.   c. a rapid increase.

Matching Words with Definitions

Following are definitions of the ten words. Clearly write or print each word next to its definition. The sentences above and on the previous page will help you decide on the meaning of each word.

1. _____   Inactive; alive but not actively growing, as if asleep

2. _____   To spread or scatter widely; distribute

3. _____   Not able to be canceled or undone; irreversible

4. _____   A rapid spread or increase

5. _____   To support; strengthen with further evidence; provide proof of

6. _____   To cause to happen quickly, suddenly, or sooner than expected

7. _____   To lift, especially with some mechanical means, like a cable

8. _____   A fake; a person who falsely claims to have some special skill or knowledge

9. _____   To branch off in different directions from the same starting point; to become different

10. _____   Illegal

CAUTION: Do not go any further until you are sure the above answers are correct. Then you can use the definitions to help you in the following practices. Your goal is eventually to know the words well enough so that you don't need to check the definitions at all.

➤ *Sentence Check 1*

Using the answer line provided, complete each item below with the correct word from the box. Use each word once.

a. **charlatan**	b. **corroborate**	c. **disseminate**	d. **diverge**	e. **dormant**
f. **hoist**	g. **illicit**	h. **irrevocable**	i. **precipitate**	j. **proliferation**

_____ 1. Children's lives often ___ from the paths their parents planned for them.

_____ 2. The "natural healer" was a ___. He knew nothing about healing—natural or otherwise.

_____ 3. I thought your vow to quit smoking was ___, but you've broken it already.

_____ 4. When I visited the art museum, my ___ creative instinct awakened. Now I've signed up for a course in sculpture.

_____ 5. Rafael's growth of four inches over the summer ___(e)d a shopping trip for new clothes.

_____ 6. In our city, the police department has special units to investigate ___ activities such as gambling and drug use.

_____ 7. The stone slabs are too heavy for us to move, so we're bringing in a forklift to ___ them onto the walkway.

_____ 8. The environmental group ___(e)d leaflets about the oil spill, describing the damage and urging people to boycott the oil company.

_____ 9. I'm afraid I can't ___ Todd's claim that he's never been in trouble with the law. The fact is that he's been in jail several times.

_____ 10. Sadly, the ___ of homeless dogs and cats has become so great that about seventeen million of them are killed in U.S. animal shelters each year.

NOTE: Now check your answers to these questions by turning to page 175. Going over the answers carefully will help you prepare for the next two practices, for which answers are not given.

➤ *Sentence Check 2*

Using the answer lines provided, complete each item below with **two** words from the box. Use each word once.

_____
_____ 1–2. The map ___s my belief that just before the lake, the highway___s into two roads, which go off in opposite directions.

_____
_____ 3–4. When criminals go to prison, their illegal careers don't necessarily lie ___. Many of them collaborate° to carry on ___ activities in prison, including theft and bribery.

_____
_____ 5–6. When the movers tried to ___ our piano to a second-floor window, a cable broke, and the piano crashed onto the sidewalk. We know this was inadvertent°, but our decision to sue the moving company is ___.

_____   7–8. Employees were ordered not to ___ any information about the fire at
_____   the factory; the news might scare off stockholders and ___ bankruptcy.

_____   9–10. After a retirement community was built in Morristown, there was a ___
_____   of ___s in the area, peddling "miracle" cures for all kinds of ills—some
                                      of which were not only useless but actually a detriment° to health.

➤ *Final Check:* A Get-Rich-Quick Scam

Here is a final opportunity for you to strengthen your knowledge of the ten words. First read the following
selection carefully. Then fill in each blank with a word from the box at the top of the previous page.
(Context clues will help you figure out which word goes in which blank.) Use each word once.

It's said that "there's a sucker born every minute." In retrospect°, after the events of last

summer, I think most of them must live in my hometown, Glenville. I, along with nearly everyone

else in town, was taken in by a (1)_____—a swindler who made us believe

he could help us get rich quick.

This con artist, whose name was Chester Turner, supposedly came into town to open a real

estate office. After buying up lots of cheap land, he hinted to some of the town's leading citizens

that there would soon be an incredible (2)_____ of people wanting to buy

land in Glenville. Naturally, those who received this interesting information promptly

(3)_____(e)d it throughout town, and soon we were all buzzing about it.

When people questioned Turner about the value of town land, he would hint that there was oil in

Glenville by asking, "What if there were energy lying (4)_____ under the

ground in the area, just waiting to spurt out?"

An oil find, we all agreed, would (5)_____ a skyrocketing of land

prices. Our suspicions about oil seemed to be (6)_____(e)d by some "oil

company executives" talking in the local diner. According to their waitress, they planned to have

cranes (7)_____ the oil derricks any day and then to pump out millions of

gallons of the precious liquid. Soon people were pounding on Turner's door, begging him to sell

them land in Glenville.

After Turner left town with all our money, there were rumors that he and his "oil men" had

been arrested for (8)_____ activities in another state. Although we had all

been of one mind when Turner was around, our views now (9)_____(e)d.

Most of us just kissed our money goodbye, though we berated° ourselves for trusting Turner.

Some people, however, clung to a belief that they could somehow get Turner to give their money

back. They couldn't accept the fact that the loss of their money was (10)_____.

Scores	Sentence Check 2 _____%	Final Check _____%

Enter your scores above and in the vocabulary performance chart on the inside back cover of the book.

ante-, anti-	extra-
chron, chrono-	ject
-cide	liber, liver
de-	vit, viv
dorm	voc, vok

Ten Word Parts in Context

Common word parts—also known as *prefixes, suffixes,* and *roots*—are used in forming many words in English. Figure out the meanings of the following ten word parts by looking *closely* and *carefully* at the context in which they appear. Then, in the space provided, write the letter of the meaning closest to that of each word part.

1 **ante-, anti-**

___ The word part *ante-* or *anti-* means

- Before you enter Mel's living room, you pass through a small **anteroom**, where guests can leave their coats.
- A clever saying warns us not to **anticipate** trouble before it happens: "Worrying casts tomorrow's clouds over today's sunshine."

   a. after.   b. free.   c. before.

2 **chron, chrono-**

___ The word part *chron* or *chrono-* means

- An acute illness is short and usually severe. By contrast, a **chronic** illness lasts a long period of time.
- A résumé should list jobs in reverse **chronological** order—that is, the most recent job should be listed first.

   a. time.   b. outside.   c. alive.

3 **-cide**

___ The word part *-cide* means

- Do the **pesticides** used in farming kill only pests? Or are they also harmful to humans?
- **Genocide** isn't simply the murder of a number of people. It's the intentional killing of a particular racial, cultural, or political group.

   a. alive.   b. kill.   c. freedom.

4 **de-**

___ The word part *de-* means

- When the two trains ran into each other, one was **derailed**, but the other stayed on the tracks.
- A good kitchen fan can **deodorize** the room by drawing away strong cooking odors, such as those of onion and garlic.

   a. voice.   b. preceding.   c. removal.

5 **dorm**

___ The word part *dorm* means

- The volcano has been **dormant** for years, but it may awaken soon.
- The **dormouse**, or "sleeping mouse," got its name because it hibernates through the winter.

   a. lively.   b. separation.   c. sleep.

6 **extra-**

___ The word part *extra-* means

- Ling studies hard for his classes, but he's also involved in **extracurricular** activities, including soccer and chess.
- **Extrasensory** perception is the ability, or seeming ability, to communicate in ways that do not involve the physical senses.

   a. enclosed.   b. throw.   c. beyond.

7 **ject**

- The pilot **ejected** from the plane shortly before the crash. Fortunately, his parachute opened in time to save his life.
- The farther away a **projector** is, the larger the picture it throws onto the screen.

__ The word part *ject* means   a. throw.   b. keep.   c. call.

8 **liber, liver**

- Freddy is very **liberal** with advice. He tells all his relatives and friends how they should run their lives.
- According to the Bible, Moses **delivered** the people of Israel from slavery in Egypt.

__ The word part *liber* or *liver* means   a. alive.   b. free.   c. outside.

9 **vit, viv**

- My elderly aunt still has great **vitality**: she works in a bakery part-time and walks two or three miles every day.
- People who **survive** a disaster sometimes feel guilty because they lived while others died.

__ The word part *vit* or *viv* means   a. life.   b. separation.   c. death.

10 **voc, vok**

- My father listens to **vocal** music as if it were being performed only by instruments. He doesn't listen to the singers' words at all.
- At the end of the service, the rabbi, stretching out his arms and raising his voice, **invoked** God to bless the congregation.

__ The word part *voc* or *vok* means   a. memory.   b. voice.   c. time.

Matching Word Parts with Definitions

Following are definitions of the ten word parts. Clearly write or print each word part next to its definition. The sentences above and on the previous page will help you decide on the meaning of each word part.

1. _____ Life, lively

2. _____ Outside, beyond

3. _____ Time

4. _____ Free, freedom

5. _____ Away, separation, removal

6. _____ Before, preceding

7. _____ Voice, call

8. _____ Sleep

9. _____ Throw, toss

10. _____ Kill, killing, killer

CAUTION: Do not go any further until you are sure the above answers are correct. Then you can use the definitions to help you in the following practices. Your goal is eventually to know the word parts well enough so that you don't need to check the definitions at all.

➤ *Sentence Check 1*

Using the answer line provided, complete each *italicized* word in the sentences below with the correct word part from the box. Use each word part once.

a. **ante-, anti-**	b. **chron**	c. **-cide**	d. **de-**	e. **dorm**
f. **extra-**	g. **ject**	h. **liber**	i. **vit, viv**	j. **voc**

_____ 1. At the Italian restaurant, we had a(n) (. . . *pasto*) ___ of olives, cheeses, and other appetizers before the main dish.

_____ 2. I was very tired when I got home from work, but a short nap (*re . . . ed*) ___ me.

_____ 3. The veterinarian asked Rosa to hold her cat firmly while he gave it an (*in . . . ion*) ___ to protect it from rabies.

_____ 4. A microwave oven is perfect for (. . . *frosting*) ___ frozen foods in a hurry.

_____ 5. The conference was held at a college campus, so participants slept in the (. . . *itories*) ___ instead of going to hotels.

_____ 6. In a crisis, people sometimes perform (. . . *ordinary*) ___ feats of strength, like lifting an automobile off a crash victim.

_____ 7. Modern inventions have (. . . *ated*) ___ us from many household chores. For instance, the dryer frees us from having to hang laundry on a clothesline.

_____ 8. (*Regi . . .*) ___ means the killing of a king. A famous instance is Charles I of England, who was beheaded in 1649.

_____ 9. Leah has an amazing (. . . *abulary*) ___ for a two-year-old. She was just telling me the difference between "Mr. Crocodile" and "Mr. Alligator."

_____ 10. An (*ana . . . ism*) ___ is someone or something that seems to belong to an earlier time and is out of place in the present. San Francisco's cable cars are an example.

NOTE: Now check your answers to these questions by turning to page 175. Going over the answers carefully will help you prepare for the next two practices, for which answers are not given.

➤ *Sentence Check 2*

Using the answer lines provided, complete each *italicized* word in the sentences below with the correct word part from the box. Use each word part once.

_____ 1–2. Angela chose medicine as her (. . . *ation*) ___ because when she was
_____ twelve years old, she had a(n) (. . . *id*) ___ dream that convinced her it was her calling to heal people.

_____ 3–4. Many people believe that (*homi . . .*) ___ will remain a(n) (. . . *ic*) ___
_____ problem in American society until our ubiquitous° handguns are made illegal. So long as guns can be obtained almost anywhere, people will be tempted to use them.

_____ 5–6. The attic bedroom has three windows, called (. . . *ers*) ___. They're set
_____   at an angle to the roof, so they look as if they are partly (. . . *tached*)
                               ___ from the rest of the house.

_____ 7–8. The queen's closest advisers were at (. . . *ty*) ___ to enter the throne
_____   room freely. All others had to wait in the (. . . *chamber*) ___ before
                               they were allowed to see her.

_____ 9–10. In science fiction stories, (. . . *terrestrials*) ___ such as E.T. are often
_____   able to communicate by (*pro . . . ing*) ___ their thoughts into Earth
                               people's minds. Real scientists, however, scoff° at this idea, thinking
                               such communication impossible.

➤ *Final Check:* Holiday Blues

Here is a final opportunity for you to strengthen your knowledge of the ten word parts. First read the
following selection carefully. Then complete each *italicized* word in the parentheses below with a word
from the box at the top of the previous page. (Context clues will help you figure out which word part goes
in which blank.) Use each word part once.

Tensions and sadness greatly (. . . *tract*) (1)_____ from many people's

enjoyment of the winter holidays. For those who are (. . . *ically*) (2)_____

depressed, the holiday season can intensify the problem.

The (. . . *ordinary*) (3)_____ expectations that many have for the

holidays often (*e . . . e*) (4)_____ sad feelings. For instance, (. . . *cipation*)

(5)_____ of the traditional family gatherings may awaken (. . . *ant*)

(6)_____ feelings of disappointment that one's family is not as warm or

close as it "should" be. In the hopes of (*in . . . ing*) (7)_____ more happiness

into the season or of (*re . . . alizing*) (8)_____ family relationships, people

may squander° their money on extravagant, ostentatious° gifts meant to impress their relatives.

The financial burden then adds to the holiday problems.

Not everyone is resilient° enough to bear all this pressure. In fact, (*sui . . .*)

(9)_____ rates increase around the holidays. Some despondent° people,

however, wisely seek counseling in hopes of (. . . *ating*) (10)_____

themselves from the holiday blues.

| *Scores*   Sentence Check 2 _____% | Final Check _____% |

Enter your scores above and in the vocabulary performance chart on the inside back cover of the book.

UNIT ONE: Review

The box at the right lists twenty-five words from Unit One. Using the clues at the bottom of the page, fill in these words to complete the puzzle that follows.

berate
charlatan
despondent
dexterous
dissident
diverge
dormant
embellish
facetious
hoist
illicit
impetuous
inane
lethargy
maudlin
optimum
regress
resilient
scoff
scrupulous
squander
squelch
ubiquitous
venerate
vicarious

ACROSS

1. Humorous; playful or joking
3. To return to an earlier, generally worse, condition or behavior
5. To branch off in different directions from the same starting point
6. To criticize or scold harshly
7. To silence or suppress; crush
10. Without sense or meaning; foolish
11. Able to recover quickly from harm, illness, or misfortune
12. To make fun of
14. Downhearted; hopeless
15. A great lack of energy; inactivity due to laziness
16. Skillful in using the hands or body
18. Experienced through the imagination
21. Done or acting in a hurry, with little thought; impulsive
22. A fake; a person who falsely claims to have some special skill or knowledge
23. Best possible; most desirable

DOWN

2. Existing or seeming to exist everywhere at the same time
4. To decorate; beautify by adding details
5. A person opposed to established ideas or beliefs
8. To lift, especially with some mechanical means
9. Careful about moral standards; conscientious
13. To respect deeply; revere
14. Inactive; alive but not actively growing, as if asleep
17. To spend or use wastefully or thoughtlessly
19. Illegal
20. Tearfully sentimental; over-emotional

UNIT ONE: *Test 1*

Choose the word that best completes each item and write it in the space provided.

_____ 1. If you grow up in a large family, it helps to be ___. Since you are so rarely alone, it's nice if you can enjoy the company.

   a. ambiguous   b. sporadic   c. gregarious   d. rudimentary

_____ 2. Because I had witnessed the accident, one driver asked me to ___ his claim that the other driver had gone through a red light.

   a. collaborate   b. estrange   c. corroborate   d. juxtapose

_____ 3. Some college students ___ campaign information for a favorite professor who was running for state senator.

   a. disseminated   b. diverged   c. hoisted   d. squandered

_____ 4. Asians tend to ___ the elderly, but in America, age does not necessarily bring respect.

   a. precipitate   b. venerate   c. juxtapose   d. squelch

_____ 5. Aren't you tired of the ___ chatter that goes on between news stories on the "happy talk" news shows?

   a. despondent   b. illicit   c. inane   d. sensory

_____ 6. If Bart's parents leave him alone with his sister for even thirty seconds, he ___ a fight with her.

   a. subsidizes   b. collaborates   c. instigates   d. hoists

_____ 7. When driving to Melissa's house, go left at the fork in the road, the point where the road ___ into two.

   a. berates   b. scoffs   c. diverges   d. precipitates

_____ 8. Overcrowding in early factories provided an ideal environment for the ___ of bacteria, resulting in epidemics of tuberculosis.

   a. proliferation   b. detriment   c. discretion   d. retrospect

_____ 9. Our brains interpret our ___ impressions for us. For instance, the images of things we look at must go to the brain so we can actually "see" them.

   a. inadvertent   b. scrupulous   c. sensory   d. resilient

_____ 10. I thought the handyman was being ___ when he said he had to cut a much bigger hole in my wall in order to fix the little hole, but that's exactly what he did.

   a. dexterous   b. facetious   c. ubiquitous   d. maudlin

(Continues on next page)

_____ 11. I tried to ___ the laugh rising in my throat, but the sight of my boss looking all over his desk for the glasses he had pushed up on his head was too funny.

     a. squelch   b. venerate   c. berate   d. juxtapose

_____ 12. Grandfather was known for being ___. Once he spent twenty-five cents for the trolley in order to go back to a store and return the extra nickel that he had received in change.

     a. illicit   b. scrupulous   c. dormant   d. vicarious

_____ 13. The nineteenth-century French writer Alfred de Musset said, "Know that there is often hidden in us a(n) ___ poet, always young and alive." It is up to us to awaken that creative part of ourselves.

     a. inane   b. facetious   c. illicit   d. dormant

PART B
Write **C** if the italicized word is used **correctly**. Write **I** if the word is used **incorrectly**.

_____ 14. Valerie's idea of a great book is one with a *maudlin* story that has the reader laughing from start to finish.

_____ 15. Meeting my husband in the cafeteria for lunch was *inadvertent*. We had planned it over breakfast.

_____ 16. If I get plenty of sleep, I'm pretty *resilient*. Otherwise, I'm slow to bounce back from illness.

_____ 17. I'm not surprised that Lucy is protesting the governor's new welfare policy. She is known for being a *dissident*.

_____ 18. On my first day of work, I had to sit in the back room and *berate* prices on hundreds of products.

_____ 19. In wood shop, we had to learn *rudimentary* skills before we could actually make something.

_____ 20. The tattooed lady, a believer in reincarnation, had her arm *embellished* with the words "I'll be back."

_____ 21. The music store owner was arrested for selling tapes which he had bought from an *illicit* source.

_____ 22. Rumors that the bank was losing money *precipitated* a panic. Hundreds of depositors demanded their savings.

_____ 23. My aunt and uncle are rich but *ostentatious*. Judging by their modest possessions, you'd never know how much money they really have.

_____ 24. People still *scoff* at the many wonderful designs drawn by Leonardo da Vinci almost five hundred years ago of such future inventions as the airplane, parachute, and submarine.

_____ 25. Use *discretion* about where to consult with your doctor. If you run into him or her at church or the supermarket, it's not appropriate to ask about your warts or athlete's foot.

Score (Number correct) _____ x 4 = _____ %

UNIT ONE: *Test 2*

PART A
Complete each item with a word from the box. Use each word once.

a. **ambiguous**	b. **charlatan**	c. **euphoric**	d. **infallible**	e. **irrevocable**
f. **juxtapose**	g. **lethargy**	h. **regress**	i. **relinquish**	j. **subsidize**
k. **vicarious**	l. **zealot**	m. **zenith**		

_____ 1. Some people who reach the ___ of their careers find that "it's lonely at the top."

_____ 2. To provide contrast, the photographer ___(e)d the men in their dark suits and the women in their pale dresses.

_____ 3. After a big picnic meal in the warm sun, a(n) ___ came over me, so I took a nap under a sassafras tree.

_____ 4. "If you don't maintain a B average," said the coach, "you ___ your right to be on this team."

_____ 5. Literature and drama allow us to experience problems in a(n) ___ way, giving us painless opportunities to shape our real-life views.

_____ 6. The minister asked business leaders to ___ his Elderly Assistance Program because church donations didn't cover all the costs.

_____ 7. Kay's family was ___ when she arrived home, alive and well, three hours late. She had missed her plane, the one that had crashed.

_____ 8. Jason sounds so sure of himself that he gives people the impression he is ___. But he makes mistakes too, just like the rest of us.

_____ 9. The state trooper warned my brother, "Your driver's license is not ___. If you get one more speeding ticket, you will lose your license for a year."

_____ 10. Mrs. Angelo was shocked to learn that the "doctor" she had been seeing for three years was a(n) ___. In reality, he had attended medical school for only two semesters.

_____ 11. When I asked my sister whether my seven kids and I could visit her for a week, her response was so ___ that I'm not sure if she said yes or no.

_____ 12. The Bradleys won't go on vacation until their new puppy is fully trained. They're afraid that if he stays at the kennel for a week, he will ___ and start ruining the rugs again.

_____ 13. After her first husband died from alcohol-related causes, Carry Nation became an anti-drinking ___. One year, as she crusaded around the country against alcohol, she destroyed twenty saloons with a hatchet.

(Continues on next page)

PART B

Write **C** if the italicized word is used **correctly**. Write **I** if the word is used **incorrectly**.

_____ 14. Ana naturally became *despondent* when she learned that she had won a free trip to Honolulu.

_____ 15. A tightrope walker must be both *dexterous* and unafraid of heights.

_____ 16. Billy *estranged* people with his warm conversation and friendly manner.

_____ 17. Earth happens to be a place where oxygen is *ubiquitous*, making the planet suitable for many forms of life.

_____ 18. My father is so *impetuous* that he can't even place a lunch order without studying the menu for fifteen minutes.

_____ 19. "In *retrospect*," said the chairman of the board, "I think the next five years will be our most successful ever."

_____ 20. Professor Sherman wants to *collaborate* on a new science textbook. He always prefers working with a coauthor.

_____ 21. When the survivor of the shipwreck grabbed the rope, he was *hoisted* up out of the water to the helicopter.

_____ 22. During my childhood, we made *sporadic* visits to my grandparents' house. Not a Sunday passed that we didn't see them.

_____ 23. Donald *squanders* his money so quickly that a few days after receiving his paycheck, he's asking me for a loan.

_____ 24. All members of the town council agreed that playgrounds were a *detriment* to the community, so they approved funding for three more to be built next year.

_____ 25. The hotel offers the *optimum* in accommodations. The only guests who ever return there (with friends and relations) are the roaches.

Score   (Number correct) _____ x 4 = _____ %

Enter your score above and in the vocabulary performance chart on the inside back cover of the book.

UNIT ONE: Test 3

PART A
Complete each sentence in a way that clearly shows you understand the meaning of the **boldfaced** word. Take a minute to plan your answer before you write.

    Example: I was being **facetious** when I said that *my parrot can tell the future. In fact, he's always wrong*.

1. An **illicit** way to make a living is _____

_____.

2. A common **detriment** to good health is _____

_____.

3. Rhetta **squandered** her money on _____

_____.

4. A **zealot** in the environmental movement would never _____

_____.

5. Being **gregarious**, Stephanie wants to celebrate her birthday by _____

_____.

6. I was **despondent** because _____

_____.

7. An **inane** way to study for final exams is to _____

_____.

8. At the mall, my **impetuous** friend _____

_____.

9. A good way to **estrange** your parents is to _____

_____.

10. In **retrospect**, I realized that _____

_____.

(Continues on next page)

PART B

After each **boldfaced** word are a *synonym* (a word that means the same as the boldfaced word), an *antonym* (a word that means the opposite of the boldfaced word), and a word that is neither. On the answer line, write the letter of the word that is the antonym.

Example: __b__ **inadvertent**   a. accidental   b. intentional   c. playful

_____ 11. **berate**   a. scold   b. invite   c. praise

_____ 12. **rudimentary**   a. foolish   b. advanced   c. elementary

_____ 13. **detriment**   a. advantage   b. contradiction   c. obstacle

_____ 14. **inane**   a. inexpensive   b. sensible   c. silly

_____ 15. **dexterous**   a. skillful   b. spiritual   c. clumsy

PART C

Use five of the following ten words in sentences. Make it clear that you know the meaning of each word you use. Feel free to use the past tense or plural form of a word.

a. **ambiguous**	b. **charlatan**	c. **hoist**	d. **infallible**	e. **irrevocable**
f. **ostentatious**	g. **proliferation**	h. **scoff**	i. **scrupulous**	j. **ubiquitous**

16. _____

_____

17. _____

_____

18. _____

_____

19. _____

_____

20. _____

_____

Score   (Number correct) _____ x 5 = _____ %

Enter your score above and in the vocabulary performance chart on the inside back cover of the book.

UNIT ONE: *Test 4 (Word Parts)*

PART A

Listed in the left-hand column below are ten common word parts, along with words in which the parts are used. In each blank, write in the letter of the correct definition on the right.

Word Parts	Examples	Definitions
____ 1. **ante-, anti-**	anteroom, anticipate	a. Time
____ 2. **chron-, chrono-**	chronic, chronological	b. Voice, call
____ 3. **-cide**	pesticide, genocide	c. Away, separation, removal
____ 4. **de-**	derail, deodorize	d. Life, lively
____ 5. **dorm**	dormant, dormouse	e. Kill, killing, killer
____ 6. **extra-**	extracurricular, extrasensory	f. Free, freedom
____ 7. **ject**	eject, projector	g. Throw, toss
____ 8. **liber, liver**	liberal, deliver	h. Before, preceding
____ 9. **viv, vit**	vitality, survive	i. Sleep
____ 10. **voc, vok**	vocal, invoke	j. Outside, beyond

PART B

Using the answer line provided, complete each *italicized* word in the sentences below with the correct word part from the box. Not every word part will be used.

a. **ante-**	b. **chron**	c. **-cide**	d. **de-**	e. **dorm**
f. **extra-**	g. **ject**	h. **liver**	i. **vit**	j. **vok**

_____ 11. A passenger train's (. . . *itory*) ___ car has sleeping facilities for the train's crew.

_____ 12. The chorus line was so wonderfully (*syn . . . ized*) ___—the dancers kept perfect time, seeming to move as one person.

_____ 13. In the refining process, white rice and white bread lose much of their (. . . *amin*) ___ content.

_____ 14. Ventriloquists must be able to (*pro . . .*) ___ their voices to the audience while keeping their mouths closed.

_____ 15. Airplane passengers used to be let off outdoors. Now they usually (. . . *plane*) ___ onto a ramp that leads directly into the terminal.

(Continues on next page)

PART C
Use your knowledge of word parts to determine the meaning of the **boldfaced** words. On the answer line, write the letter of each meaning.

_____ 16. He **antedated** his check to the IRS.

      a. dated correctly   b. dated earlier than the actual date   c. wrote too late

_____ 17. A new **bactericide** was being developed in the laboratory.

      a. something that destroys bacteria   b. a picture of bacteria   c. a dish of bacteria

_____ 18. She had an **extrauterine** pregnancy.

      a. within the uterus   b. with a normal uterus   c. out of the uterus

_____ 19. My friend Kareem would like to **liberate** all the animals in the zoo.

      a. adopt   b. kill   c. set free

_____ 20. The singer always **vocalized** before a concert.

      a. exercised her voice   b. took a nap   c. moved around on-stage

Score   (Number correct) _____ x 5 = _____ %

Enter your score above and in the vocabulary performance chart on the inside back cover of the book.

Unit Two

Chapter 7

equivocate	propensity
fortuitous	reprehensible
impeccable	sham
liaison	solace
predisposed	solicitous

Chapter 8

attrition	oblivious
circumvent	reticent
cohesive	robust
grievous	sanction
inundate	vociferous

Chapter 9

bolster	relegate
depreciate	replete
indiscriminate	sedentary
inquisitive	tenet
nebulous	terse

Chapter 10

autonomy	recourse
bureaucratic	reiterate
mandate	tantamount
ostracize	tenacious
raucous	utopia

Chapter 11

clandestine	indigenous
contingency	liability
egocentric	prolific
exonerate	reinstate
incongruous	superfluous

Chapter 12

a-, an-	pan-
bibl-, biblio-	prim, prime
fid	rect
-ism	sym-, syn-
nov	ver

equivocate	propensity
fortuitous	reprehensible
impeccable	sham
liaison	solace
predisposed	solicitous

Ten Words in Context

In the space provided, write the letter of the meaning closest to that of each **boldfaced** word. Use the context of the sentences to help you figure out each word's meaning.

1 **equivocate**
(ē-kwĭv′ə-kāt′)
-verb

• I can't get my boss to tell me whether or not he intends to give me a raise. When I ask him, he **equivocates**, saying, "You've been doing good work, Bob."

• Hank doesn't want to come right out and tell Barb he doesn't love her. If she asks, he **equivocates** by telling her something like "You know how I feel."

__ *Equivocate* means   a. to be blunt.   b. to be unclear.   c. to deny.

2 **fortuitous**
(fôr-tōō′ə-təs)
-adjective

• The birth of triplets wasn't entirely **fortuitous**. The mother had taken a fertility drug, which often causes multiple births.

• It was strictly **fortuitous** that Vince found his missing class notes. They happened to drop out of his dictionary when it fell to the floor.

__ *Fortuitous* means   a. accidental.   b. predictable.   c. overdue.

3 **impeccable**
(ĭm-pĕk′ə-bəl)
-adjective

• My aunt always looks stylish but never overdressed. Her taste in clothes is **impeccable**.

• When she auditioned for the play, Julie gave an **impeccable** performance. She read the lines perfectly.

__ *Impeccable* means   a. flawless.   b. deceptive.   c. faulty.

4 **liaison**
(lē′ə-zōn′)
-noun

• The president of the Student Council acts as a **liaison** between the students and the administration.

• Because she is bilingual, Elsa often serves as a **liaison** between the Spanish- and English-speaking personnel in her office.

__ *Liaison* means   a. a follower.   b. a caregiver.   c. a link.

5 **predisposed**
(prē′dĭs-pōzd′)
-adjective

• Terry didn't want to move in the first place, so she was **predisposed** to hate the new apartment.

• As a Mel Gibson fan, I'm **predisposed** to enjoy any movie he stars in.

__ *Predisposed* means   a. unlikely.   b. likely.   c. pretending.

6 **propensity**
(prə-pĕn′sĭ-tē)
-noun

• Because Ivan has a **propensity** to gain weight, he watches what he eats.

• Cheryl is aware of her **propensity** to blab, so she warns her friends not to tell her anything they wouldn't want repeated.

__ *Propensity* means   a. a coincidence.   b. a readiness.   c. a concern.

7 **reprehensible**
(rĕp′rĭ-hĕn′sə-bəl)
-adjective

- The Riordans never discipline their son. No matter how **reprehensible** his behavior is, they just say, "Kids will be kids."
- The company's failure to clean up the oil spill was **reprehensible** and drew harsh criticism.

__ *Reprehensible* means   a. shameful.   b. misleading.   c. uncertain.

8 **sham**
(shăm)
-noun

- Karen's apparent affection for Raul is a **sham**. He's rich, and she cares only about his money.
- When the city inspectors came, the restaurant kitchen was sparkling. However, such cleanliness was a **sham**—the place is usually filthy.

__ *Sham* means   a. something false.   b. something confusing.   c. something accidental.

9 **solace**
(sŏl′ĭs)
-noun

- After a family quarrel, Tamara finds **solace** in the privacy and quiet of her own room.
- When I need **solace** because of some upsetting experience, I find that stroking my cat can be very comforting.

__ *Solace* means   a. excitement.   b. perfection.   c. relief.

10 **solicitous**
(sə-lĭs′ə-təs)
-adjective

- The waiter was overly **solicitous**. He kept interrupting our conversation to ask, "Is everything all right here?"
- **Solicitous** toward her elderly neighbor, Marie calls every day to see how he is feeling and if he needs anything.

__ *Solicitous* means   a. distant.   b. attentive.   c. patient.

Matching Words with Definitions

Following are definitions of the ten words. Clearly write or print each word next to its definition. The sentences above and on the previous page will help you decide on the meaning of each word.

1. _____   A natural preference or tendency

2. _____   Deserving of blame, criticism, or disapproval

3. _____   Happening by chance, by accident, or at random; lucky

4. _____   Comfort in sorrow or misfortune; consolation

5. _____   A person who serves as a connection between individuals or groups; a go-between

6. _____   To be deliberately vague in order to mislead

7. _____   Faultless; perfect

8. _____   Showing or expressing concern, care, or attention

9. _____   Tending toward or open to something beforehand

10. _____   A pretense or counterfeit; something meant to deceive

CAUTION: Do not go any further until you are sure the above answers are correct. Then you can use the definitions to help you in the following practices. Your goal is eventually to know the words well enough so that you don't need to check the definitions at all.

➤ *Sentence Check 1*

Using the answer line provided, complete each item below with the correct word from the box. Use each word once.

a. **equivocate**	b. **fortuitous**	c. **impeccable**	d. **liaison**	e. **predisposed**
f. **propensity**	g. **reprehensible**	h. **sham**	i. **solace**	j. **solicitous**

_____ 1. When my grandmother died, I found ___ in the thought that she had lived a long, happy life.

_____ 2. Jan writes at least three drafts of every paper so that the final result will be ___. She wants each assignment to be perfect.

_____ 3. The boss is in a rotten mood today, so he's not ___ to tolerate any mistakes.

_____ 4. My brother and I are both grown up, but Mom is still ___ about our health. She says, "You'll always be my babies."

_____ 5. Many people consider rape such a(n) ___ crime that they think the penalties should be as harsh as possible.

_____ 6. The "going-out-of-business" sale was a ___. A year later, the store was still open.

_____ 7. It's hard to believe that Stacy, with her ___ for flashy clothes and nightlife, has become a missionary.

_____ 8. Unexpectedly, I ran into an old friend who had just started her own business. The ___ meeting led to a job offer for me.

_____ 9. Olive acted as a ___ between her divorced parents, but she finally insisted that they deal with each other directly.

_____ 10. The job candidate ___(e)d when he said he'd been "working out West." Actually, he'd been a ski bum for three years.

NOTE: Now check your answers to these questions by turning to page 175. Going over the answers carefully will help you prepare for the next two practices, for which answers are not given.

➤ *Sentence Check 2*

Using the answer lines provided, complete each item below with **two** words from the box. Use each word once.

_____
_____ 1–2. When Shirley said she was sick of Len's ___ to flirt with other women, he ___(e)d by making an ambiguous° statement: "I promise you'll never catch me flirting again."

_____
_____ 3–4. The woman wasn't permitted to visit her husband, a political prisoner, so it gave her some ___ to have a minister act as a ___ between them.

_____
_____ 5–6. Even before I met my father's nurse, I was ___ to like her, because I had heard how ___ she was toward him.

_____ 7–8. It was strictly ___ that no one was killed when the chemical plant
_____ exploded. The explosion, however, was no matter of chance, but the
result of ___ carelessness on the part of an employee.

_____ 9–10. The candidate's lifestyle seemed ___, but it was all a ___. He was a
_____ drinker and a womanizer and was mixed up in all kinds of illicit°
activities involving drugs and bribes.

➤ _Final Check:_ A Phony Friend

Here is a final opportunity for you to strengthen your knowledge of the ten words. First read the following selection carefully. Then fill in each blank with a word from the box at the top of the previous page. (Context clues will help you figure out which word goes in which blank.) Use each word once.

When my grandfather, Henry Altman, died, he left me a large sum of money. This was very surprising because he and my father had become estranged° years before, after a quarrel, and the old man had never even seen me. I was sad that he had died before we could meet.

Soon after the news of my inheritance, a young man named Seth showed up to offer me his sympathy. Seth said he had been a friend of my grandfather's and that when the old man had become ill, he'd asked Seth to act as a (1)_____ between himself and the granddaughter he'd never met. "It's too late for Henry," said Seth, "but I think he'd want me to offer you my friendship. In his later years, he regretted his earlier (2)_____ to quarrel with his family."

Believing that Seth had been my grandfather's friend made me (3)_____ to like him, and it gave me (4)_____ to speak to someone who had known my grandfather. Still, I was puzzled because Seth didn't seem able to give me much information. For example, when I asked some questions about Grandfather's second wife, Seth seemed to (5)_____, saying, "All I can say is that she was quite a woman." On the other hand, Seth appeared genuinely (6)_____ about my welfare, and his manners were (7)_____. I had never met anyone so perfectly polite.

I really didn't know what to make of him until, one day, I had a(n) (8)_____ meeting with an old school friend I hadn't seen in years. When I described Seth, my friend looked startled and said, "I know that guy. He's a phony, a complete (9) _____. He's after the money, and I bet he never even knew your grandfather."

When I checked, my friend's story was corroborated° by reports of how Seth had tricked several other women out of their inheritances. The next time he called, I told him I knew about his (10)_____ behavior and would notify the police if he ever tried to contact me again.

Scores   Sentence Check 2 _____%   Final Check _____%

Enter your scores above and in the vocabulary performance chart on the inside back cover of the book.

attrition	oblivious
circumvent	reticent
cohesive	robust
grievous	sanction
inundate	vociferous

Ten Words in Context

In the space provided, write the letter of the meaning closest to that of each **boldfaced** word. Use the context of the sentences to help you figure out each word's meaning.

1 attrition
(ə-trĭsh′ən)
-*noun*

- Sports teams are constantly looking for new talent to replace players lost through **attrition**—those who retire, quit because of injuries, and so on.
- Colleges try not to have a high rate of **attrition**. They want students to stay until graduation rather than drop out early.

__ *Attrition* means   a. an increase in numbers.   b. a natural loss of individuals.   c. ill health.

2 circumvent
(sŭr′kəm-vĕnt′)
-*verb*

- If we take this roundabout route, we can **circumvent** the rush-hour traffic and get home early.
- I had to swerve to the right to **circumvent** a huge pothole.

__ *Circumvent* means   a. to avoid.   b. to meet head-on.   c. to make smaller.

3 cohesive
(kō-hēs′ĭv)
-*adjective*

- For a **cohesive** pie dough, one that doesn't fall apart, be sure to add enough liquid.
- A family needs to be **cohesive**—to stay together even when stresses and strains threaten to tear it apart.

__ *Cohesive* means   a. connected.   b. popular.   c. large.

4 grievous
(grēv′əs)
-*adjective*

- The death of a beloved pet is a **grievous** loss for a child.
- The assassination of a great leader, such as Mahatma Gandhi or Martin Luther King, Jr., often does **grievous** harm to a society.

__ *Grievous* means   a. preventable.   b. unavoidable.   c. terrible.

5 inundate
(ĭn′ŭn-dāt′)
-*verb*

- During the heavy rains, the river overflowed and **inundated** the fields, destroying all the crops.
- After his brief announcement, the President was **inundated** with questions from reporters.

__ *Inundate* means   a. to flood.   b. to strengthen.   c. to go around.

6 oblivious
(ə-blĭv′ē-əs)
-*adjective*

- The driver continued into the intersection, apparently **oblivious** to the fact that the light had turned red.
- It's easy to spot lovers. They are the ones who, **oblivious** to everyone else present, see only each other.

__ *Oblivious to* means   a. angry about.   b. not noticing.   c. overwhelmed by.

7 reticent
(rĕt′ə-sənt)
-*adjective*

- Paul is very **reticent** about his first marriage; he never talks about his former wife or what led to their divorce.
- It's odd that many people who love to gossip about someone else are so **reticent** about their own lives.

__ *Reticent* means   a. dishonest.   b. quiet.   c. unaware.

8 robust
(rō-bŭst′)
-*adjective*

- Once an energetic, **robust** man, Mr. Rand has been considerably weakened by illness.
- A number of weight lifters who were previously **robust** have ruined their health and vigor by taking steroids.

__ *Robust* means   a. very noisy.   b. sickly.   c. strong and well.

9 sanction
(săngk′shən)
-*verb*

- By greeting the dictator with extreme courtesy and fanfare, the legislature seemed to **sanction** his policies.
- Many people whose children attend religious schools would like the government to **sanction** the use of public funds to help pay for their education.

__ *Sanction* means   a. to grant approval of.   b. to criticize severely.   c. to remember.

10 vociferous
(vō-sĭf′ər-əs)
-*adjective*

- When male loons sense that their territory is being invaded, they give **vociferous** cries of challenge.
- The principal became angry and **vociferous**, shouting at students who tried to sneak out of the fire drill.

__ *Vociferous* means   a. distant.   b. mild.   c. loud.

Matching Words with Definitions

Following are definitions of the ten words. Clearly write or print each word next to its definition. The sentences above and on the previous page will help you decide on the meaning of each word.

1. _____   To authorize, allow, or approve

2. _____   To cover, as by flooding; overwhelm with a large number or amount

3. _____   To avoid by going around or as if by going around; to escape from, prevent, or stop through cleverness

4. _____   Quiet or uncommunicative; reluctant to speak out

5. _____   Healthy and strong; vigorous

6. _____   Sticking or holding together; unified

7. _____   Noisy; expressing feelings loudly and intensely

8. _____   A gradual natural decrease in number; becoming fewer in number

9. _____   Causing grief or pain; very serious or severe

10. _____   Unaware; failing to notice

CAUTION: Do not go any further until you are sure the above answers are correct. Then you can use the definitions to help you in the following practices. Your goal is eventually to know the words well enough so that you don't need to check the definitions at all.

➤ Sentence Check 1

Using the answer line provided, complete each item below with the correct word from the box. Use each word once.

a. **attrition**	b. **circumvent**	c. **cohesive**	d. **grievous**	e. **inundate**
f. **oblivious**	g. **reticent**	h. **robust**	i. **sanction**	j. **vociferous**

_____ 1. The chatty, slow-moving clerk at the checkout counter seemed ___ to the fact that the line of impatient customers was growing longer and longer.

_____ 2. A quiet, polite discussion may be better than a(n) ___ argument, but some people get more satisfaction out of yelling and shouting.

_____ 3. In many places, the law doesn't ___ gambling—but the officials don't do much to stop it, either.

_____ 4. A half-hour of aerobic exercise every other day will help you stay ___.

_____ 5. People sometimes do odd things to ___ regulations. In New York, when saloons were illegal, one owner called his place "O'Neal's Baloon."

_____ 6. If you want your essay to be ___, stick to your point.

_____ 7. Alzheimer's disease is a disaster for the patient and a(n) ___ burden for the family.

_____ 8. Some days we're ___(e)d with junk mail—the mailbox is crammed full and overflowing with it.

_____ 9. The cutting down of the rain forests has caused a dangerous rate of ___ among species that live in those forests.

_____ 10. Some people who could benefit from counseling avoid seeing a therapist because they are ___ about private matters.

NOTE: Now check your answers to these questions by turning to page 175. Going over the answers carefully will help you prepare for the next two practices, for which answers are not given.

➤ Sentence Check 2

Using the answer lines provided, complete each item below with **two** words from the box. Use each word once.

_____
_____ 1–2. Craig is ___(e)d with bills, but he keeps on squandering° money. He's ___ to his financial problems.

_____
_____ 3–4. The company doesn't ___ the policy of laying off workers. It believes that the optimum° way to reduce the staff is by ___: employees who quit or retire simply aren't replaced.

_____
_____ 5–6. Child abuse is a(n) ___ crime, but children are often ___ about it. Their silence may prevent them from collaborating° with the police or the courts to bring the abusers to justice.

_____   7–8. Although my brother was ___ enough to meet the army's standards for
_____   enlisting, his eyesight was too poor. He tried to ___ this problem by
                                           memorizing the eye chart.

_____   9–10. The teacher of the Cooking for Health class was ___ about avoiding
_____   egg yolks. "You don't need yolks for a(n) ___ batter!" he shouted. "The
                                           whites will hold it together."

➤ *Final Check:* Coco the Gorilla

Here is a final opportunity for you to strengthen your knowledge of the ten words. First read the following selection carefully. Then fill in each blank with a word from the box at the top of the previous page. (Context clues will help you figure out which word goes in which blank.) Use each word once.

Illegal killings of gorillas are reducing their numbers far faster than would be expected from normal (1)_____. Here is the story of one gorilla family.

Carrying spears and knives, hunters entered an African game preserve, where it was unlawful to kill or capture wildlife. When they spotted a young gorilla, they closed in. Ten adult gorillas, members of a(n) (2)_____ family group, attempted to shield the infant. The men quickly killed all the adults. As if (3)_____ to the infant's screams, the men strapped his hands and feet to bamboo poles with wire, then carried him down the mountain on which he'd been born.

After several weeks, Dian Fossey, an American studying gorillas in the wild, learned that the young gorilla had been taken to park officials. She found him in a cage so small that he had no room to stand or turn. He was clearly frightened and nearly dead—thirsty, starving, and with infected wounds at his ankles and wrists. Fossey could hardly believe that the officials could (4)_____ such reprehensible° cruelty.

When she demanded an explanation from the park's chief official, he seemed (5)_____ about the animal. Finally, however, he admitted that he had made an illegal deal with a German zoo. In return for a new car, he had arranged for the gorilla's capture. Fossey was (6)_____ in insisting that the infant be released into her care. The official agreed on the condition that the infant be shipped to the zoo as soon as his health returned.

For several months, Fossey cared for the infant, now named Coco, who would cling to her for comfort. When he became more (7)_____, he began to romp and explore. In an effort to (8)_____ the agreement to send Coco to the zoo, Fossey (9)_____(e)d government officials with letters, begging them to step in and arrange for him to be returned to the wild. In the end, though, the little gorilla was taken away from her—a(n) (10)_____ hardship for both of them. Gorillas can live into their 50s, but Coco died in the zoo at the age of 12.

Scores   Sentence Check 2 _____%   Final Check _____%

Enter your scores above and in the vocabulary performance chart on the inside back cover of the book.

CHAPTER

9

bolster	relegate
depreciate	replete
indiscriminate	sedentary
inquisitive	tenet
nebulous	terse

Ten Words in Context

In the space provided, write the letter of the meaning closest to that of each **boldfaced** word. Use the context of the sentences to help you figure out each word's meaning.

1 **bolster**
(bōl′stər)
-verb

- The front porch was sagging, so we had to **bolster** it with cinder blocks until it could be repaired.
- When Lisa was in the hospital, visits from friends **bolstered** her spirits.

__ *Bolster* means a. to reach.   b. to replace.   c. to support.

2 **depreciate**
(dĭ-prē′shē-āt′)
-verb

- As soon as you drive a new car off the lot, it **depreciates**; it's immediately worth less than you paid for it.
- The property **depreciated** when the city built a sewage plant nearby.

__ *Depreciate* means a. to become better. b. to become less valuable. c. to become definite.

3 **indiscriminate**
(ĭn′dĭ-skrĭm′ĭ-nĭt)
-adjective

- Some people end up hopelessly in debt because of **indiscriminate** spending, so be selective about what and how much you buy.
- I confess to an **indiscriminate** love of chocolate. I don't distinguish between plain old Hershey bars and fancy imported chocolates—I adore them all.

__ *Indiscriminate* means a. healthy.   b. unenthusiastic.   c. unselective.

4 **inquisitive**
(ĭn-kwĭz′ə-tĭv)
-adjective

- **Inquisitive** students usually do better than those who are less curious and less eager to learn.
- Small children are naturally **inquisitive**. They wonder about the world around them, and they are constantly asking "Why?"

__ *Inquisitive* means a. hard-working. b. particular.   c. questioning.

5 **nebulous**
(nĕb′yə-ləs)
-adjective

- When I ask Leonard what he wants for his birthday, he never gives me any specific ideas. He just gives a **nebulous** answer like "Oh, something interesting."
- "Don't give **nebulous** answers on the exam," said the history instructor. "Be specific."

__ *Nebulous* means a. indefinite.   b. long.   c. specific.

6 **relegate**
(rĕl′ə-gāt′)
-verb

- At family gatherings, we kids were always **relegated** to the kitchen table while the adults ate in the dining room.
- When we have overnight guests, my parents give them my room and **relegate** me to a cot in the attic.

__ *Relegate* means a. to send.   b. to punish.   c. to reward.

7 replete
(rĭ-plēt′)
-*adjective*

- The show was **replete** with dazzling effects, including gorgeous scenery, glittering costumes, dramatic lighting, and thrilling music.
- The book of household hints got an excellent review. "It's **replete** with good advice," the critic said, "a real treasure."

__ *Replete* means   a. replaced.   b. filled.   c. followed.

8 sedentary
(sĕd′′n-tĕr′ē)
-*adjective*

- People in **sedentary** occupations, such as bus drivers and writers, need to make a special effort to exercise.
- My lifestyle is so **sedentary** that the longest walk I ever take is from my living room couch to the front seat of my car.

__ *Sedentary* means   a. involving much walking.   b. involving stress.   c. involving much sitting.

9 tenet
(tĕn′ĭt)
-*noun*

- A basic **tenet** of Islam is "There is no God but Allah, and Muhammed is his prophet."
- This world might be a paradise if everyone lived by such **tenets** as "Never cause suffering."

__ *Tenet* means   a. a principle.   b. a ritual.   c. a prediction.

10 terse
(tûrs)
-*adjective*

- I was hurt by Roger's **terse** response to my invitation. All he said was "No thanks."
- A British humor magazine once gave this **terse** advice to people about to marry: "Don't."

__ *Terse* means   a. dishonest.   b. unclear.   c. short.

Matching Words with Definitions

Following are definitions of the ten words. Clearly write or print each word next to its definition. The sentences above and on the previous page will help you decide on the meaning of each word.

1. _____   To fall or decrease in value or price; to lower the value of

2. _____   Not chosen carefully; not based on careful selection

3. _____   Marked by much sitting; requiring or taking little exercise

4. _____   A belief or principle held to be true by an individual or group

5. _____   Brief and clear; effectively concise

6. _____   To hold up, strengthen, or reinforce; support with a rigid object

7. _____   Curious; eager to learn

8. _____   Plentifully supplied; well-filled

9. _____   Vague; unclear

10. _____   To assign to a less important or less satisfying position, place, or condition

CAUTION: Do not go any further until you are sure the above answers are correct. Then you can use the definitions to help you in the following practices. Your goal is eventually to know the words well enough so that you don't need to check the definitions at all.

➤ *Sentence Check 1*

Using the answer line provided, complete each item below with the correct word from the box. Use each word once.

a. **bolster**	b. **depreciate**	c. **indiscriminate**	d. **inquisitive**	e. **nebulous**
f. **relegate**	g. **replete**	h. **sedentary**	i. **tenet**	j. **terse**

_____ 1. John considers Arlene rude because her comments are usually ___, but I prefer her brief, clear answers to his long-winded ones.

_____ 2. Pat's TV viewing is ___. He just watches whatever happens to be on.

_____ 3. When a sofa leg broke, we ___(e)d that end of the sofa with a pile of books.

_____ 4. Houses and antiques often increase in value, but most other things, like cars, computers, and appliances, tend to ___.

_____ 5. A large sign in the boys' treehouse stated their club's main ___: "No Girls or Snakes Allowed!!!"

_____ 6. The refrigerator was ___ with all kinds of marvelous foods for the party.

_____ 7. The catcher worried that unless he started playing better, he'd be ___(e)d to the minor leagues.

_____ 8. Before I entered college, my thoughts about a career were ___, but now I have a much clearer idea of what work I want to do.

_____ 9. When we were children, my active sister was always playing tag or jumping rope. I was more ___, preferring to spend hour after hour just sitting and reading.

_____ 10. The book *Answers to 1,001 Interesting Questions* sounds like the perfect gift for a(n) ___ person.

NOTE: Now check your answers to these questions by turning to page 176. Going over the answers carefully will help you prepare for the next two practices, for which answers are not given.

➤ *Sentence Check 2*

Using the answer lines provided, complete each item below with **two** words from the box. Use each word once.

_____
_____ 1–2. My car manual's instructions for changing the spark plugs are so ___ that by the time I figure out exactly how to do it, my car will have ___(e)d a few thousand dollars more.

_____
_____ 3–4. Dad was a construction worker, but as soon as he reached 60— though he was as robust° as ever—his company ___(e)d him to a(n) ___ desk job.

_____ 5–6. The guides at the Leaning Tower of Pisa are inundated° with questions from ___ travelers: "Why is it leaning?" "How far is it leaning?" "Is it being ___(e)d to keep it from falling any further?"

_____   7–8. Folk wisdom is ___ with contradictory sayings and ___s. It's fun to
_____   juxtapose° pairs such as "He who hesitates is lost" and "Look before
                          you leap."

_____   9–10. Stan is not exactly a ___ speaker, which is why he's earned the
_____   nickname "Motor Mouth." What's more, his conversation is totally
                          ___; he uses no discretion° but just says anything that comes to mind.

➤ _Final Check:_ Our Annual Garage Sale

Here is a final opportunity for you to strengthen your knowledge of the ten words. First read the following selection carefully. Then fill in each blank with a word from the box at the top of the previous page. (Context clues will help you figure out which word goes in which blank.) Use each word once.

It's almost September—time for our annual garage sale. Our unwanted items keep piling up in the basement, which is now so full that we've had to (1)_____ some of the collection to the garage. Though the sale is a lot of work, the sight of all those piles and boxes (2)_____s our determination to go through with it.

This proliferation° of stuff has left us with a huge number of possessions for sale, from tools and spools to baskets and gaskets. This year, for example, we have an old bike that some zealot° for exercise might buy and a soft chair and footstool for a more (3)_____ customer. Our ad states our main (4)_____: "Something for everyone!" Maybe that's a bit (5)_____, but we don't want to be specific. We just want to disseminate° the general idea that our sale will be (6)_____ with treasures.

Last year, one customer took a quick look and departed with the (7)_____ comment "Nothing but junk." However, most people seem to take a completely (8)_____ approach to shopping. They're predisposed° to spend their money on anything, including rusty baking pans and broken lamps. Then there are the (9)_____ shoppers who want us to tell them every detail about every item: How old is it? What did we pay for it? Will it increase or (10)_____ in value?

Friends have foolishly asked us where in the world we get all this junk to sell year after year— an inane° question, because the answer is simple. We shop at garage sales.

Scores	Sentence Check 2 _____%	Final Check _____%

Enter your scores above and in the vocabulary performance chart on the inside back cover of the book.

autonomy	recourse
bureaucratic	reiterate
mandate	tantamount
ostracize	tenacious
raucous	utopia

Ten Words in Context

In the space provided, write the letter of the meaning closest to that of each **boldfaced** word. Use the context of the sentences to help you figure out each word's meaning.

1 autonomy
(ô-tŏn′ə-mē)
-noun

- In 1776, the American colonists, tired of being ruled by England, fought for their **autonomy**.
- Children as young as age two begin to want some **autonomy**. The term "terrible twos" reflects their struggle for independence.

___ *Autonomy* means   a. assistance.   b. freedom from control.   c. self-sacrifice.

2 bureaucratic
(byōŏr′ə-krăt′ĭk)
-adjective

- **Bureaucratic** organizations can become so bogged down in regulations that almost no work gets done.
- "This family is more **bureaucratic** than the federal government!" Mac complained to his parents. "You have rules for everything."

___ *Bureaucratic* means   a. over-regulated.   b. old-fashioned.   c. independent.

3 mandate
(man′dāt′)
-noun

- All the union members voted for the strike, giving their leaders a clear **mandate**.
- The senator received so many letters supporting his position on gun control that he felt he had the **mandate** of the people.

___ *Mandate* means   a. a criticism.   b. a delay.   c. an authorization.

4 ostracize
(ŏs′trə-sīz′)
-verb

- Children who look or act "different" are often **ostracized** by their classmates. No one will play with them or even talk to them.
- When Sabrina ran off with her sister's husband, she was **ostracized** by the entire family and all her friends. No one would have anything to do with her.

___ *Ostracize* means   a. to reject.   b. to feel sorry for.   c. to control.

5 raucous
(rô′kəs)
-adjective

- The audience at the rock concert was so **raucous** that we feared the noise and commotion would lead to violence.
- At the horror movie, the audience's behavior became **raucous**. Everyone was shouting at the characters on the screen and pretending to shriek with fright.

___ *Raucous* means   a. persistent.   b. disorderly.   c. angry.

6 recourse
(rē′kôrs)
-noun

- "Unless you pay your bill," the company threatened, "we'll have no **recourse** but to sue you."
- "We'll try treating you with medication," the doctor explained. "If that isn't effective, the only **recourse** will be surgery."

___ *Recourse* means   a. a way to get help.   b. a problem.   c. a question.

7 reiterate
(rē-ĭt'ə-rāt')
-verb

- The agency director stated, "I have said this before, but let me **reiterate**: Unless we receive the funds to hire more staff, the children of this city will continue to suffer."

- I hate it when a speaker **reiterates** the same point over and over, as if the listeners weren't paying attention or were just too stupid to understand.

___ *Reiterate* means   a. to repeat.   b. to forget.   c. to exclude.

8 tantamount
(tănt'ə-mount')
-adjective

- Charging three dollars for a cup of coffee is **tantamount** to robbery.

- My mother's refusal to let me have the car was **tantamount** to forbidding me to go to the beach.

___ *Tantamount to* means   a. the result of.   b. just like.   c. independent of.

9 tenacious
(tə-nā'shəs)
-adjective

- The cat's grip on the ledge was **tenacious**, but we weren't sure how long she could keep hanging on so firmly.

- My aunt's **tenacious** determination to recover may have pulled her through her illness.

___ *Tenacious* means   a. grasping strongly.   b. weak and ineffective.   c. slowly shrinking.

10 utopia
(yoō-tō'pē-ə)
-noun

- In 1888, Edward Bellamy wrote about a **utopia** where everyone would have a comfortable income, work only until the age of 45, and then enjoy leisure.

- Everyone has a different idea of **utopia**. A situation that seems perfect to me might make you miserable.

___ *Utopia* means   a. a city.   b. a self-government.   c. a paradise.

Matching Words with Definitions

Following are definitions of the ten words. Clearly write or print each word next to its definition. The sentences above and on the previous page will help you decide on the meaning of each word.

1. _____   An ideal or perfect place or state; a place achieving social or political perfection

2. _____   Noisy and disorderly; boisterous

3. _____   A source of help, security, or strength; something to turn to

4. _____   Insisting on strict rules and routine, often to the point of hindering effectiveness

5. _____   To state again or repeatedly

6. _____   Independence; self-government

7. _____   A group's expressed wishes; clear signal to act; vote of confidence

8. _____   To expel or exclude from a group

9. _____   Equal in effect or value; the same as

10. _____   Holding firmly; persistent; stubborn

CAUTION: Do not go any further until you are sure the above answers are correct. Then you can use the definitions to help you in the following practices. Your goal is eventually to know the words well enough so that you don't need to check the definitions at all.

➤ *Sentence Check 1*

Using the answer line provided, complete each item below with the correct word from the box. Use each word once.

a. **autonomy**	b. **bureaucratic**	c. **mandate**	d. **ostracize**	e. **raucous**
f. **recourse**	g. **reiterate**	h. **tantamount**	i. **tenacious**	j. **utopia**

_____ 1. My job gives me a great deal of ___. I can set my own hours, work at home when I like, and make many decisions on my own.

_____ 2. In high school, Felipe was ___(e)d because of his political views, but in college he found many people who shared his opinions.

_____ 3. When you write a letter of complaint, begin by stating what you want the company to do about the problem. Then ___ this request at the end.

_____ 4. Our local supermarket is so expensive that shopping there is ___ to throwing your money away.

_____ 5. The children on the school bus were so ___ that the driver got a headache from all the noise.

_____ 6. Helen's smoking was a ___ habit; she wasn't able to give it up until she watched her brother die of lung cancer.

_____ 7. Idealists have sometimes tried to establish ___s, but these communities have always failed. I wonder if it is possible to achieve perfection.

_____ 8. While most college instructors are flexible, some are very ___, allowing no exceptions to the rules regardless of the circumstances.

_____ 9. In a landslide election, the voters' ___ is clear. If the vote has been close, though, it's difficult to tell what "the people" really want.

_____10. In the past, workers often had no ___ when employers discriminated against them. Today, however, they can seek help from the Equal Employment Opportunity Commission.

NOTE: Now check your answers to these questions by turning to page 176. Going over the answers carefully will help you prepare for the next two practices, for which answers are not given.

➤ *Sentence Check 2*

Using the answer lines provided, complete each item below with **two** words from the box. Use each word once.

_____ 1–2. One concept of a(n) ___ is a society in which each individual maintains
_____   his or her ___ yet collaborates° with others to achieve the good for all.

_____ 3–4. "My company is so ___," Nick complained, "that we are buried in
_____   paperwork. Sometimes we have to ___ the same information on five different forms."

_____ 5–6. If elected officials ignore the ___ of the people, citizens always have
_____   the ___ of voting those officials out of office.

_____ 7–8. Our neighbor has a ___ belief in superstitions. For instance, she insists
_____   that our owning a black cat is ___ to asking for grievous° misfortune.

_____ 9–10. The kids' basketball league ___(e)d one team because of the
_____   reprehensible° behavior of its players. They engaged in ___ horseplay
                                   on the court, instigated° fights, and constantly tried to circumvent° the
                                   rules. Now the other teams refuse to play them.

➤ *Final Check:* **A Debate on School Uniforms**

Here is a final opportunity for you to strengthen your knowledge of the ten words. First read the following
selection carefully. Then fill in each blank with a word from the box at the top of the previous page.
(Context clues will help you figure out which word goes in which blank.) Use each word once.

At Monday's student council meeting, the officers debated about whether or not students
should be required to wear uniforms.

Barbara, president of the senior class, stated that as an elected representative of the students,
she wouldn't vote to change the dress code without a clear (1)_____ from the
students calling for such a change. "Personally," she said, "I think that forcing people to wear
certain clothing robs them of their (2)_____. What is school supposed to
teach us, if not the ability to think and act independently? Besides," she added, "the school
administration is (3)_____ enough. We don't need any more rules and
regulations."

Ray, vice-president of the junior class, disagreed. "The current situation is
(4)_____ to a three-ring circus," he said. "Students compete to see who can
look most clownish. Some of the outfits are nearly blinding. Other kids are such snobs about their
ostentatious° designer clothes that they (5)_____ kids who can't afford to
keep up with them. I'm not saying that uniforms would change the school into a(n)
(6)_____. No place is perfect. I just think that if we want school to be more
fair, our best (7)_____ is a strict dress code."

At that, several students burst into (8)_____ disagreement, yelling and
pounding on their desks. After several minutes of vociferous° chaos, the meeting came to order,
and Barbara was called on again.

(9)_____ in her opinion, she insisted, "I understand what you're saying,
Ray, but I want to (10)_____ a point I made earlier. Uniforms do away with
one aspect of personal choice, and one of my tenets° is that personal choice is precious."

Scores	Sentence Check 2 _____%	Final Check _____%

Enter your scores above and in the vocabulary performance chart on the inside back cover of the book.

clandestine	indigenous
contingency	liability
egocentric	prolific
exonerate	reinstate
incongruous	superfluous

Ten Words in Context

In the space provided, write the letter of the meaning closest to that of each **boldfaced** word. Use the context of the sentences to help you figure out each word's meaning.

1 clandestine
(klăn-dĕs′tĭn)
-*adjective*

• In a **clandestine** meeting in an alley, Steve sold his employer's valuable anti-aging formula to a competitor.
• The famous "Underground Railroad" was not an actual railroad: it was a **clandestine** network that took escaped slaves to safety in the years before the Civil War.

___ *Clandestine* means   a. popular.   b. unnecessary.   c. concealed.

2 contingency
(kən-tĭn′jən-sē)
-*noun*

• Faye thought her company might transfer her to another city. With that **contingency** in mind, she decided to rent a house rather than buy one.
• We believe in providing for every **contingency**. We have a list of emergency phone numbers, a first-aid kit, and a box of candles in case of a power failure.

___ *Contingency* means   a. a possibility.   b. an advantage.   c. a desire.

3 egocentric
(ē′gō-sĕn′trĭk)
-*adjective*

• Denise is completely **egocentric**. Whatever event takes place, she thinks only of how it will affect her personally.
• "We've talked enough about me," said the **egocentric** author to a friend. "Now let's talk about you. What do you think of my new book?"

___ *Egocentric* means   a. self-involved.   b. unselfish.   c. self-educated.

4 exonerate
(ĕg-zŏn′ər-āt′)
-*verb*

• Saul was suspected of robbing a bank, but he was **exonerated** when the hidden camera's photos clearly showed someone else holding up the teller.
• Politicians accused of illegal activities always seem to say the same thing: that they'll be **exonerated** when all the facts are known.

___ *Exonerate* means   a. to be harmed.   b. to be found guilty.   c. to be found not guilty.

5 incongruous
(ĭn-kŏng′grōō-əs)
-*adjective*

• The cuckoo lays eggs in other birds' nests. This practice can result in the **incongruous** sight of one large cuckoo chick among several tiny baby robins.
• It wasn't really **incongruous** for a former general to join the peace movement. He had seen the horrors of war.

___ *Incongruous* means   a. contradictory.   b. unnecessary.   c. not noticeable.

6 indigenous
(ĭn-dĭj′ə-nəs)
-*adjective*

• Kangaroos are **indigenous** only to Australia. They have never been found living anyplace else in the world.
• Corn was not **indigenous** to Europe, so Europeans had never seen or heard of it until their explorers first reached the New World and found it growing there.

___ *Indigenous* means   a. important.   b. native.   c. welcomed.

7 liability
(lī′ə-bĭl′ə-tē)
-noun

- My shyness with strangers would be a **liability** in any job that involved meeting the public, such as sales.
- When Juanita returned to school at age 40, she was afraid her age would be a **liability**. Instead, she found that it gave her an advantage over younger students.

__ *Liability* means   a. an asset.   b. a handicap.   c. a necessity.

8 prolific
(prō-lĭf′ĭk)
-adjective

- Rabbits deserve their reputation for being **prolific**. A female can produce three families each summer.
- Haydn was a **prolific** composer. He wrote, among many other musical works, 104 symphonies.

__ *Prolific* means   a. creating abundantly.   b. working secretly.   c. important.

9 reinstate
(rē′ĭn-stāt′)
-verb

- Michiko left work for a year to stay home with her new baby. When she returned, she was relieved and happy to be **reinstated** in her former job.
- The college had canceled the course in folklore, but the demand was so great that the classes had to be **reinstated**.

__ *Reinstate* means   a. to recognize.   b. to appreciate.   c. to put back.

10 superfluous
(soŏ-pûr′floō-əs)
-adjective

- In the phrase "rich millionaire," the word *rich* is **superfluous**. All millionaires are rich.
- Lately, business at the store has been so slow that the three clerks have almost nothing to do. Two of them seem **superfluous**.

__ *Superfluous* means   a. unnecessary.   b. ordinary.   c. required.

Matching Words with Definitions

Following are definitions of the ten words. Clearly write or print each word next to its definition. The sentences above and on the previous page will help you decide on the meaning of each word.

1. _____   Something that acts as a disadvantage; a drawback

2. _____   Done in secret; kept hidden

3. _____   Out of place; having parts that are not in harmony or that are inconsistent

4. _____   A possible future event that must be prepared for or guarded against; possibility

5. _____   Living, growing, or produced naturally in a particular place; native

6. _____   Beyond what is needed, wanted, or useful; extra

7. _____   Producing many works, results, or offspring; fertile

8. _____   To clear of an accusation or charge; prove innocent

9. _____   Self-centered; seeing everything in terms of oneself

10. _____   To restore to a previous position or condition; bring back into being or use

CAUTION: Do not go any further until you are sure the above answers are correct. Then you can use the definitions to help you in the following practices. Your goal is eventually to know the words well enough so that you don't need to check the definitions at all.

➤ *Sentence Check 1*

Using the answer line provided, complete each item below with the correct word from the box. Use each word once.

a. **clandestine**	b. **contingency**	c. **egocentric**	d. **exonerate**	e. **incongruous**
f. **indigenous**	g. **liability**	h. **prolific**	i. **reinstate**	j. **superfluous**

_____ 1. Agnes is only five feet tall, but her boyfriend is six-foot-four. They make a(n) ___-looking couple.

_____ 2. Sharon and Ben have ___(e)d a Jewish family tradition they hadn't observed for years: lighting candles on the Sabbath.

_____ 3. Bad handwriting isn't a serious ___ in an age of computers.

_____ 4. Here, squirrels are red or gray, but I used to live in a state where black squirrels were ___.

_____ 5. Although our city has never been struck by an earthquake, it has emergency plans for just such a ___.

_____ 6. Two students were blamed for starting the fire in the physics lab, but they were ___(e)d when it was found that the cause was faulty electrical equipment.

_____ 7. Flies are amazingly ___. Within a five-month breeding period, one female can produce thousands of offspring.

_____ 8. Because a submarine is able to hide underwater, it can be very useful in ___ operations.

_____ 9. "Your writing is too wordy," the instructor had written on my paper. "Eliminate all those ___ words and phrases."

_____ 10. Nancy is so ___ that when I told her my car had been stolen, her only reaction was, "Does this mean you can't drive me to work tomorrow?"

NOTE: Now check your answers to these questions by turning to page 176. Going over the answers carefully will help you prepare for the next two practices, for which answers are not given.

➤ *Sentence Check 2*

Using the answer lines provided, complete each item below with **two** words from the box. Use each word once.

_____
_____ 1–2. People who spend Christmas in Florida often find the decorations ___. Santa Clauses, sleighs, reindeer, and fir trees somehow seem ___ to the North and look odd juxtaposed° with palm trees and tropical flowers.

_____
_____ 3–4. When a million dollars mysteriously vanished, the company decided to fire its accountant. But he was ___(e)d and ___(e)d in his position when the cause was traced to a computer malfunction.

_____   5–6. The ___ author has just come out with her fiftieth novel. Although she
_____   publishes numerous books, her writing style remains tight, with no ___
                                          words.

_____   7–8. The foreman is so ___ that he has become a ___ to the company.
_____   Concerned only with his own needs, he's oblivious° to the needs of the
                                          workers.

_____   9–10. The ship's captain seemed to be losing his mental balance. Fearing that
_____   he might become completely insane, the crew held a(n) ___ meeting to
                                           discuss what to do in that ___.

➤ *Final Check:* My Large Family

Here is a final opportunity for you to strengthen your knowledge of the ten words. First read the following selection carefully. Then fill in each blank with a word from the box at the top of the previous page. (Context clues will help you figure out which word goes in which blank.) Use each word once.

For many years I didn't realize that my family was larger than normal. That's because enormous families somehow seemed (1)_____ to our neighborhood. I don't know what made people on our block so (2)_____, but the Harrisons, on one side of us, had nine kids; and the Montoyas, on the other side, had twelve. When Mom said she was going to have her eleventh child, the ten of us wondered if another baby wasn't (3)_____: one more than necessary. Still, I think we enjoyed one another as much as any family I know. Naturally, we had our battles, but though they were sometimes intense, they never lasted long, and it didn't take much to (4)_____ yourself in a brother's or a sister's good graces. If nothing else worked, you could always (5)_____ yourself by blaming whatever had happened on another sibling who wasn't home at the moment. Also, we learned to cooperate. When you have to get along with so many different people, you learn not to be (6)_____. A self-centered person wouldn't have lasted ten minutes in my home.

Of course, there were times when the size of our family was a (7)_____. With all those people around, any kind of (8)_____ activity was just about impossible—there was simply no place to hide and no way to keep a secret. Our numbers could be a disadvantage to others, as well. Once, a new neighbor, not realizing how many of us there were, offered to take us all for ice cream. With amusement, he watched the (9)_____ sight of nine children and one toddler trying to squeeze into an ordinary passenger car. Although he obviously hadn't been prepared for such a(n) (10)_____, it didn't squelch° his plans. He just grinned and said, "Okay, we'll go in shifts."

	Scores Sentence Check 2 _____% Final Check _____%

Enter your scores above and in the vocabulary performance chart on the inside back cover of the book.

CHAPTER

12

a-, an-	pan-
bibl-, biblio-	prim, prime
fid	rect
-ism	sym-, syn-
nov	ver

Ten Word Parts in Context

Figure out the meanings of the following ten word parts by looking *closely* and *carefully* at the context in which they appear. Then, in the space provided, write the letter of the meaning closest to that of each word part.

1 a-, an-

- Harold is completely **apolitical**. He never votes and never even seems to know who the candidates are.
- Aspirin is an **analgesic**, or painkiller. If you take it, you will soon be without pain.

___ The word part *a-* or *an-* means   a. true.   b. without.   c. new.

2 bibl-, biblio-

- The first book printed from movable type was the Gutenberg **Bible**.
- Mr. Steffen was a noted **bibliophile**, so when his collection of books was sold, many other book lovers crowded the auction room.

___ The word part *bibl-* or *biblio-* means   a. book.   b. religious doctrine.   c. belief.

3 fid

- People think of dogs as trusty companions. This is reflected in the traditional name "**Fido**," which means "faithful one."
- From the viewpoint of a particular religion, an **infidel** is a person who does not believe in that faith.

___ The word part *fid* means   a. first.   b. loyalty.   c. real.

4 -ism

- **Totalitarianism** is a system of government in which a dictator rules and the state controls every aspect of people's lives.
- William Penn came to America in the 1600s to establish the principles of his religion, **Quakerism**.

___ The word part *-ism* means   a. a set of beliefs.   b. a lack of something.   c. a rank.

5 nov

- People are always trying to sell us something new. This year's **novelty** seems to be trading cards with pictures of mud wrestlers.
- Anya is an **innovative** cook, always thinking of creative, unusual combinations, like sweet potatoes and oranges.

___ The word part *nov* means   a. important.   b. original.   c. realistic.

6 pan-

- As the name implies, the **Pan-American** games involve athletes from all the Americas—North America, Central America, and South America.
- Some people turn to drugs in hopes of finding a **panacea**, a remedy for all the problems in their lives.

___ The word part *pan-* means   a. new.   b. true.   c. entire.

7 prim, prime

___ The word part *prim* or *prime* means

- When you go deep into a forest, you can imagine yourself back in **primeval** times, long before humans appeared on the scene.
- "**Prime**" beef is the highest-quality cut. Unfortunately, it's also highest in fat and in price.

a. first.   b. true.   c. entire.

8 rect

___ The word part *rect* means

- The pool, a large **rectangle**, was surrounded by bushes in rows as straight as the sides of the pool itself.
- We sometimes learn best by trying something new, making a mistake, and then figuring out how to **rectify** the error.

a. real.   b. recent.   c. straight.

9 sym-, syn-

___ The word part *sym-* or *syn-* means

- A **syndrome** is a collection of **symptoms** that normally accompany a particular disease.
- We'd better **synchronize** our watches before the race starts. Let's set them all right now, at exactly 1:46.

a. truth.   b. together.   c. faith.

10 ver

___ The word part *ver* means

- I thought Jesse was lying about having seen a UFO, but when neighbors showed up, they **verified** his story.
- A **verdict** should be an honest statement of how members of the jury have judged a case.

a. together.   b. orderly.   c. true.

Matching Word Parts with Definitions

Following are definitions of the ten word parts. Clearly write or print each word part next to its definition. The sentences above and on the previous page will help you decide on the meaning of each word part.

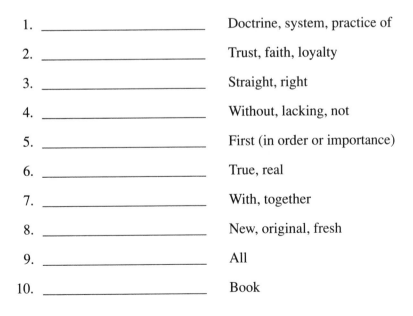

1. _____   Doctrine, system, practice of

2. _____   Trust, faith, loyalty

3. _____   Straight, right

4. _____   Without, lacking, not

5. _____   First (in order or importance)

6. _____   True, real

7. _____   With, together

8. _____   New, original, fresh

9. _____   All

10. _____   Book

CAUTION: Do not go any further until you are sure the above answers are correct. Then you can use the definitions to help you in the following practices. Your goal is eventually to know the word parts well enough so that you don't need to check the definitions at all.

➤ *Sentence Check 1*

Using the answer line provided, complete each *italicized* word in the sentences below with the correct word part from the box. Use each word part once.

a. **a-, an-**	b. **bibl-, biblio-**	c. **fid**	d. **-ism**	e. **nov**
f. **pan-**	g. **prim, prime**	h. **rect**	i. **sym-, syn-**	j. **ver**

_____   1. Vicki has gotten an A on every paper and test in her biology class, so she is (*con . . . ent*) ___ that she'll get an A for the course.

_____   2. I don't know how the magician did it, but he held up the (. . . *y*) ___ card I was thinking of.

_____   3. From the top of the mountain, Cliff was able to take pictures of a breathtaking (. . . *orama*) ___. The entire valley was spread out before him.

_____   4. The (. . . *ary*) ___ grades are generally considered to be kindergarten and first grade.

_____   5. When people say "as the crow flies," they mean in a straight line, a (*di . . .*) ___ route from one place to another.

_____   6. Psychologists often use (. . . *therapy*) ___ to help troubled children. When children read books about others in similar situations, they may be able to work through their own problems.

_____   7. (. . . *onyms*) ___ are words with the same meaning. But even words that are very close in meaning may suggest different things—for example, *break* and *shatter*.

_____   8. (*Hindu . . .*) ___ includes a principle called reincarnation: the belief that when we die, our souls return to earth to exist in new bodies.

_____   9. When she received the (. . . *onymous*) ___ note from "an admirer," Jenny was just itching to know who sent it.

_____   10. Ted and Sara are trying to decide if it's worthwhile trying to (*re . . . ate*) ___ their rickety old farmhouse, or if it would make more sense just to tear it down and build a new one.

NOTE: Now check your answers to these questions by turning to page 176. Going over the answers carefully will help you prepare for the next two practices, for which answers are not given.

➤ *Sentence Check 2*

Using the answer lines provided, complete each *italicized* word in the sentences below with the correct word part from the box. Use each word part once.

_____   1–2. The (. . . *ary*) ___ principle of (. . . *theism*) ___ is that God is the entire
_____   universe and all things and beings within it. In other words, God is ubiquitous°.

_____ 3–4. When they collaborated° on a term paper about (*Naz . . .*) ___, Eddie
_____ and Dina compiled a long (*. . . graphy*) ___ of books dealing with
Hitler, the Nazis, and World War II.

_____ 5–6. A (*. . . phony*) ___ orchestra consists of about a hundred musicians. If
_____ that many people are going to play together as a cohesive° unit, they
must follow the (*di . . . ion*) ___ of the conductor.

_____ 7–8. Animals are said to be (*. . . moral*) ___, having no concept of right or
_____ wrong, but that isn't always (*. . . ified*) ___ by their behavior. For
instance, a dog may slink around guiltily after chewing on the rug.

_____ 9–10. My uncle feels he is on the verge of developing an (*in . . . ative*) ___
_____ gadget that will make a fortune. To keep his idea from being stolen, he
is (*con . . . ing*) ___ in only a few people he really trusts.

➤ *Final Check:* **Alex's Search**

Here is a final opportunity for you to strengthen your knowledge of the ten word parts. First read the following selection carefully. Then complete each *italicized* word in the parentheses below with a word from the box at the top of the previous page. (Context clues will help you figure out which word part goes in which blank.) Use each word part once.

Although Alex was brought up in a Catholic family, he himself never adopted (*Catholic . . .*)
(1)_____, but set off on a search for his own ideas. He read the (*. . . e*)
(2)_____ thoroughly and visited many places where people gather together to
worship—churches, (*. . . agogues*) (3)_____, mosques, and temples—but he
was not attracted by the tenets° of any organized religion. Finally, he developed what he thought
was a (*. . . el*) (4)_____ idea: that God exists in all of nature, in trees, rivers,
and even stones. As he learned more about the beliefs of early humans and more (*. . . itive*)
(5)_____ societies, though, he found that this concept—(*. . . theism*)
(6)_____—was not really new and had existed for a long time and in many
places.

All this estranged° Alex from his parents, who felt that his idea was tantamount° to
(*. . . theism*) (7)_____, the same as saying there is no God at all. They saw
him as an *(in . . . el)* (8)_____ who had abandoned the faith of his own
people, and they begged him to (*. . . ify*) (9)_____ this grievous° error and
return to the Catholic church. Alex, however, argued that since no one could (*. . . ify*)
(10)_____ religious principles scientifically, people should accept the fact
that some beliefs may differ from their own.

Scores Sentence Check 2 _____% Final Check _____%

Enter your scores above and in the vocabulary performance chart on the inside back cover of the book.

UNIT TWO: Review

The box at the right lists twenty-five words from Unit Two. Using the clues at the bottom of the page, fill in these words to complete the puzzle that follows.

attrition
bolster
egocentric
equivocate
exonerate
inquisitive
inundate
liability
liaison
ostracize
prolific
raucous
recourse
reinstate
reiterate
replete
reticent
robust
sham
solace
solicitous
tenet
terse
utopia
vociferous

ACROSS

2. Expressing feelings loudly
4. A gradual natural decrease in number; becoming fewer
6. Showing or expressing concern, care, or attention
7. Something that acts as a disadvantage; drawback
8. Plentifully supplied
10. To hold up, strengthen, or reinforce
11. Curious; eager to learn
18. To restore to a previous position or condition
19. Comfort in sorrow or misfortune; consolation
21. An ideal or perfect place or state
23. Self-centered; seeing everything in terms of oneself
24. To clear of an accusation or charge; prove innocent
25. Quiet or uncommunicative; reluctant to speak out

DOWN

1. Healthy and strong; vigorous
3. To be deliberately vague in order to mislead
5. A person who serves as a connection between individuals or groups
9. Producing many works, results, or offspring; fertile
12. A pretense or counterfeit; something meant to deceive
13. Brief and clear
14. To expel or exclude
15. Noisy and disorderly
16. To state again or repeatedly
17. A source of help, security, or strength; something to turn to
20. To cover, as by flooding; overwhelm with a large number or amount
22. A belief or principle held to be true by an individual or group

UNIT TWO: Test 1

PART A
Choose the word that best completes each item and write it in the space provided.

_____ 1. Peter has a(n) ___ to tell people what they want to hear. As a result, he's engaged to three women.

    a. utopia   b. propensity   c. attrition   d. contingency

_____ 2. My high-school pals and I were a ___ group. We stuck together through good times and bad.

    a. prolific   b. bureaucratic   c. cohesive   d. terse

_____ 3. In almost any job, being unable to read is a definite ___.

    a. recourse   b. mandate   c. tenet   d. liability

_____ 4. Felipe seems so ___ today that it's hard to believe he was close to death only two months ago.

    a. robust   b. terse   c. indigenous   d. superfluous

_____ 5. When I asked my father if he liked my new dress, he ___, saying, "That green is a terrific color."

    a. inundated   b. equivocated   c. ostracized   d. depreciated

_____ 6. Although Marian is open and talkative when the two of us are alone, she is ___ around other people.

    a. reticent   b. replete   c. prolific   d. predisposed

_____ 7. At age 10, my cousin still has a ___ belief in Santa Claus. She becomes upset at any suggestion that he doesn't exist.

    a. sedentary   b. tenacious   c. tantamount d. nebulous

_____ 8. The math instructor ___ his explanation of the problem several times because his students were having difficulty understanding it.

    a. depreciated   b. reiterated   c. exonerated   d. circumvented

_____ 9. Because of the ___ nature of drug dealing, it is very difficult to stop.

    a. terse   b. clandestine   c. solicitous   d. fortuitous

_____ 10. The table at the coffee shop was wobbly, and the muffins were hard as rocks. So we used one of the muffins to ___ the short leg of the table.

    a. inundate   b. exonerate   c. bolster   d. depreciate

_____ 11. Janet opened her own business because she hated the ___ system at her last job. But she soon found herself making just as many strict rules to keep her own workers in line.

    a. bureaucratic   b. solicitous   c. impeccable   d. vociferous

(Continues on next page)

_____ 12. The managers at Brian's company refused to ___ the early-retirement plan proposed by the union because they felt the plan would cost too much.

      a. ostracize   b. sanction   c. inundate   d. circumvent

_____ 13. A modern American wedding is ___ with customs originally intended to ensure the couple's fertility, including having a wedding cake, throwing rice, and tying shoes to the back of the car.

      a. tantamount   b. inquisitive   c. replete   d. grievous

PART B
Write **C** if the italicized word is used **correctly**. Write **I** if the word is used **incorrectly**.

_____ 14. Food, air, and water are *superfluous* to human life.

_____ 15. A big sign in the college library read, "*Raucous* Study Only."

_____ 16. Theo's behavior toward his sister is *reprehensible*. He shouldn't be allowed to mistreat her so.

_____ 17. For many people, hearing a boyfriend or girlfriend say, "I just want to be friends" is *tantamount* to total rejection.

_____ 18. Some people invest in art and antiques, hoping that their investments will eventually *depreciate*.

_____ 19. After sitting in a small office all day, Ingrid enjoyed more *sedentary* activities, such as racquetball or tennis.

_____ 20. In my grandmother's nursing home, only one nurse was *solicitous*. The others gave her almost no care.

_____ 21. Frannie's conversation is so *nebulous* that I always know exactly what she thinks and feels about a subject.

_____ 22. After getting no satisfaction at the car dealership, Mom decided that her best *recourse* would be the president of the company.

_____ 23. When Clarence arrived at camp, he was immediately *ostracized* by the other campers. He was thrilled to be so warmly welcomed.

_____ 24. A tall tree *indigenous* to Australia has been successfully transplanted to the edge of the Sahara Desert, where it keeps the desert from spreading.

_____ 25. My cousin is so *egocentric* that when the family got together for his sister's graduation, he assumed the gathering was in honor of his new job as manager of a fast-food restaurant.

Score   (Number correct) _____ x 4 = _____ %

Enter your score above and in the vocabulary performance chart on the inside back cover of the book.

UNIT TWO: Test 2

PART A
Complete each item with a word from the box. Use each word once.

a. **circumvent**	b. **exonerate**	c. **grievous**	d. **inundate**	e. **mandate**
f. **oblivious**	g. **predisposed**	h. **prolific**	i. **sham**	j. **solace**
k. **tenet**	l. **utopia**	m. **vociferous**		

_____ 1. I hate mornings. My idea of a(n) ___ would be a world in which no job or class began before noon.

_____ 2. The local election made the voters' ___ clear: Build more neighborhood parks.

_____ 3. People who ignore their elderly parents do them a(n) ___ wrong.

_____ 4. We tried to ___ the construction area by taking the other highway, but that road was being repaired too.

_____ 5. The main ___ of the "Girls Are Great" club is that girls can do anything boys can do.

_____ 6. Gerry was accused of stealing a wallet but was ___(e)d when the wallet was found in another student's locker.

_____ 7. Because his father and grandfather both had heart disease, my cousin worries that he may be ___ to the same disorder.

_____ 8. Susan signed in and began work, ___ to the fact that she had forgotten to change from her bedroom slippers into her shoes.

_____ 9. When the Bakers' young daughter died last year, they found ___ with a support group of other parents who had also lost a child.

_____ 10. After telling a reader to kick her boyfriend out, the newspaper advice columnist was ___(e)d with thousands of letters saying she was wrong.

_____ 11. When three-year-old Ginger doesn't get what she wants, her protests are so ___ that you can hear her all over the neighborhood.

_____ 12. The invitation we sent my parents to attend a friend's birthday party was a(n) ___. We were actually giving a surprise party in honor of their anniversary.

_____ 13. The most ___ woman on record is a Russian peasant who lived in the early 1700s. She gave birth to sixty-nine children—sixteen pairs of twins, seven sets of triplets, and four sets of quadruplets.

(Continues on next page)

PART B
Write **C** if the italicized word is used **correctly**. Write **I** if the word is used **incorrectly**.

_____ 14. My meeting with Phil was *fortuitous*. We had planned to meet ever since he registered for the conference in my hometown.

_____ 15. Doris calls herself *inquisitive* because she likes to ask people so many questions, but personally, I think she's just plain nosy.

_____ 16. My brother's choice of friends is *indiscriminate*. He refuses to associate with people whose idea of a good time is stealing a car.

_____ 17. The student expelled for drug possession was *reinstated* in school only after completing a rehabilitation program.

_____ 18. My uncle is quite *terse*. He talks for at least an hour every time I call him.

_____ 19. In the overcrowded school, math classes were *relegated* to trailers behind the gym.

_____ 20. Sally's appearance was *impeccable*. Even her fingernails were dirty.

_____ 21. Our company has grown by leaps and bounds through *attrition*.

_____ 22. Although they planned an outdoor wedding, Heather and Tony wanted to be prepared for any *contingency*. So they rented a large tent, in case of rain.

_____ 23. As a *liaison* between the hospital staff and patients' families, Jon helped provide information about patients' conditions in language their families could understand.

_____ 24. When she went away to college, Beth established her *autonomy* by calling her parents every day and asking their advice on each decision she faced, no matter how small.

_____ 25. It seems *incongruous* that the Taylors, who are so health-conscious, should allow their children to sit in front of the TV for hours each day, munching on chips and cookies.

Score   (Number correct) _____ x 4 = _____ %

Enter your score above and in the vocabulary performance chart on the inside back cover of the book.

UNIT TWO: Test 3

PART A

Complete each sentence in a way that clearly shows you understand the meaning of the **boldfaced** word. Take a minute to plan your answer before you write.

Example: On our picnic, we carried a basket **replete** with ____*a complete meal and plenty of snacks*____ .

1. A very **terse** answer to the question "Did you have fun at the dentist's office?" is " _____
   _____ ."

2. A loud voice would probably be a **liability** in _____
   _____ .

3. One good way to **bolster** a friend's spirits is to _____
   _____ .

4. Marcie has a tendency to be **vociferous**. When the waitress brought her the wrong food, for example,
   _____
   _____ .

5. Reverend Patterson's appearance is **incongruous** with my image of a minister. He wears _____
   _____ .

6. When Barb's grandfather died, she found **solace** in _____
   _____ .

7. Vanessa is so **egocentric** that _____
   _____ .

8. I have a **propensity** to _____
   _____ .

9. One way to **circumvent** rush-hour traffic is to _____
   _____ .

10. My idea of a **utopia** is _____
    _____ .

(Continues on next page)

PART B

After each **boldfaced** word are a *synonym* (a word that means the same as the boldfaced word), an *antonym* (a word that means the opposite of the boldfaced word), and a word that is neither. On the answer line, write the letter of the word that is the antonym.

Example: __b__ **fortuitous**   a. accidental   b. planned   c. risky

____ 11. **reprehensible**   a. forbidden   b. admirable   c. blameworthy

____ 12. **robust**   a. healthy   b. dangerous   c. weak

____ 13. **prolific**   a. infertile   b. large   c. fruitful

____ 14. **oblivious**   a. exciting   b. aware   c. unaware

____ 15. **nebulous**   a. clear   b. large   c. vague

PART C

Use five of the following ten words in sentences. Make it clear that you know the meaning of each word you use. Feel free to use the past tense or plural form of a word.

a. **autonomy**	b. **clandestine**	c. **depreciate**	d. **exonerate**	e. **inquisitive**
f. **raucous**	g. **reiterate**	h. **relegate**	i. **sedentary**	j. **sham**

16. _____

_____

17. _____

_____

18. _____

_____

19. _____

_____

20. _____

_____

Score   (Number correct) _____ x 5 = _____%

UNIT TWO: Test 4 (Word Parts)

PART A
Listed in the left-hand column below are ten common word parts, along with words in which the parts are used. In each blank, write in the letter of the correct definition on the right.

Word Parts	Examples	Definitions
____ 1. **a-, an-**	apolitical, analgesic	a. First (in order or importance)
____ 2. **bibl-, biblio-**	Bible, bibliophile	b. All
____ 3. **fid**	Fido, infidel	c. Without, lacking, not
____ 4. **-ism**	totalitarianism, Quakerism	d. New, original, fresh
____ 5. **nov**	novelty, innovative	e. Straight, right
____ 6. **pan**	Pan-American, panacea	f. Doctrine, system, practice of
____ 7. **prim, prime**	primeval, prime	g. Trust, faith, loyalty
____ 8. **rect**	rectangle, rectify	h. Book
____ 9. **sym-, syn-**	symptom, synchronize	i. True, real
____ 10. **ver**	verify, verdict	j. With, together

PART B
Using the answer line provided, complete each *italicized* word in the sentences below with the correct word part from the box. Not every word part will be used.

a. **an-**	b. **biblio-**	c. **fid**	d. **-ism**	e. **nov**
f. **pan-**	g. **prime**	h. **rect**	i. **syn-**	j. **ver**

_____ 11. My uncle, a(n) (. . . *phile*) ___, collects rare and beautiful books.

_____ 12. Zen (*Buddh . . .*) ___ stresses meditation and self-reliance.

_____ 13. (. . . *orexia*) "___" means a lack of appetite for food.

_____ 14. The (. . . *-American*) ___ Highway runs from Alaska to Chile, linking all the Americas.

_____ 15. Musical comedies are a(n) (. . . *thesis*) ___ of several arts, bringing together dancing, singing, and acting.

(Continues on next page)

PART C

Use your knowledge of word parts to determine the meaning of the **boldfaced** words. On the answer line, write the letter of each meaning.

_____ 16. Jessica was a **novice** at carpentry.

      a. an expert   b. a beginner   c. a worker

_____ 17. The book is an outdated **primer** on chemistry.

      a. a first book   b. an argument   c. a workbook

_____ 18. The church teaches **rectitude**.

      a. righteousness   b. patience   c. the masses

_____ 19. The jurors doubted the **veracity** of the defense attorney's witness.

      a. memory   b. intentions   c. honesty

_____ 20. The President's wife is his friend and **confidant**.

      a. an admirer   b. the mother of his children   c. a person one trusts
                                                                        enough to tell secrets to

Score (Number correct) _____ x 5 = _____%

Unit Three

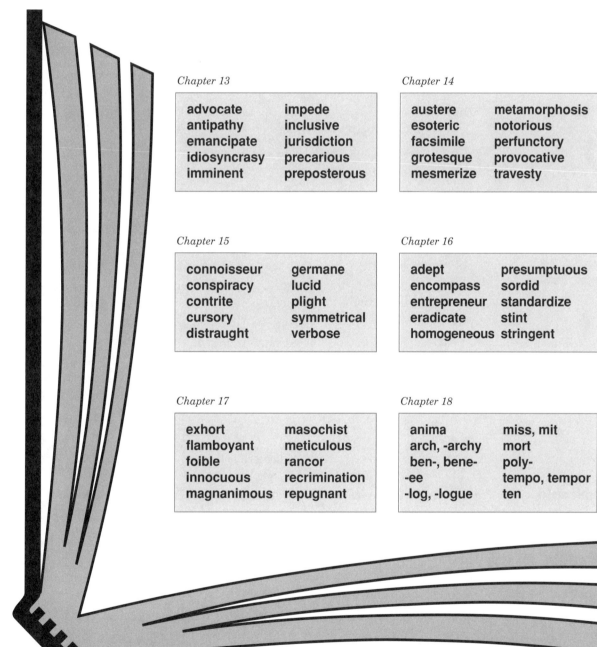

Chapter 13

advocate	impede
antipathy	inclusive
emancipate	jurisdiction
idiosyncrasy	precarious
imminent	preposterous

Chapter 14

austere	metamorphosis
esoteric	notorious
facsimile	perfunctory
grotesque	provocative
mesmerize	travesty

Chapter 15

connoisseur	germane
conspiracy	lucid
contrite	plight
cursory	symmetrical
distraught	verbose

Chapter 16

adept	presumptuous
encompass	sordid
entrepreneur	standardize
eradicate	stint
homogeneous	stringent

Chapter 17

exhort	masochist
flamboyant	meticulous
foible	rancor
innocuous	recrimination
magnanimous	repugnant

Chapter 18

anima	miss, mit
arch, -archy	mort
ben-, bene-	poly-
-ee	tempo, tempor
-log, -logue	ten

CHAPTER

13

advocate	impede
antipathy	inclusive
emancipate	jurisdiction
idiosyncrasy	precarious
imminent	preposterous

Ten Words in Context

In the space provided, write the letter of the meaning closest to that of each **boldfaced** word. Use the context of the sentences to help you figure out each word's meaning.

1 advocate
(ăd′və-kāt′)
-verb

- One author was refused permission to give a speech on campus because he **advocates** violence as a means of social reform.
- Some gardeners consider chemicals and pesticides harmful; instead, they **advocate** using "organic" methods of growing fruits and vegetables.

__ *Advocate* means   a. to oppose.   b. to promote.   c. to understand.

2 antipathy
(ăn-tĭ′pə-thē)
-noun

- Bud's parents didn't understand why he hated school until they found that the reason for his **antipathy** was poor eyesight: he couldn't see the chalkboard.
- I can't believe that my sister is going to marry Frank. Just a few months ago, she showed complete **antipathy** toward him.

__ *Antipathy* means   a. a strong dislike.   b. a lack of concern.   c. a preference.

3 emancipate
(ē-măn′sĭ-pāt′)
-verb

- The salesman promised that his amazing machine—a vacuum cleaner, floor polisher, and carpet shampooer in one—would **emancipate** us from hours of backbreaking housework.
- When the Allies entered Germany at the end of World War II, they **emancipated** many foreigners and political prisoners who had been used as slave laborers in German industries.

__ *Emancipate* means   a. to encourage.   b. to administer justice.   c. to free.

4 idiosyncrasy
(ĭd′ē-ō-sĭng′krə-sē)
-noun

- My uncle asks very personal questions, but please don't be offended—it's just an **idiosyncrasy** of his. He doesn't realize how odd it seems to others.
- For as long as I've known Clara, she's had the unusual **idiosyncrasy** of dressing only in black.

__ *Idiosyncrasy* means   a. a personal habit.   b. a dangerous habit.   c. a selfish habit.

5 imminent
(ĭm′ə-nənt)
-adjective

- We canceled the picnic because a thunderstorm seemed **imminent**.
- As word spread that the king's death was **imminent**, the people began to gather at the palace gates. They wanted to be nearby when he died.

__ *Imminent* means   a. over.   b. delayed.   c. likely to occur soon.

6 impede
(ĭm-pēd′)
-verb

- Muddy roads **impeded** the progress of the trucks bringing food to the refugees.
- The construction work at the mall **impeded** shoppers, who had to step around piles of planks, cables, crates, tools, and sacks of cement.

__ *Impede* means   a. to oppress.   b. to hinder.   c. to include.

7 **inclusive**
(ĭn-kloo′sĭv)
-adjective

• The medical center's annual fee is **inclusive**, covering all visits, tests, treatments, and other services.

• The newspaper's coverage of the trial was **inclusive**; day by day, it printed a word-for-word transcript of the courtroom proceedings.

___ *Inclusive* means   a. complete.   b. lacking something.   c. about to start.

8 **jurisdiction**
(joor′ĭs-dĭk′shən)
-noun

• Shakespeare's theater, the Globe, was built across the river from London. Officials had forbidden theaters in London, but the other side of the river was beyond their **jurisdiction**.

• The United States has no **jurisdiction** over foreign embassies on American soil; those embassies are under the authority of their own governments.

___ *Jurisdiction* means   a. advice.   b. beliefs.   c. control.

9 **precarious**
(prē-kâr′ē-əs)
-adjective

• The icy roads made travel **precarious**.

• The old, worn-out electrical wiring in the building puts all the residents in a **precarious** position. At any moment, it could fail, causing a fire.

___ *Precarious* means   a. unsafe.   b. illegal.   c. unusual.

10 **preposterous**
(prē-pŏs′tər-əs)
-adjective

• Louis always comes up with **preposterous** get-rich-quick schemes. Now he wants to open a doughnut shop in Antarctica.

• The discovery of x-rays in 1895 was followed by some **preposterous** ideas and fears. For example, merchants in England sold "x-ray-proof" underwear.

___ *Preposterous* means   a. risky.   b. exciting.   c. ridiculous.

Matching Words with Definitions

Following are definitions of the ten words. Clearly write or print each word next to its definition. The sentences above and on the previous page will help you decide on the meaning of each word.

1. _____   To delay or slow; get in the way of

2. _____   Including much or everything; broad or complete in coverage

3. _____   To speak or write in favor of; support

4. _____   The authority to administer justice; authority; range or extent of authority

5. _____   A strong dislike or distaste; hatred

6. _____   To set free from slavery, captivity, or oppression

7. _____   Contrary to nature or reason and thus laughable; absurd

8. _____   A personal peculiarity; quirk

9. _____   Dangerous; risky; dangerously uncertain

10. _____   About to happen

CAUTION: Do not go any further until you are sure the above answers are correct. Then you can use the definitions to help you in the following practices. Your goal is eventually to know the words well enough so that you don't need to check the definitions at all.

➤ *Sentence Check 1*

Using the answer line provided, complete each item below with the correct word from the box. Use each word once.

a. **advocate**	b. **antipathy**	c. **emancipate**	d. **idiosyncrasy**	e. **imminent**
f. **impede**	g. **inclusive**	h. **jurisdiction**	i. **precarious**	j. **preposterous**

_____ 1. For someone allergic to insect bites, beekeeping would be a(n) ___ occupation.

_____ 2. Nutritionists today ___ a diet low in fats and high in fiber.

_____ 3. The caterer's services were really ___: food, wine, flowers, decorations, coat check, music, and master of ceremonies.

_____ 4. When the jury's verdict was ___, the lawyers, reporters, and spectators hastily returned to the courtroom.

_____ 5. I swore that nothing would keep me from getting to Gloria's wedding on time, but I was ___(e)d by a traffic jam.

_____ 6. One aim of the modern women's liberation movement is to ___ women from job and wage discrimination.

_____ 7. Since the bank robbery had involved crossing state lines, the federal government had ___ in the case.

_____ 8. Burt has a(n) ___ for everything that isn't "100 percent American." He thinks it makes him a patriot, but I think a dislike of foreigners or foreign ways shows ignorance.

_____ 9. When my little boy said there was a frog in his glass of milk, I laughed at his ___ idea—until I looked and saw that a frog really was there.

_____ 10. Tamiko always takes off her shoes off before entering the house. Ralph thought this was just a(n) ___ of hers, but he later learned that it's a Japanese custom.

NOTE: Now check your answers to these questions by turning to page 176. Going over the answers carefully will help you prepare for the next two practices, for which answers are not given.

➤ *Sentence Check 2*

Using the answer lines provided, complete each item below with **two** words from the box. Use each word once.

_____
_____ 1–2. One member of the school board ___s a more ___ high school curriculum, with courses in subjects such as parenting and preserving the environment as well as the more traditional academic subjects.

_____
_____ 3–4. Chet refuses to use a telephone. For most people, this ___ would certainly ___ their attempts to have a social life, but Chet isn't very gregarious° anyway.

_____ 5–6. Being outdoors in an electrical storm is a(n) ___ situation. When a
_____   storm is ___, the optimum° strategy is to go indoors and stay there.

_____ 7–8. During the Civil War, President Lincoln's administration could not
_____   actually ___ the slaves because his government had no ___ in the
                             South.

_____ 9–10. Ellen's ___ toward Jack is based on her ___ but tenacious° belief that
_____   he's an evil alien from a distant planet.

➤ *Final Check:* Ann's Love of Animals

Here is a final opportunity for you to strengthen your knowledge of the ten words. First read the following selection carefully. Then fill in each blank with a word from the box at the top of the previous page. (Context clues will help you figure out which word goes in which blank.) Use each word once.

Perhaps more than anyone else I know, Ann cares about animals. Her affection for them is all-

(1)_____, extending even to animals others find less appealing, such as rats,

which she keeps as pets. Because she loves animals, Ann hates to see them caged. She objects to

anything that (2)_____s any creature's movements. This explains a(n)

(3)_____ of hers: she lets her pet white rats run freely throughout her

apartment.

Ann's view of cages has also led to a strong (4)_____ toward zoos.

If Ann had (5)_____ over all the zoos in the world, she would make

them illegal and (6)_____ all the animals from their captivity. Many

people will argue that zoos protect animals, but Ann scoffs° at this idea, saying it's

(7)_____ because animals often die when they are being trapped for zoos

or shipped to zoos. She believes that the most (8)_____ life in the wild is

preferable to the safest life in captivity.

Of course, Ann realizes that her utopia°—a society with no cages or zoos—is far from

(9)_____. Nevertheless, her spirit has not been squelched°, and she

continues to (10)_____ freeing the animals in the hope that someday the

zoos will close their gates forever.

Scores Sentence Check 2 _____%	Final Check _____%

Enter your scores above and in the vocabulary performance chart on the inside back cover of the book.

CHAPTER

14

austere	metamorphosis
esoteric	notorious
facsimile	perfunctory
grotesque	provocative
mesmerize	travesty

Ten Words in Context

In the space provided, write the letter of the meaning closest to that of each **boldfaced** word. Use the context of the sentences to help you figure out each word's meaning.

1 **austere**
(ô-stîr′)
-*adjective*

- Ms. Stone's appearance was **austere**. She wore plain, quiet clothing with no jewelry, and she never used makeup.
- The walls in Alan's den are white and nearly bare, and his white furniture has simple lines. This **austere** decor gives the room a pleasantly calm mood.

__ *Austere* means   a. very ugly.   b. very plain.   c. very youthful.

2 **esoteric**
(ĕs′ə-tĕr′ĭk)
-*adjective*

- The instruction manuals that come with computer software often use such **esoteric** terms that they seem to be written in a foreign language.
- The poetry of Ezra Pound, filled with references to ancient Greek culture, is too **esoteric** for most readers.

__ *Esoteric* means   a. difficult to understand.   b. shallow.   c. unfavorable.

3 **facsimile**
(făk-sĭm′ə-lē)
-*noun*

- When a **facsimile** of an old Sears-Roebuck catalogue was published recently, it became a bestseller. People enjoyed seeing what was for sale a century ago.
- The word *fax* is short for **facsimile**. With a fax machine, you can send a precise image of a document across the country electronically in seconds.

__ *Facsimile* means   a. an original.   b. a distorted version.   c. an accurate copy.

4 **grotesque**
(grō-tĕsk′)
-*adjective*

- Most people found the movie character E.T. adorable, but I thought the little alien was **grotesque**, with its weird combination of babyish features and old, wrinkled skin.
- The clown made **grotesque** faces, squinting his eyes, pulling down the corners of his mouth, and sticking out his tongue.

__ *Grotesque* means   a. strange-looking.   b. hard to understand.   c. charming.

5 **mesmerize**
(mĕz′mə-rīz′)
-*verb*

- The intense eyes of the woman in the photograph **mesmerized** me. I couldn't take my eyes off the picture.
- When driving at night, you can become **mesmerized** by the lines on the road or by other cars' headlights or taillights. To avoid a hypnotic state, keep your eyes moving from front to side to rearview mirror.

__ *Mesmerize* means   a. to amuse.   b. to fascinate.   c. to distort.

6 **metamorphosis**
(mĕt′ə-môr′fĕ-sĭs)
-*noun*

- A caterpillar's transformation into a butterfly is a well-known example of **metamorphosis**.
- In Franz Kafka's famous story "The **Metamorphosis**," a man wakes up on his thirtieth birthday to discover that he has turned into an enormous insect.

__ *Metamorphosis* means   a. a change in form.   b. a disaster.   c. a scientific theory.

7 notorious
(nō-tôr′ē-əs)
-adjective

- Batman and Robin matched wits with the Joker and the Penguin, who were **notorious** for their evil deeds.
- The campus cafeteria is **notorious** for bitter coffee, soggy vegetables, limp salads, and mystery meat.

__ *Notorious* means   a. regarded negatively.   b. regarded with curiosity.   c. ignored.

8 perfunctory
(pər-fŭnk′tə-rē)
-adjective

- The doctor's examination was **perfunctory**. He seemed to be just going through the motions without taking any interest in the patient.
- Most of the candidates were passionate on the subject of nuclear weapons, but one spoke in a very **perfunctory** way, apparently bored with the topic.

__ *Perfunctory* means   a. uninterested.   b. enthusiastic.   c. exaggerated.

9 provocative
(prō-vŏk′ə-tĭv)
-adjective

- "A good essay is **provocative**," said our English instructor. "It gets the reader interested and attentive from the very first paragraph."
- To arouse the viewers' curiosity, the television ad began with a **provocative** image: a spaceship landing on a baseball field, at home plate.

__ *Provocative* means   a. predictable.   b. difficult to understand.   c. attention-getting.

10 travesty
(trăv′ĭs-tē)
-noun

- The fraternity skit, a **travesty** of college life, exaggerated and ridiculed many campus activities.
- The musical comedy version of *Hamlet* was a **travesty**. The critics and audience agreed that it made a mockery of Shakespeare's profound tragedy.

__ *Travesty* means   a. a joking, disrespectful imitation.   b. an exact copy.   c. a simple version.

Matching Words with Definitions

Following are definitions of the ten words. Clearly write or print each word next to its definition. The sentences above and on the previous page will help you decide on the meaning of each word.

1. _____   To hypnotize or fascinate; hold spellbound
2. _____   A great or complete change; transformation
3. _____   A crude, exaggerated, or ridiculous representation; mockery
4. _____   Done only as a routine, with little care or interest; performed with no interest or enthusiasm
5. _____   Known widely but unfavorably; having a bad reputation
6. _____   Tending to arouse interest or curiosity
7. _____   An exact copy or reproduction
8. _____   Intended for or understood by only a certain group; beyond the understanding of most people
9. _____   Without decoration or luxury; severely simple
10. _____   Distorted or strikingly inconsistent in shape, appearance, or manner

CAUTION: Do not go any further until you are sure the above answers are correct. Then you can use the definitions to help you in the following practices. Your goal is eventually to know the words well enough so that you don't need to check the definitions at all.

➤ *Sentence Check 1*

Using the answer line provided, complete each item below with the correct word from the box. Use each word once.

a. **austere**	b. **esoteric**	c. **facsimile**	d. **grotesque**	e. **mesmerize**
f. **metamorphosis**	g. **notorious**	h. **perfunctory**	i. **provocative**	j. **travesty**

_____ 1. The trial was a ___ of justice because several of the jurors had been bribed.

_____ 2. The ___ killer known as Jack the Ripper brutally murdered at least five prostitutes in London in 1888.

_____ 3. To capture readers' attention, an author sometimes begins an article with a(n) ___ question, such as, "Which do you think is more dangerous, climbing stairs or parachuting out of an airplane?"

_____ 4. In some modern paintings, human figures are distorted into such ___ shapes that it's hard to recognize facial features and body parts.

_____ 5. Lining the music school's hallway are framed ___s of handwritten pages of music by great composers.

_____ 6. Legal documents are usually worded in such ___ language that most people need a lawyer to translate the "legalese" into plain English.

_____ 7. As I stood looking at the grandfather clock, I became ___(e)d by the shiny pendulum that swung back and forth, back and forth, back and forth.

_____ 8. Usually the therapist showed great interest in her patients, but today she was too worried about her own family to give more than ___ responses.

_____ 9. Our dormitory room is rather ___, with cement-block walls and bare floors, but we've made it less stark by hanging colorful posters and adding bright bedspreads and cushions.

_____10. The magician David Copperfield does a trick called "___." One person is chained and locked in a box. When the box is opened, that person is gone and someone else is chained there instead.

NOTE: Now check your answers to these questions by turning to page 176. Going over the answers carefully will help you prepare for the next two practices, for which answers are not given.

➤ *Sentence Check 2*

Using the answer lines provided, complete each item below with **two** words from the box. Use each word once.

_____ 1–2. The political cartoon showed the judge as a(n) ___ figure, with a huge
_____ belly and a gaping mouth. To me it's unfair— a ___ of journalistic ethics.

_____ 3–4. The cat burglar in the film, ___ for stealing expensive jewelry,
_____ committed all his robberies wearing a(n) ___ outfit: a black T-shirt, plain black pants, black shoes, and black gloves.

_____   5–6. The novel has a(n) ___ opening scene, in which a young woman and
_____   her parrot sneak out of a house on a ladder. The novel goes on to ___
                               the reader with one spellbinding episode after another.

_____   7–8. Former principals had made only ___ efforts to rid the school of drugs,
_____   but the new principal attacked the problem head-on. As a result, the
                               school has undergone a ___ from "hooked" to "clean."

_____   9–10. At the jewelers' convention, ___s of several famous gems were on
_____   display. I enjoyed seeing them, but I didn't understand the accompanying
                                ___ explanation of the technical methods used to produce the copies.

➤ *Final Check:* A Costume Party

Here is a final opportunity for you to strengthen your knowledge of the ten words. First read the following
selection carefully. Then fill in each blank with a word from the box at the top of the previous page.
(Context clues will help you figure out which word goes in which blank.) Use each word once.

On the afternoon of a friend's New Year's Eve costume party, I made only a(n)
(1)_____ effort to put a costume together. Unenthusiastic about spending
much time on this, I wanted to do something as simple as possible, even if the effect would be
rather (2)_____. I decided on a ghost costume—just a plain sheet with
eyeholes cut out. Since all my sheets are green, I had to be the ghost of a frog.

The party began for me with a rather (3)_____ encounter: the door
was opened by Elizabeth Taylor, wearing her famous sixty-nine-carat diamond—or at least a very
good (4)_____ of it. Then, when I went inside, the first men I saw were
two (5)_____ pirates, Blackbeard and Captain Hook. I listened in on their
conversation, expecting to be (6)_____(e)d by fascinating tales of cut-throat
adventures; instead I heard only the (7)_____ language of two math majors.

Giving up any hope of understanding their remarks, I looked around for my own friends. But
their (8)_____ from ordinary people to famous or odd people was so
complete that I couldn't recognize anyone. Most of the costumes were in good taste. One, though,
struck me as a (9)_____: a person dressed as Abraham Lincoln—a
President I venerate° for his character and leadership—was wearing a bull's-eye target, in crude
mockery of President Lincoln's assassination. Another person looked frighteningly
(10)_____, with a mouth twisted to one side and three eyes, all of different
sizes.

In the course of the evening, I also met Cleopatra, Shakespeare, and Snoopy, among others. I
may never again spend time at a gathering replete° with so many celebrities.

Scores Sentence Check 2 _____%	Final Check _____%

Enter your scores above and in the vocabulary performance chart on the inside back cover of the book.

CHAPTER

15

connoisseur	germane
conspiracy	lucid
contrite	plight
cursory	symmetrical
distraught	verbose

Ten Words in Context

In the space provided, write the letter of the meaning closest to that of each **boldfaced** word. Use the context of the sentences to help you figure out each word's meaning.

1 **connoisseur**
(kŏn′ə-sûr′)
-noun

• My sister is a **connoisseur** of Southern novels. She's read dozens of them, and she knows all about the authors and their different styles.

• Curtis has broad knowledge of French wines—where they are made, when they are at their best, and exactly how each one tastes. He's a true **connoisseur**.

__ *Connoisseur* means a. a doubter. b. an authority. c. a leader.

2 **conspiracy**
(kən-spĭr′ə-sē)
-noun

• The **conspiracy** to overthrow the government was started by two of the premier's own advisors.

• Although only Lee Harvey Oswald was arrested for the assassination of President Kennedy, many believe there was a **conspiracy** to kill the President.

__ *Conspiracy* means a. a plot. b. an idea. c. an announcement.

3 **contrite**
(kən-trīt′)
-adjective

• Dolores was especially **contrite** about tearing her sister's dress because she'd borrowed it without permission.

• Judges are often more lenient with offenders who truly regret their crimes. A criminal who seems genuinely **contrite** may get a shorter sentence.

__ *Contrite* means a. angry. b. confused. c. sorry.

4 **cursory**
(kûr′sə-rē)
-adjective

• Leah spent a full week studying for the exam. Joyce, however, gave her text-book only a **cursory** review, flipping through the pages an hour before the test.

• This morning, the mechanic was short of time and gave my car only a **cursory** inspection. He said he'd check it thoroughly later and then give me an estimate.

__ *Cursory* means a. thorough. b. hurried. c. wordy.

5 **distraught**
(dĭ-strôt′)
-adjective

• The parents of the little girl who wandered off in the crowded mall were **distraught** until she was found.

• As the snowstorm got worse and worse and my wife still hadn't arrived home from work, I became increasingly **distraught**.

__ *Distraught* means a. anxious. b. busy. c. forgetful.

6 **germane**
(jər-mān′)
-adjective

• Stacy went to the law library to look up information that might be **germane** to her client's case.

• It bothered Christine when her new boss asked if she had a boyfriend. That information certainly wasn't **germane** to her work.

__ *Germane* means a. damaging. b. related. c. foreign.

84

7 **lucid**
(loo'sĭd)
-adjective

- I usually find computer manuals horribly unclear, but this one is **lucid**.
- The scientist's explanation of the greenhouse effect was so **lucid** that the entire audience was able to grasp it.

___ *Lucid* means   a. easy to understand.   b. repetitious.   c. fair to both sides.

8 **plight**
(plīt')
-noun

- The **plight** of the homeless can be somewhat relieved by decent shelters.
- There were reports of a cave-in at the mine, but it was too soon to know much about the **plight** of the trapped miners.

___ *Plight* means   a. a delayed situation.   b. an unlikely situation.   c. an unfortunate situation.

9 **symmetrical**
(sĭ-mĕ'trĭ-kəl)
-adjective

- The children's sandcastle was **symmetrical**, with a wall on each side and a tower and flag at each end.
- No one's face is perfectly **symmetrical**. For example, one eye is usually slightly higher than the other, and the left and right sides of the mouth differ.

___ *Symmetrical* means   a. unique.   b. beautiful.   c. balanced.

10 **verbose**
(vər-bōs')
-adjective

- The **verbose** senator said, "At this point in time, we have an urgent and important need for more monetary funds to declare unconditional war on drugs and combat this evil and harmful situation." The reporter wrote, "The senator said we urgently need more money to fight drugs."
- Gabe is the most **verbose** person I know. He always uses ten words when one would do.

___ *Verbose* means   a. loud.   b. wordy.   c. self-important.

Matching Words with Definitions

Following are definitions of the ten words. Clearly write or print each word next to its definition. The sentences above and on the previous page will help you decide on the meaning of each word.

1. _____   Very troubled; distressed

2. _____   Using or containing too many words

3. _____   Done quickly with little attention to detail; not thorough

4. _____   Having to do with the issue at hand; relevant

5. _____   Clearly expressed; easily understood

6. _____   Truly sorry for having done wrong; repentant

7. _____   Well proportioned; balanced; the same on both sides

8. _____   An expert in fine art or in matters of taste

9. _____   A situation marked by difficulty, hardship, or misfortune

10. _____   A secret plot by two or more people, especially for a harmful or illegal purpose

CAUTION: Do not go any further until you are sure the above answers are correct. Then you can use the definitions to help you in the following practices. Your goal is eventually to know the words well enough so that you don't need to check the definitions at all.

➤ *Sentence Check 1*

Using the answer line provided, complete each item below with the correct word from the box. Use each word once.

a. **connoisseur**	b. **conspiracy**	c. **contrite**	d. **cursory**	e. **distraught**
f. **germane**	g. **lucid**	h. **plight**	i. **symmetrical**	j. **verbose**

_____ 1. Claire was truly sorry for having started the argument with Sal. To show how ___ she felt, she sent him a special note of apology.

_____ 2. Everyone is greatly concerned about the ___ of the hostages. We're not even certain they're still alive.

_____ 3. The garden is ___, with the same flowers and shrubs, arranged in the same pattern, on each side of a central path.

_____ 4. A ___ of Asian art told me that my Chinese vase is very old, quite rare, and valuable.

_____ 5. In writing, it is actually easier to be ___ than to make the effort to cut out the unnecessary words.

_____ 6. During the Revolutionary War, Benedict Arnold, an American officer, was involved in a ___ to help the British win.

_____ 7. The instructor and the other students became irritated when Susan kept asking questions that weren't ___ to the class discussion.

_____ 8. My parents had expected my sister home by ten o'clock. By the time she finally walked in at two in the morning, they were very ___.

_____ 9. Ved's instructor was so pleased with his clear explanation of a difficult theory that she wrote on his paper, "Wonderfully ___!"

_____ 10. My husband is no help when I'm trying to buy a new dress. Whatever I show him, he gives it a ___ glance and says, "That's fine. Let's buy it and get out of here."

NOTE: Now check your answers to these questions by turning to page 176. Going over the answers carefully will help you prepare for the next two practices, for which answers are not given.

➤ *Sentence Check 2*

Using the answer lines provided, complete each item below with **two** words from the box. Use each word once.

_____
_____ 1–2. In the novel *Rosemary's Baby*, Rosemary becomes more and more ___ as she realizes that her husband and friends are involved in a ___ against her.

_____
_____ 3–4. Ms. Lewis is a ___ of Native American crafts. She can identify the tribe of the artist after just a ___ examination of a necklace or piece of pottery.

_____ 5–6. The drunk driver is ___ about causing the accident, but his regret won't
_____   give Marsha solace° or ease her ___. She is permanently disabled.

_____ 7–8. The professor said, "It seems ___ to our discussion of the Age of
_____   Reason to mention that ___ architecture was typical. Balance was
                              valued—both in art and in the individual."

_____ 9–10. Using too many superfluous° words can make something more difficult
_____   to understand. Thus if the essay had not been so ___, it would have
                               been more ___.

➤ *Final Check:* The Missing Painting

Here is a final opportunity for you to strengthen your knowledge of the ten words. First read the following
selection carefully. Then fill in each blank with a word from the box at the top of the previous page.
(Context clues will help you figure out which word goes in which blank.) Use each word once.

It wasn't until noon that Daniel Cobb noticed the painting was missing. He was immediately
(1)_____. As a (2)_____ of art, he well knew this was
a grievous° loss—the painting was enormously valuable. He was so upset that when he phoned the
police, he could not think or talk clearly enough to give a (3)_____ description
of his unfortunate (4)_____. Instead, he found himself rambling so much that
he was afraid the police would think he was just a (5)_____ old fool.

Nevertheless, the police soon arrived at Cobb's home, which was magnificent—a fine old
mansion in a (6)_____ style, with a row of columns on each side of the
front door. Leading the police to the room from which the painting had been taken, Cobb began to
explain. "Last night," he said, "my wife and I gave a dinner party for art experts. We showed them
our entire collection. I remember that they gave the missing painting special attention. At least, a
few of them seemed to give it more than a merely (7)_____ examination. I
can only assume that we are the victims of a (8)_____. Our guests must have
plotted to sneak into the house during the night and take the painting."

As Cobb finished speaking, his wife entered the room, having just returned from town. She
was clearly alarmed by the presence of the police. After Cobb quickly explained, however, she
started to laugh. "Today's Monday," she finally said.

"I hardly see how that's (9)_____ to our problem!" her husband responded.

"Remember, we told the Leeworth Art Association it could exhibit the painting today, for its
annual show. That's where I've been. I brought the painting there early this morning."

Cobb looked embarrassed but relieved that his guests had been exonerated° by his wife's story.
"Accept my sincere apology for having bothered you. I am most (10)_____,"
he said to the police officers. "Please stay and have some lunch."

Scores Sentence Check 2 _____%	Final Check _____%	

Enter your scores above and in the vocabulary performance chart on the inside back cover of the book.

adept	presumptuous
encompass	sordid
entrepreneur	standardize
eradicate	stint
homogeneous	stringent

Ten Words in Context

In the space provided, write the letter of the meaning closest to that of each **boldfaced** word. Use the context of the sentences to help you figure out each word's meaning.

1 **adept**
(ə-dĕpt′)
-adjective

- People enjoy visiting my parents, who are **adept** at making guests feel welcome and at home.
- Justin is an **adept** liar. He always looks so innocent and sincere that everyone believes his lies.

___ *Adept* means   a. skillful.   b. profitable.   c. awkward.

2 **encompass**
(ĕn-kŭm′pəs)
-verb

- Our professor's broad knowledge of history **encompasses** details of life in ancient Egypt, Greece, and Rome.
- Tomorrow's test will be difficult because it **encompasses** all the material covered this semester.

___ *Encompass* means   a. to suggest.   b. to omit.   c. to include.

3 **entrepreneur**
(ŏn′trə-prə-nûr′)
-noun

- Glenville has no shopping center, but the city is growing so quickly that smart **entrepreneurs** are sure to start up new businesses there soon.
- My ten-year-old neighbor is already an **entrepreneur**. He set up a lemonade stand last summer and sold homemade cookies at Halloween.

___ *Entrepreneur* means   a. a promoter.   b. an overconfident person.   c. a conformist.

4 **eradicate**
(ĭ-răd′ĭ-kāt′)
-verb

- In recent years, smallpox has been **eradicated**—the first time in history that humans have been able to wipe out a disease.
- What makes so many people feel they must **eradicate** all signs of aging? Why should we have to get rid of our wrinkles and gray hair?

___ *Eradicate* means   a. to reveal.   b. to regulate strictly.   c. to erase.

5 **homogeneous**
(hō′mō-jē′nē-əs)
-adjective

- The student body at Eastman College appears quite **homogeneous**, but there are significant social and economic differences among the students.
- "Homogenized" milk has been made **homogeneous**. This means that it's treated so it will be of uniform consistency, rather than having the cream rise to the top.

___ *Homogeneous* means   a. strictly controlled.   b. the same throughout.   c. of high quality.

6 **presumptuous**
(prē-zŭmp′chŏo-əs)
-adjective

- It was **presumptuous** of Eric to announce his engagement to Phyllis before she had actually agreed to marry him.
- If you ask personal questions at a job interview, you'll be thought **presumptuous**. So, for example, don't ask the interviewer, "What are they paying you?"

___ *Presumptuous* means   a. too forward.   b. skilled.   c. cautious.

7 sordid
(sôr′dĭd)
-adjective

- Supermarket tabloids sell well because many people want to know the **sordid** details of celebrities' addictions and messy divorces.
- The reformed criminal now lectures at high schools on how to avoid the mistakes that led him into a **sordid** life as a drug dealer.

__ *Sordid* means   a. proud.   b. ugly.   c. natural.

8 standardize
(stăn′dĕr-dīz′)
-verb

- When the company **standardized** its pay scale, the salary for each type of job became identical throughout all the departments.
- If Jessica begins selling her homemade soup, she'll have to **standardize** the ingredients. Now she just puts in whatever she has on hand, so the soup is never the same from one day to the next.

__ *Standardize* means   a. to do away with.   b. to make consistent.   c. to vary.

9 stint
(stĭnt)
-noun

- My **stint** serving hamburgers and fries at a fast-food restaurant convinced me that I needed to get a college degree.
- After traveling during her **stint** in the Navy, Alise wanted a job that would let her continue to see the world.

__ *Stint* means   a. an assigned job.   b. a risky undertaking.   c. future work.

10 stringent
(strĭn′jənt)
-adjective

- Professor Jasper has the most **stringent** standards in the department. Passing her course is difficult; getting an A is next to impossible.
- Elected officials should be held to a **stringent** code of ethics, requiring them to avoid even the appearance of wrongdoing.

__ *Stringent* means   a. different.   b. flexible.   c. demanding.

Matching Words with Definitions

Following are definitions of the ten words. Clearly write or print each word next to its definition. The sentences above and on the previous page will help you decide on the meaning of each word.

1. _____   A person who organizes, manages, and takes the risk of a business undertaking
2. _____   Highly skilled; expert
3. _____   A period of work or service
4. _____   Too bold; overly confident
5. _____   To get rid of altogether; wipe out
6. _____   Strictly controlled or enforced; strict; severe
7. _____   To make uniform; cause to conform to a model
8. _____   To include; contain
9. _____   Made up of similar or identical parts; uniform throughout
10. _____   Indecent; morally low; corrupt

CAUTION: Do not go any further until you are sure the above answers are correct. Then you can use the definitions to help you in the following practices. Your goal is eventually to know the words well enough so that you don't need to check the definitions at all.

➤ *Sentence Check 1*

Using the answer line provided, complete each item below with the correct word from the box. Use each word once.

a. **adept**	b. **encompass**	c. **entrepreneur**	d. **eradicate**	e. **homogeneous**
f. **presumptuous**	g. **sordid**	h. **standardize**	i. **stint**	j. **stringent**

_____ 1. It's ___ of Amy to assume she's got the job when others are still being interviewed.

_____ 2. It takes years of study and practice to become ___ at acupuncture.

_____ 3. More ___ than the love affair itself were the lies Sally told her husband to conceal it from him.

_____ 4. My grandfather held many jobs during his life. He even did a(n) ___ as a circus performer.

_____ 5. Joyce and Steven's adopted son was abused in an earlier home. They're working hard to ___ the lingering effects on him of that experience.

_____ 6. The town is so close-knit and ___ that newcomers feel out of place. Many of the residents are even related.

_____ 7. The articles in our small newspaper ___ local and statewide news, but not national or international events.

_____ 8. My sister applied to several colleges, some with very high admission standards for their students and others with less ___ requirements.

_____ 9. Doug has just opened an auto repair shop. Now that he's a(n) ___, he can join the National Association for the Self-Employed.

_____ 10. Should the high school curriculum be ___(e)d throughout the state? Or should each school district be free to design its own courses?

NOTE: Now check your answers to these questions by turning to page 176. Going over the answers carefully will help you prepare for the next two practices, for which answers are not given.

➤ *Sentence Check 2*

Using the answer lines provided, complete each item below with **two** words from the box. Use each word once.

_____
_____ 1–2. To succeed, ___s must be ___ at organization and management. In addition, they must be resilient° enough to deal with the ups and downs of running a business.

_____
_____ 3–4. During Nate's ___ as a teacher at a military academy, he felt that the ___ rules impeded° his easygoing, flexible approach.

_____ 5–6. After serving a prison term for theft, Charlie is contrite°. He's decided to begin a new life as an honest citizen and ___ all traces of his ___ past.

_____ 7–8. I've been working at the daycare center only one week, so this
_____   suggestion may be ___, but I think the center's program should ___
                                activities geared to shy children as well as ones for gregarious° kids.

_____ 9–10. At a small alternative school, all children were at first put into one large
_____   class. Later the children were divided into smaller, more ___ classes. In
                                 addition, administrators decided to ___ the curriculum so that all
                                 students in one grade would use the same texts.

➤ *Final Check:* An Ohio Girl in New York

Here is a final opportunity for you to strengthen your knowledge of the ten words. First read the following selection carefully. Then fill in each blank with a word from the box at the top of the previous page. (Context clues will help you figure out which word goes in which blank.) Use each word once.

Soon after Gina moved from her small Ohio town to New York City, she became so discouraged that she nearly returned home. It was easy to see why she was despondent°: New York had the glamor and excitement that she had expected, but not the high-paying jobs. However, Gina decided to stay in the big city and put in a(n) (1)_____ as a waitress in a coffee shop while hoping for something better to turn up. She had been offered only one higher-paying job, as an exotic dancer in a bar, but she felt that this kind of work was too (2)_____.

At least she enjoyed the coffee shop. For someone used to a small, (3)_____ town, the customers seemed to come in an enormous variety. Also, the low salary forced her to stick to a(n) (4)_____ budget. As a result of this financial situation, she was becoming (5)_____ at making one dollar go as far as two did before.

One day, Gina met a customer who had recently opened a video rental store. This (6)_____ was about to open a second store, and he sometimes discussed his plans with Gina. Although she worried that he might think it (7)_____ of a waitress to offer a suggestion about the video business, Gina told him a thought she had about how he might (8)_____ his rental system. He could ask all his customers to fill out the same form. Then a single computer file could (9)_____ all the information. Customers would be signed up automatically for both stores at once. To Gina's relief, the customer didn't scoff° at her idea; in fact, he thanked her for the advice.

Sometime later, he stopped in at the coffee shop to say he needed a capable person to manage his new store. He offered Gina the job. Within a year, she was the manager of three video stores and earning an excellent salary. She was euphoric°, but her happiness would never fully (10)_____ her memories of those tough first months in New York.

Scores   Sentence Check 2 _____%   Final Check _____%

Enter your scores above and in the vocabulary performance chart on the inside back cover of the book.

CHAPTER

17

exhort	masochist
flamboyant	meticulous
foible	rancor
innocuous	recrimination
magnanimous	repugnant

Ten Words in Context

In the space provided, write the letter of the meaning closest to that of each **boldfaced** word. Use the context of the sentences to help you figure out each word's meaning.

1 exhort
(ĕg-zôrt′)
-verb

- The school counselor gave an impassioned speech to the parents, in which she **exhorted** them to make every effort to keep their children off drugs.
- On the eve of the invasion, the general **exhorted** the troops to fight bravely for their homeland.

___ *Exhort* means   a. to accuse.   b. to praise.   c. to urge.

2 flamboyant
(flăm-boi′ənt)
-adjective

- Lily can't resist **flamboyant** clothes. She'd wear a hot-pink dress with gold satin trim to a funeral.
- With his sequined suits, glittering jewelry, and silver piano, Liberace was probably the world's most **flamboyant** pianist.

___ *Flamboyant* means   a. flashy.   b. self-centered.   c. concerned with details.

3 foible
(foi′bəl)
-noun

- Serious character flaws—such as abusiveness—are hard to overlook, but **foibles**—such as drinking soup through a straw—can often be easily tolerated.
- I accept my husband's **foible** of leaving clothes lying around because it lets me be messy without feeling guilty.

___ *Foible* means   a. a serious problem.   b. a minor failing.   c. a complaint.

4 innocuous
(ĭn-nŏk′yoo-əs)
-adjective

- Although most children engage in **innocuous** pranks on Halloween, some get out of hand and do serious damage.
- Experts at the Poison Information Center can tell you if a household substance is harmful or **innocuous**.

___ *Innocuous* means   a. without bad effects.   b. expensive.   c. satisfying.

5 magnanimous
(măg-năn′ə-məs)
-adjective

- At age 5, Jonathan is already learning to be **magnanimous**. He forgives and hugs his baby sister even when she hits him on the head with a wooden block.
- Last Thanksgiving, someone at work drew a funny picture of our boss as an enormous turkey. When the boss saw it, he was **magnanimous**—he laughed, said it was terrific, and even hung it up over his desk.

___ *Magnanimous* means   a. big-hearted.   b. consistent.   c. resentful.

6 masochist
(măs′ə-kĭst)
-noun

- Psychologists are trying to understand why **masochists** obtain satisfaction from suffering.
- "A **masochist's** idea of a good time," said the comedian, "is getting hit by a truck on the way home from having all his teeth pulled."

___ *Masochist* means   a. someone filled with hatred.   b. someone who enjoys being hurt.   c. someone who enjoys hurting others.

7 **meticulous**
(mə-tĭk′yōo-ləs)
-*adjective*

• When you proofread your own writing, be **meticulous**—check every detail.

• My roommate is **meticulous** about his appearance. He never has a wrinkle in his clothing nor a hair out of place.

___ *Meticulous* means   a. precise.   b. bold.   c. unconcerned.

8 **rancor**
(răn′kər)
-*noun*

• The **rancor** between my uncles has lasted for twenty years, ever since Uncle Dmitri married the woman to whom Uncle Sergei had proposed.

• When there is long-lasting **rancor** between divorced parents, their children may also start to share this bitterness.

___ *Rancor* means   a. a minor fault.   b. deep hostility.   c. secrecy.

9 **recrimination**
(rĭ-krĭm′ə-nā′shən)
-*noun*

• The couple's session with the marriage counselor failed miserably; it began with the husband and wife hurling accusations at each other, and it never progressed beyond these **recriminations**.

• When Lainie's father and her teacher met to discuss Lainie's poor grades, they exchanged **recriminations**—each accused the other of not helping her do better.

___ *Recrimination* means   a. an urgent plea.   b. a detailed suggestion.   c. an accusation in reply.

10 **repugnant**
(rĭ-pŭg′nənt)
-*adjective*

• My parents find some of my eating habits **repugnant**, but I see nothing offensive about mixing peas and ketchup into mashed potatoes.

• A snake is **repugnant** to many people—"Slimy!" they say, shivering with distaste. However, snakes are not at all slimy, and most are harmless.

___ *Repugnant* means   a. disgusting.   b. amusing.   c. remarkable.

Matching Words with Definitions

Following are definitions of the ten words. Clearly write or print each word next to its definition. The sentences above and on the previous page will help you decide on the meaning of each word.

1. _____   Intense hatred or ill will; long-lasting resentment

2. _____   Harmless; inoffensive

3. _____   Offensive; distasteful; repulsive

4. _____   A person who gains satisfaction from suffering physical or psychological pain

5. _____   Very showy; strikingly bold

6. _____   A minor weakness or character flaw; a minor fault in behavior

7. _____   An accusation made in response to an accuser; countercharge

8. _____   To urge with argument or strong advice; plead earnestly

9. _____   Noble in mind and spirit; especially generous in forgiving

10. _____   Extremely careful and exact; showing great attention to details

CAUTION: Do not go any further until you are sure the above answers are correct. Then you can use the definitions to help you in the following practices. Your goal is eventually to know the words well enough so that you don't need to check the definitions at all.

➤ *Sentence Check 1*

Using the answer line provided, complete each item below with the correct word from the box. Use each word once.

a. **exhort**	b. **flamboyant**	c. **foible**	d. **innocuous**	e. **magnanimous**
f. **masochist**	g. **meticulous**	h. **rancor**	i. **recrimination**	j. **repugnant**

_____ 1. Why is it that bats seem so ___? Do we think a flying mouselike creature is distasteful, or do we associate bats with vampires?

_____ 2. It was ___ of the Greens to forgive the driver who ran over their dog.

_____ 3. Battered women who stay with their abusive partners aren't necessarily ___s; they don't enjoy being hurt, but often they can't see any way to escape.

_____ 4. Although nail-biting is only a ___, it can become maddening to a companion who observes it day after day.

_____ 5. Before the football game, the coach gave a fiery pep talk. He___(e)d the players to fight for the honor of the team and the school.

_____ 6. To an allergic person, foods that are normally ___, such as milk or wheat, can cause discomfort and even serious illness.

_____ 7. The long-standing ___ between the two women finally came to an end when one of them fell and the other rushed over to help her.

_____ 8. The angry neighbors traded ___s: "Your wild kids trampled all over my flower bed!" "Well, your crazy dog dug up my lawn!"

_____ 9. Some jobs needn't be done in a(n) ___ way. For instance, why sweep every speck of dust off a floor that's only going to get dirty again in an hour?

_____ 10. On New Year's Day in Philadelphia, string bands called "Mummers" strut their stuff in ___ costumes designed to outshine all other bands in the parade.

NOTE: Now check your answers to these questions by turning to page 176. Going over the answers carefully will help you prepare for the next two practices, for which answers are not given.

➤ *Sentence Check 2*

Using the answer lines provided, complete each item below with **two** words from the box. Use each word once.

_____
_____ 1–2. My second-grade teacher had stringent° standards. For one thing, she ___(e)d us to be ___ about our handwriting. "Dot every *i*," she would say, "and cross every *t*."

_____
_____ 3–4. In a small business, it's important never to instigate° quarrels or let ___ develop. People must learn to be ___ and forgive each other's errors.

_____
_____ 5–6. Many find the thought of a ___ seeking out and enjoying suffering to be as ___ as the idea of causing someone else to suffer.

_____   7–8. Walter is certainly odd. Still, most of his ___s—like wearing bedroom
_____   slippers to work and leaving bags of pretzels all over the office—are so
                                  ___ that nobody really minds them.

_____   9–10. When Martha put on a bright red sequined dress with huge rhinestone
_____   earrings, ___s flew back and forth between her and her sister. "You
                                   look preposterous° in that outfit," her sister said. "It's much too ___."
                                   Martha replied, "Well, _your_ clothes are the most boring I've ever seen."

➤ _Final Check:_ How Neat Is Neat Enough?

Here is a final opportunity for you to strengthen your knowledge of the ten words. First read the following
selection carefully. Then fill in each blank with a word from the box at the top of the previous page.
(Context clues will help you figure out which word goes in which blank.) Use each word once.

　　　Experts say that differences about money and sex are not the only causes of marital problems.
If one spouse is a slob and the other is (1)_____, there is bound to be trouble.

　　　At first, newlyweds tend to be (2)_____, readily forgiving each other's
(3)_____s. The wife says it's "sweet" that her husband made the bed while she
was still in it and "cute" that he grabbed her plate to wash it when she picked up her sandwich to
take a bite. "You're so helpful," she coos. And he manages a smile when she dumps her too-
expensive, too-(4)_____ gold sequined dress in the middle of the bedroom
floor. "We've sure got a high-priced, flashy rug," he jokes.

　　　But the honeymoon ends, and the idiosyncrasies° that once seemed (5)_____
start to be seriously annoying. He begins to think, "Since my housekeeping is so impeccable°, why
isn't she picking up my good habits? Why must I wade through dirty pantyhose to reach the closet?
Why is there spaghetti sauce on the kitchen ceiling fan again?" He (6)_____s her to
have some self-respect and stop living like a pig.

　　　And she begins to wonder about him: Why does he insist on dusting the tops of the door
frames when no one can see them? So what if she squeezes the toothpaste from the middle of the
tube—why should he find that harmless habit so (7)_____? Maybe he's a
(8)_____—why else would he be so happy down on his knees, scrubbing the
bathroom floor with a toothbrush (one of the "old" ones that he replaced after using it for a week).

　　　Soon the accusations and (9)_____s start. She yells, "You're a zealot°
for neatness—that's all you care about. You spend more time holding that vacuum cleaner than
you spend holding me!" He responds, "If you weren't so sloppy, I'd hold you more often. As it is,
I have to climb over a mountain of junk just to get near you!"

　　　Eventually, as the two of them continue arguing with each other and berating° each other, their
feelings of (10)_____ become so strong that a breakup is imminent.° It
won't be long before another relationship, so to speak, bites the dust.

Scores　Sentence Check 2 _____%	Final Check _____%

Enter your scores above and in the vocabulary performance chart on the inside back cover of the book.

anima	miss, mit
arch, -archy	mort
ben-, bene-	poly-
-ee	tempo, tempor
-log, -logue	ten

Ten Word Parts in Context

Figure out the meanings of the following ten word parts by looking *closely* and *carefully* at the context in which they appear. Then, in the space provided, write the letter of the meaning closest to that of each word part.

1 anima

- During the worst part of her illness, Trina lay quietly in bed. We knew she was recovering when she sat up and began to talk in an **animated** way.
- I never understood why pet rocks were popular. They were **inanimate** objects, and who wants a "pet" that doesn't move or even breathe?

__ The word part *anima* means

   a. good.   b. experience.   c. life.

2 arch, -archy

- Many fictional heroes have an **archenemy**. For instance, Sherlock Holmes's main opponent was the evil Dr. Moriarty.
- Among Amish people, the family is a **patriarchy**. The father rules the household, and the women and children are expected to obey.

__ The word part *arch* or *-archy* means

   a. chief.   b. sender.   c. receiver.

3 ben-, bene-

- Southern California has a **benign** climate—sunny and warm.
- For Cheryl, day care has been **beneficial**. She's much less shy now.

__ The word part *ben-* or *bene-* means

   a. experience.   b. deadly.   c. good.

4 -ee

- The mayor had to appoint a new chief of police. The first **appointee** became unavailable—he was serving a two-year sentence in prison.
- Today's **employees** expect to receive benefits as well as a salary.

__ The word part *-ee* means

   a. a ruler.   b. someone who receives.   c. someone who sends.

5 -log, -logue

- It's almost impossible to have a **dialog** with Aaron because he does all the talking.
- The play opened with a **prologue**: before the action began, one of the characters came onstage and made a speech to the audience.

__ The word part *-log* or *-logue* means

   a. speaking.   b. time.   c. send.

6 miss, mit

- The United Nations sends peacekeeping **missions** to trouble spots around the world, although not all of these efforts succeed.
- I use a telephone every day, but to tell you the truth, I really have no idea how it **transmits** sound across a distance.

__ The word part *miss* or *mit* means

   a. send.   b. well.   c. hold.

7 **mort**

- Ms. Patterson took her class to visit a **mortician**, who explained how he prepares a body for burial.
- Shakespeare's works are said to have achieved **immortality**: they will never die, since they will be read and performed forever.

___ The word part *mort* means   a. death.   b. breath.   c. name.

8 **poly-**

- A **polytechnic** school is one which teaches many different sciences and industrial arts.
- **Polygamy** is a form of marriage in which a person can have a number of spouses at the same time.

___ The word part *poly-* means   a. difficult.   b. time.   c. many.

9 **tempo, tempor**

- The chorus sang the difficult piece slowly at first. When they seemed sure of all the notes, the director speeded up the **tempo**.
- The trailer in the Langs' yard is there only **temporarily**, until the repairs to their house are finished and they can move back in.

___ The word part *tempo* or *tempor* means   a. holding.   b. time.   c. number.

10 **ten**

- **Detention** is a common punishment in elementary and high school. Students who misbehave are kept for an hour or so at the end of the day.
- **Tenant** farmers hold the right to work someone else's land; they pay rent in cash or with a portion of the produce.

___ The word part *ten* means   a. spirit.   b. keep.   c. divide.

Matching Word Parts with Definitions

Following are definitions of the ten word parts. Clearly write or print each word part next to its definition. The sentences above and on the previous page will help you decide on the meaning of each word part.

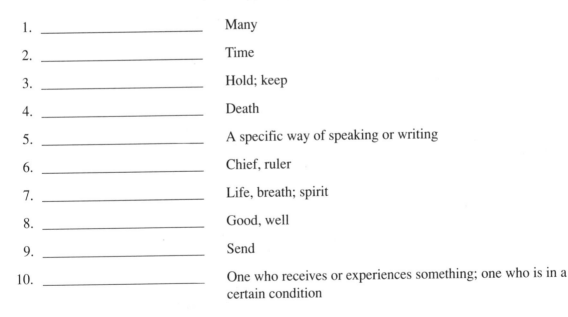

1. _____   Many

2. _____   Time

3. _____   Hold; keep

4. _____   Death

5. _____   A specific way of speaking or writing

6. _____   Chief, ruler

7. _____   Life, breath; spirit

8. _____   Good, well

9. _____   Send

10. _____   One who receives or experiences something; one who is in a certain condition

CAUTION: Do not go any further until you are sure the above answers are correct. Then you can use the definitions to help you in the following practices. Your goal is eventually to know the word parts well enough so that you don't need to check the definitions at all.

➣ Sentence Check 1

Using the answer line provided, complete each *italicized* word in the sentences below with the correct word part from the box. Use each word part once.

a. anima	b. arch, -archy	c. ben-, bene-	d. -ee	e. -logue
f. miss, mit	g. mort	h. poly-	i. tempo, tempor	j. ten

_____ 1. A high-ranking angel is called a(n) (. . . *angel*) ___.

_____ 2. A(n) (. . . *factor*) ___ has been good enough to give the city blankets to pass out to the homeless.

_____ 3. The (. . . *ality*) ___ rate is the death rate—that is, the percentage of people in a group who die in a given time or from a particular cause.

_____ 4. I enjoy (*trave* . . . *s*) ___ on TV. It's interesting to hear people talk about their travels.

_____ 5. Certain (. . . *ets*) ___, such as the belief in the sanctity of marriage, are held by many religions.

_____ 6. When the bell rang and the teacher said "Class is (*dis* . . . *ed*) ___," that was enough to send the children hurtling into the hallway like popcorn exploding from a popper.

_____ 7. There was suspicion that the evil dictator had been murdered, but a (*post* . . . *em*) ___ examination showed that he had died of natural causes.

_____ 8. A(n) (. . . *graph*) ___, or "lie detector," records several physical responses of the person hooked up to it, including heart rate, breathing rate, and blood pressure.

_____ 9. Many cartoons today are not made very well. The (. . . *tion*) ___ is so poor that the characters don't seem to be alive—they don't move smoothly and naturally.

_____ 10. "We are here to nominate candidates for president of the Liars' Club," said the club's current president. "Remember that the (*nomin* . . . *s*) ___ should be exceptionally honest."

NOTE: Now check your answers to these questions by turning to page 176. Going over the answers carefully will help you prepare for the next two practices, for which answers are not given.

➣ Sentence Check 2

Using the answer lines provided, complete each *italicized* word in the sentences below with the correct word part from the box. Use each word part once.

_____
_____ 1–2. The (*cata* . . .) ___ of unusual gifts includes a plastic skunk named "Rosebud" which (*e* . . . *s*) ___ a rose-scented air freshener.

_____
_____ 3–4. Our parish priest was especially (. . . *volent*) ___ and wise. I wasn't surprised to hear that he eventually became a(n) (. . . *bishop*) ___.

_____ 5–6. The owner of the safe-deposit box had to relinquish° it to the police.
_____ The (con . . . ts) ___ are now being held (. . . arily) ___ by the district
attorney, until the trial.

_____ 7–8. Our visitor from (. . . nesia) ___, a country of many islands, told us
_____ about the plight° of (refug . . . s) ___ who had to flee from one island
after it was struck by a hurricane.

_____ 9–10. The story of Frankenstein's monster is about a doctor who had the
_____ presumptuous° belief that a mere (. . . al) ___ could achieve godlike
power and (. . . te) ___ a lifeless body.

➤ _Final Check:_ A Cult Community

Here is a final opportunity for you to strengthen your knowledge of the ten word parts. First read the
following selection carefully. Then complete each _italicized_ word in the parentheses below with a word
from the box at the top of the previous page. (Context clues will help you figure out which word part goes
in which blank.) Use each word part once.

My friend Lucy recently visited her brother Ben in British Columbia. She was shocked to

discover that Ben was living in a cult—a community of about forty followers, headed by a

(_patri . . ._) (1)_____ whom they all called Uncle. Uncle was a (. . . _ign_)

(2)_____ leader as long as his authority wasn't questioned, but he wouldn't

tolerate troublemakers or dissidents°. Uncle's followers were expected to regard him as infallible°

and to uphold the stringent° (. . . _ets_) (3)_____ of his "religion." These strict

rules included sticking to a monogamous lifestyle. Uncle himself, however, was a(n) (. . . _gamist_)

(4)_____ who chose the prettiest cult members as his wives, and he drove

around in an ostentatious° car, a gold Rolls-Royce. Several times each day, all the cult members

would be gathered to hear Uncle's (_mono . . . s_) (5)_____, speeches in

which he exhorted° them to think of eternal life, not of their brief, (. . . _ary_)

(6)_____ existence on earth. Many of them believed Uncle to be (_im . . . al_)

(7)_____. Others admitted that he might indeed die someday, but they fully

expected that his body would be (_re . . . ted_) (8)_____very soon thereafter.

Lucy's brother was a particularly strong (_devot . . ._) (9)_____ of the cult;

he believed that God had sent him on a (. . . _ion_) (10)_____ to follow Uncle.

To Lucy, however, it seemed that Ben had been mesmerized° by a charlatan°, and she wished she

knew how to break the spell that this dishonest leader had cast on her brother.

Scores	Sentence Check 2 _____%	Final Check _____%

Enter your scores above and in the vocabulary performance chart on the inside back cover of the book.

UNIT THREE: Review

The box at the right lists twenty-five words from Unit Three. Using the clues at the bottom of the page, fill in these words to complete the puzzle that follows.

| adept |
| antipathy |
| austere |
| contrite |
| cursory |
| eradicate |
| esoteric |
| exhort |
| foible |
| germane |
| grotesque |
| imminent |
| impede |
| inclusive |
| lucid |
| masochist |
| meticulous |
| notorious |
| precarious |
| rancor |
| sordid |
| stint |
| stringent |
| travesty |
| verbose |

ACROSS

2. Beyond the understanding of most people
4. About to happen
7. A minor weakness or character flaw
9. Having to do with the issue at hand; relevant
10. Known widely but unfavorably
12. Highly skilled; expert
13. Extremely careful and exact; showing great attention to details
17. Clearly expressed
19. A period of work or service
20. Using too many words
22. Done quickly with little attention to detail
23. To urge with argument or strong advice; plead earnestly
24. A strong dislike or distaste
25. Dangerous; risky

DOWN

1. Distorted or strikingly inconsistent in shape, appearance, or manner
3. Strictly controlled or enforced; strict; severe
5. A person who gains satisfaction from suffering or psychological pain
6. To get rid of; wipe out
8. Indecent; morally low
11. Including much or everything
14. A crude, exaggerated, or ridiculous representation
15. To delay or slow up; get in the way of
16. Without decoration or luxury; severely simple
18. Truly sorry for having done wrong; repentant
21. Intense hatred or ill will

UNIT THREE: Test 1

PART A
Choose the word that best completes each item and write it in the space provided.

_____ 1. Working-class housing in nineteenth-century England was ___ by today's standards: crowded, dark, badly ventilated, and unsanitary.

    a. austere   b. distraught   c. sordid   d. innocuous

_____ 2. Even when textbooks are ___ throughout a school system, methods of teaching may vary greatly.

    a. standardized   b. mesmerized   c. contrite   d. symmetrical

_____ 3. The existence of nuclear weapons puts everyone in a(n) ___ situation.

    a. meticulous   b. precarious   c. magnanimous   d. flamboyant

_____ 4. As long as the thief was in Europe, American courts had no ___ over him.

    a. metamorphosis   b. connoisseur   c. jurisdiction   d. travesty

_____ 5. Because most people feel ___ toward spiders and snakes, these unpopular creatures are often featured in horror movies.

    a. idiosyncrasy   b. antipathy   c. stint   d. deprivation

_____ 6. Having lived in Italy and studied cooking there, the newspaper's food critic is a ___ of Italian cuisine.

    a. masochist   b. rancor   c. plight   d. connoisseur

_____ 7. Although the population of the United States includes a great variety of racial and ethnic backgrounds, Japan's population is largely ___.

    a. homogeneous   b. contrite   c. flamboyant   d. lucid

_____ 8. New York City drivers are ___ for failing to pay their parking fines. Currently they owe about half a billion dollars.

    a. stringent   b. symmetrical   c. notorious   d. magnanimous

_____ 9. Some people feel that a circus act in which costumed elephants dance or stand on their heads is a ___ of these intelligent animals' true nature.

    a. foible   b. recrimination   c. conspiracy   d. travesty

_____ 10. My ___ as a worker in the hotel laundry lasted only a day. It turned out that I was allergic to the soap.

    a. facsimile   b. idiosyncrasy   c. foible   d. stint

_____ 11. The Dalton Gang was ___ at robbing banks, but when five gang members greedily attempted to rob two banks in one day, four were killed and the fifth was captured.

    a. lucid   b. germane   c. adept   d. imminent

(Continues on next page)

_____ 12. The Englishman John Merrick had an illness that gave him a(n) ___ appearance, which is why he was called "The Elephant Man." Despite people's reactions to his misshapen head and body, Merrick remained affectionate and gentle.

      a. cursory   b. imminent   c. contrite   d. grotesque

_____ 13. A founder of the U.S. Steel Company was wealthy enough to have an expensive ___. It was his habit to bet a thousand dollars on which of two raindrops falling down a windowpane would reach the bottom first.

      a. masochist   b. recrimination   c. facsimile   d. idiosyncrasy

PART B
Write **C** if the italicized word is used **correctly**. Write **I** if the word is used **incorrectly**.

_____ 14. Only female black widow spiders are dangerous to humans. The bite of a male is *innocuous*.

_____ 15. The Beatles will always be famous because of their *esoteric* music.

_____ 16. When my knee aches, I know that a change in the weather is *imminent*.

_____ 17. Marsha, as *verbose* as always, signed her letter only "Best," instead of "Best wishes."

_____ 18. Ramps *impede* people in wheelchairs by allowing them to enter buildings more easily.

_____ 19. Lois and Manny were divorced three years ago, and they still feel such *rancor* that they refuse to speak to each other.

_____ 20. Two former characters on *Saturday Night Live* are *masochists* who brag to each other about their painful experiences.

_____ 21. Sue always drives her *flamboyant* gray subcompact when she goes to the city because no one would bother to steal it.

_____ 22. Valentine hearts are perfectly *symmetrical*, but the left and right sides of a human heart differ in shape and size.

_____ 23. Ricardo writes thoughtful essays and then spoils them by handing in a *meticulous* final draft filled with spelling and typing errors.

_____ 24. My *cursory* studying for final exams includes an in-depth review of my notes and of underlined portions of my textbooks.

_____ 25. I didn't think I'd enjoy the dance concert, but I was *mesmerized* from start to finish by the wonderful movement and music.

Score	(Number correct) _____ x 4 = _____%

Enter your score above and in the vocabulary performance chart on the inside back cover of the book.

UNIT THREE: Test 2

PART A
Complete each item with a word from the box. Use each word once.

a. **advocate**	b. **conspiracy**	c. **contrite**	d. **emancipate**	e. **eradicate**
f. **exhort**	g. **facsimile**	h. **foible**	i. **inclusive**	j. **lucid**
k. **metamorphosis**	l. **preposterous**	m. **repugnant**		

_____ 1. The furry white and green mold growing on the old tomato sauce was a(n) ___ sight.

_____ 2. Correct punctuation makes prose more ___.

_____ 3. One of my ___s is biting into many chocolates in a box until I find one I like.

_____ 4. The dictator arrested everyone involved in the ___ to overthrow him, including his wife.

_____ 5. A(n) ___ of a transcript isn't official unless it has been stamped with the seal of the school registrar.

_____ 6. The boys were ___ when they realized that their teasing had made Mary afraid to go to school the next day.

_____ 7. If the common cold were ever ___(e)d, it would be economically unhealthy for the makers of cold remedies.

_____ 8. The TV preacher ___(e)d viewers to support his ministry with whatever funds they could manage to send.

_____ 9. "It's a(n) all-___ tour," the travel agent said. "Hotel, meals, flights both ways—everything is covered in one package."

_____ 10. Environmentalists ___ stricter controls on American industry, which releases billions of pounds of pollution into the air each year.

_____ 11. After Cristina learned to read at age 30, she underwent a(n) ___. She changed from being shy to being confident, got an interesting new job, and started taking college classes at night.

_____ 12. American women have yet to be ___(e)d from domestic abuse. One in three women experiences physical mistreatment by a boyfriend or husband.

_____ 13. The man made the ___ claim that he had been taken aboard a Martian spaceship by someone who looked like Woody Allen, except that his skin was green.

(Continues on next page)

PART B
Write **C** if the italicized word is used **correctly**. Write **I** if the word is used **incorrectly**.

_____ 14. I was *distraught* when I got the raise I had asked for.

_____ 15. Vincent seemed *presumptuous* when, uninvited, he addressed his new boss by her first name.

_____ 16. Fran threw a party to celebrate her *plight*: she had been chosen for the Olympic swimming team.

_____ 17. The workshop lasted all day, but it still did not *encompass* all the information I needed to operate the computer.

_____ 18. The science museum has many *provocative* exhibits, including a giant heart that visitors can walk through.

_____ 19. Rose's "How are you?" always seems *perfunctory*, just a matter of routine courtesy, not genuine interest.

_____ 20. The restaurant looked *austere*, with its brightly colored flowered wallpaper and its thick red carpet.

_____ 21. Years ago, some shrewd *entrepreneur* got the idea of selling "pet rocks" and made a fortune when they became a fad.

_____ 22. As a teen, I used to make fun of my sister's telephone *recriminations* to her boyfriend, such as "I love you lots too."

_____ 23. The yearbook meeting got sidetracked. Our discussion of our instructors' merits and flaws wasn't *germane* to the topic of the photo layout.

_____ 24. As kids, my brother and I loved staying with our grandparents because of their *stringent* rules; they let us stay up as late as we liked and eat candy for breakfast.

_____ 25. After the waiter spilled hot coffee on her, the customer was *magnanimous*. She sued him and the restaurant for fifty million dollars.

Score (Number correct) _____ x 4 = _____ %

UNIT THREE: Test 3

PART A
Complete each sentence in a way that clearly shows you understand the meaning of the **boldfaced** word. Take a minute to plan your answer before you write.

Example: Kim must be an **adept** manager because _____*she was just promoted again*_____.

1. My parents often **exhort** me to _____
_____.

2. I was **distraught** when _____
_____.

3. My best friend has an odd **foible**: _____
_____.

4. The **magnanimous** boss _____
_____.

5. Two things I find **repugnant** are _____
_____.

6. The singer's **flamboyant** outfit consisted of _____
_____.

7. As a child, I was **contrite** after _____
_____.

8. Professor Cowens has such **stringent** standards that _____
_____.

9. One **verbose** way of saying no is "_____
_____."

10. At the party, Len told a **preposterous** story about _____
_____
_____.

(Continues on next page)

PART B

After each **boldfaced** word are a *synonym* (a word that means the same as the boldfaced word), an *antonym* (a word that means the opposite of the boldfaced word), and a word that is neither. On the answer line, write the letter of the word that is the antonym.

	Example: __a__ **distraught**	a. happy	b. troubled	c. guilty
____	11. **rancor**	a. noise	b. good will	c. bitterness
____	12. **encompass**	a. include	b. turn	c. omit
____	13. **provocative**	a. boring	b. foreign	c. interesting
____	14. **impede**	a. discover	b. aid	c. interfere with
____	15. **lucid**	a. understandable	b. unclear	c. loose

PART C

Use five of the following ten words in sentences. Make it clear that you know the meaning of each word you use. Feel free to use the past tense or plural form of a word.

a. **antipathy**	b. **cursory**	c. **eradicate**	d. **grotesque**	e. **idiosyncrasy**
f. **mesmerize**	g. **meticulous**	h. **plight**	i. **precarious**	j. **stint**

16. _____

_____

17. _____

_____

18. _____

_____

19. _____

_____

20. _____

_____

Score   (Number correct) _____ x 5 = _____ %

UNIT THREE: *Test 4 (Word Parts)*

PART A
Listed in the left-hand column below are ten common word parts, along with words in which the parts are used. In each blank, write in the letter of the correct definition on the right.

Word Parts	Examples	Definitions
____ 1. **anima**	animated, inanimate	a. Hold; keep
____ 2. **arch, -archy**	archenemy, patriarchy	b. Send
____ 3. **ben- bene-**	benign, beneficial	c. A specific way of speaking or writing
____ 4. **-ee**	appointee, employee	d. Many
____ 5. **-log, -logue**	dialog, prologue	e. One who receives or experiences something; one who is in a certain condition
____ 6. **miss, mit**	mission, transmit	f. Good, well
____ 7. **mort**	mortician, immortality	g. Chief, ruler
____ 8. **poly-**	polytechnic, polygamy	h. Time
____ 9. **tempo, tempor**	tempo, temporarily	i. Life, breath; spirit
____ 10. **ten**	detention, tenant	j. Death

PART B
Using the answer line provided, complete each *italicized* word in the sentences below with the correct word part from the box. Not every word part will be used.

a. **anima**	b. **arch**	c. **bene-**	d. **-ee**	e. **-logue**
f. **miss**	g. **mort**	h. **poly-**	i. **tempor**	j. **ten**

_____ 11. One (*mon . . .*) ___ in Persia was king for seventy years—his entire life.

_____ 12. My brother and I always loved the minister's (*. . . diction*) ___ because that final blessing meant the service was over.

_____ 13. My sister-in-law likes early American furniture, but I prefer (*con . . . ary*) ___ styles, designs that reflect today's times.

_____ 14. Shakespeare sometimes wrote an (*epi . . .*) ___ to a play, a final speech spoken by a character directly to the audience.

_____ 15. Stick insects are so named because when they don't move, they resemble (*in . . . te*) ___ twigs more than living insects.

(Continues on next page)

PART C

Use your knowledge of word parts to determine the meaning of the **boldfaced** words. On the answer line, write the letter of each meaning.

____ 16. Instead of using the perfectly good words *no* and *yes*, Evan insists on using the **polysyllabic** words *negative* and *affirmative*.

    a. having long syllables   b. having many syllables   c. hard to pronounce

____ 17. My brother has a **retentive** memory.

    a. tending to forget   b. highly selective   c. tending to hold

____ 18. Giving the **emissary** a hollow nickel containing key information, the spy told him to get the nickel to army headquarters.

    a. a king   b. a recipient   c. a messenger sent on an errand

____ 19. My wife and I donated blood today. The **donee** is a neighbor.

    a. a person receiving blood   b. a doctor   c. a chief of a blood bank

____ 20. After recovering from breaking many bones while going over Niagara Falls in a barrel, Bobby Leech was **mortally** injured in 1911 when he slipped on a banana peel.

    a. painfully   b. fatally   c. strangely

Score   (Number correct) _____ x 5 = _____ %

Enter your score above and in the vocabulary performance chart on the inside back cover of the book.

Unit Four

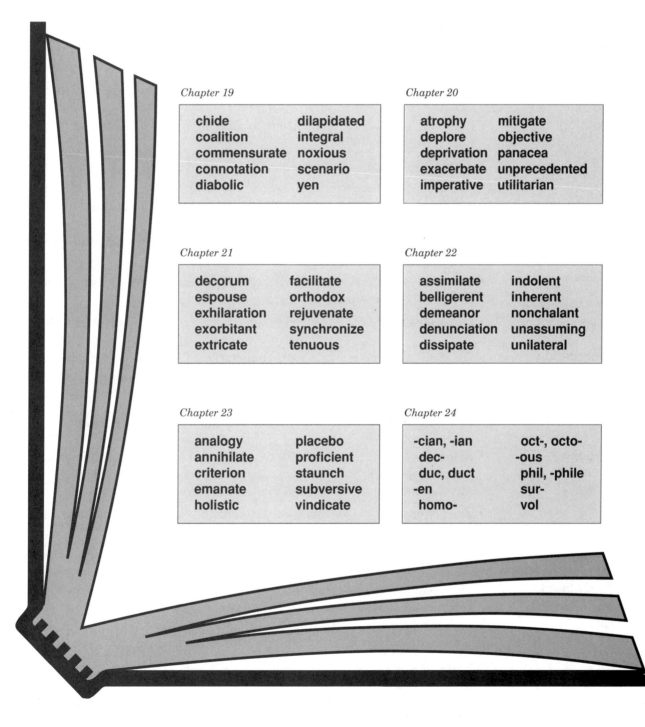

Chapter 19

chide	dilapidated
coalition	integral
commensurate	noxious
connotation	scenario
diabolic	yen

Chapter 20

atrophy	mitigate
deplore	objective
deprivation	panacea
exacerbate	unprecedented
imperative	utilitarian

Chapter 21

decorum	facilitate
espouse	orthodox
exhilaration	rejuvenate
exorbitant	synchronize
extricate	tenuous

Chapter 22

assimilate	indolent
belligerent	inherent
demeanor	nonchalant
denunciation	unassuming
dissipate	unilateral

Chapter 23

analogy	placebo
annihilate	proficient
criterion	staunch
emanate	subversive
holistic	vindicate

Chapter 24

-cian, -ian	oct-, octo-
dec-	-ous
duc, duct	phil, -phile
-en	sur-
homo-	vol

chide	dilapidated
coalition	integral
commensurate	noxious
connotation	scenario
diabolic	yen

Ten Words in Context

In the space provided, write the letter of the meaning closest to that of each **boldfaced** word. Use the context of the sentences to help you figure out each word's meaning.

1 **chide**
(chīd)
-*verb*

    Chide means

- My parents **chided** me for getting sunburned, but my blistered skin hurt a lot more than their scolding.
- Elise was right to **chide** me when I lazily threw the newspapers into the trash instead of stacking and tying them for recycling.

  a. to command.   b. to criticize.   c. to be cruel to.

2 **coalition**
(kō′ə-lĭsh′ən)
-*noun*

    Coalition means

- Four colleges formed a **coalition** to operate a shared Center of Higher Education.
- A **coalition** of one sheriff, two horse thieves, three stagecoach robbers, and a couple of crooked gamblers once made up the government of Virginia City.

  a. one part of a whole.   b. a neighborhood.   c. a partnership.

3 **commensurate**
(kə-mĕn′shoŏr-ĭt)
-*adjective*

    Commensurate with
means

- Most students who work hard will eventually see results **commensurate** with their efforts.
- The expression "make the punishment fit the crime" means that a penalty should be **commensurate** with the degree of wrongdoing.

  a. essential to.   b. delayed by.   c. consistent with.

4 **connotation**
(kŏn′ə-tā′shən)
-*noun*

    Connotation means

- For many of us, the word *sea* has a **connotation** of salty air and vast openness.
- *Sayonara*, the Japanese word for "goodbye," actually means "if it must be so" and thus has **connotations** of sadness at parting.

  a. a suggested meaning.   b. a handicap.   c. a warning.

5 **diabolic**
(dī′ə-bŏl′ĭk)
-*adjective*

    Diabolic means

- In the musical *Sweeney Todd: The Demon Barber of Fleet Street*, the barber is indeed **diabolic**: he kills his clients by cutting their throats so that his friend Mrs. Lovett can make the victims into meat pies.
- The horror story featured open graves, walking corpses, and a **diabolic** villain who turned an entire townful of people into zombies.

  a. lazy.   b. frightened.   c. devilish.

6 **dilapidated**
(də-lăp′ə-dāt′ĭd)
-*adjective*

    Dilapidated means

- The **dilapidated** house must have once been handsome. Some of its broken windows are stained glass, and the loose door hinges are fine metalwork.
- My son's teddy bear is **dilapidated**, with both ears hanging by threads and the stuffing coming out, but he won't let go of it long enough for me to repair it.

  a. out of proportion.   b. strongly desired.   c. run-down.

7 integral
(ĭn'tə-grəl)
-adjective

- Arguing seems to be an **integral** part of Laura and Nate's relationship. If they weren't fighting, they'd have nothing to say to each other.
- Voting is **integral** to democracy. Without free elections, a democratic system cannot continue to exist.

___ *Integral* means   a. essential.   b. very small.   c. predicted.

8 noxious
(nŏk'shəs)
-adjective

- When you are cleaning, never mix ammonia and bleach. The **noxious** gas they produce could land you in the hospital.
- The entire office building had to be evacuated when **noxious** fumes started coming out of the air vents and dozens of workers got sick.

___ *Noxious* means   a. potential.   b. unhealthy.   c. impossible.

9 scenario
(sĭ-nâr'ē-ō)
-noun

- "I've worked out an overall **scenario** for the movie," the screenwriter said, "but I haven't gone beyond the basic plot."
- To help governments and industries plan for the future, experts sometimes develop **scenarios** describing what might happen in the next year or decade.

___ *Scenario* means   a. an outline of possible events.   b. a budget.   c. an actual occurrence.

10 yen
(yĕn)
-noun

- Whenever I have a **yen** for a cigarette, I chew on a pencil instead.
- My **yen** for garlic bagel chips doesn't go away even after I've eaten a whole bagful.

___ *Yen* means   a. a longing.   b. a feeling of disapproval.   c. a memory.

Matching Words with Definitions

Following are definitions of the ten words. Clearly write or print each word next to its definition. The sentences above and on the previous page will help you decide on the meaning of each word.

1. _____ Harmful to life or health; poisonous

2. _____ A sequence of events that is imagined, assumed, or suggested

3. _____ Very cruel; wicked; demonic

4. _____ To scold mildly or express disapproval

5. _____ A strong desire; craving

6. _____ Necessary to the whole; belonging to the whole

7. _____ A union of individuals, groups, or nations for some specific purpose

8. _____ Corresponding in degree, number, or size; in proportion

9. _____ A secondary meaning suggested by a word, in addition to the word's dictionary definition

10. _____ Fallen into a state in which repairs are badly needed; broken down

CAUTION: Do not go any further until you are sure the above answers are correct. Then you can use the definitions to help you in the following practices. Your goal is eventually to know the words well enough so that you don't need to check the definitions at all.

➤ *Sentence Check 1*

Using the answer line provided, complete each item below with the correct word from the box. Use each word once.

a. **chide**	b. **coalition**	c. **commensurate**	d. **connotation**	e. **diabolic**
f. **dilapidated**	g. **integral**	h. **noxious**	i. **scenario**	j. **yen**

_____ 1. The doctor ___(e)d Rick for not following her advice about switching to a low-fat diet.

_____ 2. One Chinese emperor was so quick to have people executed that his officials always said their last goodbyes when they were summoned to the presence of their ___ ruler.

_____ 3. We may argue about whether character or plot is more important, but they are both ___ to any novel.

_____ 4. The New York telephone directory lists twenty different ___s, including action groups for "Korean-American Voters," "Fairness to Africa," and "A Smoke-Free City."

_____ 5. Often, to satisfy a ___, I eat something sweet, only to find that the sweetness has produced an equally strong craving for something salty.

_____ 6. "I wish I could give you a grade ___ with the excellence of your paper," the professor said. "Unfortunately, there is no such grade as A plus-plus."

_____ 7. Dictionaries usually don't give the ___s of words. These associated meanings become familiar to us only through experience.

_____ 8. My parents always know when my friend Theo has been here because his ___ old car, which has a leaky radiator, leaves a puddle of water in the driveway.

_____ 9. Cigarettes aren't bad only for smokers. "Secondhand smoke" is also ___ and can be harmful to everyone nearby.

_____ 10. I had thought up several ___s of how my widowed mother might marry again, but I never would have predicted what actually happened: she married my widowed father-in-law.

NOTE: Now check your answers to these questions by turning to page 176. Going over the answers carefully will help you prepare for the next two practices, for which answers are not given.

➤ *Sentence Check 2*

Using the answer lines provided, complete each item below with **two** words from the box. Use each word once.

_____ 1–2. When red M&Ms were discontinued, angry consumers ___(e)d the
_____ company and formed a "___ for the Restoration and Preservation of Red M&Ms." The company hastily reinstated° the red pieces.

_____ 3–4. The developers who endangered the local water supply by dumping
_____   ___ wastes in the landfill did not get a punishment that was ___ with
                            their reprehensible° act: they had to pay only a small fine.

_____ 5–6. A dark, ___ old house in our neighborhood scares local children, who
_____   feel that the quiet, unfriendly owner is some sort of ___ villain.

_____ 7–8. The TV writer was distraught°: "The producer told me to shorten the
_____   script by cutting the deathbed scene out of my ___. But how can I? It's
                            a(n)___ part of the story."

_____ 9–10. While the word "___" can refer to a strong desire for anything, to many
_____   people it has the specific ___ of a sharp longing for a particular food.

➤ *Final Check:* Halloween Troubles

Here is a final opportunity for you to strengthen your knowledge of the ten words. First read the following selection carefully. Then fill in each blank with a word from the box at the top of the previous page. (Context clues will help you figure out which word goes in which blank.) Use each word once.

Discomfort was such a(n) (1)_____ part of my childhood Halloweens that I wouldn't have recognized the holiday without it. In retrospect°, I think I must have been a masochist°. As a Dutch girl, I limped from door to door in crippling wooden shoes. As a vampire with sharp fangs, I cut my lower lip every time I said "Trick or treat." Even today the word *Halloween* carries for me (2)_____s of physical misery.

My (3)_____ for the perfect Halloween encompassed° not only scaring others, but also frightening myself. So I was willing to approach even the most scary-looking houses, ones sure to be haunted or to belong to (4)_____ witches waiting to boil children for dinner. Generally, such houses were (5)_____, with cracked windows, creaking steps, and loose shutters banging in the wind. Even scarier than those places, however, were the (6)_____s of high-school students. At any moment, these gangs might corner me and demand, "Your candy or your life." I might die if I refused to relinquish° my Baby Ruths, Hershey's Kisses, and Three Musketeers.

My candy haul was always disappointing, never (7)_____ with what I had suffered on my rounds. In addition, as soon as I returned home, my parents would order me to throw out all unwrapped candy, since it might contain some (8)_____ substance, even poison. By then, of course, I had built up a powerful and indiscriminate° (9)_____ for candy—any candy at all. So I would stuff myself with the loot that remained—and then be (10) _____(e)d for getting sick.

Scores	Sentence Check 2 _____%	Final Check _____%

Enter your scores above and in the vocabulary performance chart on the inside back cover of the book.

CHAPTER

20

atrophy	mitigate
deplore	objective
deprivation	panacea
exacerbate	unprecedented
imperative	utilitarian

Ten Words in Context

In the space provided, write the letter of the meaning closest to that of each **boldfaced** word. Use the context of the sentences to help you figure out each word's meaning.

1 **atrophy**
(ă′trə-fē)
-*verb*

- Since unused muscles **atrophy**, an arm or a leg that remains in a cast for some time becomes thinner.

- "If you watch any more of those mindless television programs," my father said, "your brain will **atrophy**."

___ *Atrophy* means   a. to grow.   b. to waste away.   c. to cause pain.

2 **deplore**
(dĭ-plôr′)
-*verb*

- Bernie **deplored** his coworkers' habit of taking home paper clips, Scotch tape, pens, and stationery from the office, a practice he felt was dishonest.

- Many people **deplore** pornography but feel we must tolerate it, because they disapprove just as strongly of censorship.

___ *Deplore* means   a. to condemn.   b. to ignore.   c. to make worse.

3 **deprivation**
(dĕp′rə-vā′shən)
-*noun*

- Children who spend their early years in institutions where they receive no love may suffer throughout life from the effects of this **deprivation**.

- Typically, women lose income after a divorce, but that is not their only **deprivation**. They also lose status, identity, and sometimes even their homes and children.

___ *Deprivation* means   a. a deficiency.   b. a feeling of disapproval.   c. a strong desire.

4 **exacerbate**
(ĕg-zăs′ər-bāt)
-*verb*

- Scratching a mosquito bite only makes it worse: the scraping **exacerbates** the itching and may even cause an infection.

- Instead of soothing the baby, the sound of the music box seemed only to **exacerbate** his crying.

___ *Exacerbate* means   a. to find the cause of.   b. to relieve.   c. to make worse.

5 **imperative**
(ĭm-pĕr′ə-tĭv)
-*adjective*

- It is **imperative** that I renew my driver's license today—it expires at midnight.

- "It is **imperative** for this letter to reach Mr. Rivera tomorrow," the boss said, "so please send it by Express Mail."

___ *Imperative* means   a. impossible.   b. difficult.   c. essential.

6 **mitigate**
(mĭt′ə-gāt)
-*verb*

- The disabilities resulting from Mr. Dobbs's stroke were **mitigated** by physical therapy, but he still has difficulty using his right arm.

- Time usually **mitigates** the pain of a lost love. When Richard's girlfriend broke their engagement, he was miserable, but now the hurt is much less.

___ *Mitigate* means   a. to relieve.   b. to worsen.   c. to reveal.

7 objective
(əb-jĕk′tĭv)
-adjective

- Scientists must strive to be totally **objective** in their observations and experiments, putting aside their personal wishes and expectations.
- All too often, we let our own prejudices prevent us from being **objective** in judging others.

__ *Objective* means   a. personal.   b. open-minded.   c. persuasive.

8 panacea
(păn′ə-sē′ə)
-noun

- My aunt considers vitamins a **panacea**. She believes that they can cure everything from chapped lips to heart disease.
- Ravi thinks his troubles would be over if he just had plenty of money. But money isn't a **panacea**; it wouldn't solve all his problems.

__ *Panacea* means   a. a belief.   b. a basic necessity.   c. a universal remedy.

9 unprecedented
(ŭn-prĕs′ə-dĕn′tĭd)
-adjective

- When Sandra Day O'Connor was named to the Supreme Court, her appointment was **unprecedented**—all the previous justices had been men.
- The spring concert was "standing room only." This was **unprecedented**, the first time in the history of the college that the concert had been sold out.

__ *Unprecedented* means   a. unheard-of.   b. unprejudiced.   c. controversial.

10 utilitarian
(yōō-tĭl′ə-târ′ē-ən)
-adjective

- One difference between "arts" and "crafts" is that crafts tend to be more **utilitarian**. They are generally created to serve a specific use.
- I prefer **utilitarian** gifts, such as pots and pans, to gifts that are meant to be just ornamental or beautiful.

__ *Utilitarian* means   a. unique.   b. practical.   c. inexpensive.

Matching Words with Definitions

Following are definitions of the ten words. Clearly write or print each word next to its definition. The sentences above and on the previous page will help you decide on the meaning of each word.

1. _____   To aggravate (a situation or condition); make more severe

2. _____   To make less severe or less intense; relieve

3. _____   Being the first instance of something; never having occurred before

4. _____   Something supposed to cure all diseases, evils, or difficulties; cure-all

5. _____   To wear down, lose strength, or become weak, as from disuse, disease, or injury (said of a body part); to wither away

6. _____   Lack or shortage of one or more basic necessities

7. _____   Necessary; urgent

8. _____   Not influenced by emotion or personal prejudice; based only on what can be observed

9. _____   Made or intended for practical use; stressing usefulness over beauty or other considerations

10. _____   To feel or express disapproval of

CAUTION: Do not go any further until you are sure the above answers are correct. Then you can use the definitions to help you in the following practices. Your goal is eventually to know the words well enough so that you don't need to check the definitions at all.

➤ *Sentence Check 1*

Using the answer line provided, complete each item below with the correct word from the box. Use each word once.

a. atrophy	b. deplore	c. deprivation	d. exacerbate	e. imperative
f. mitigate	g. objective	h. panacea	i. unprecedented	j. utilitarian

_____ 1. When we go camping and my kids have to spend a whole weekend without pizza and TV, they think they are undergoing some great ___.

_____ 2. The last time I had a migraine headache, I tried draping a cold, wet cloth over my eyes to ___ the pain and nausea, but they only got worse.

_____ 3. First-aid instructions usually advise against moving an accident victim, because movement can ___ an injury.

_____ 4. The election of John F. Kennedy, a Catholic, to the presidency was ___ in American history—he was the first Catholic president.

_____ 5. No one could ___ drinking and driving more than Elena; her son was killed by a drunk driver.

_____ 6. Although an Oscar is not meant to be ___, one Academy Award winner uses his as a paperweight.

_____ 7. If you find it difficult to be ___ about your own writing, try asking a classmate to read it over and give you an unbiased opinion.

_____ 8. Our city has many different crime-related problems, but the mayor has only one solution to offer: more police officers on the streets. She believes an enlarged police force is a ___.

_____ 9. When told that Ms. Thomas was in conference and could not be disturbed, the caller said urgently, "It's ___ that I speak to her. Her house is on fire."

_____ 10. In Burma, some women lengthen their necks by stretching them with copper coils. This practice damages the muscles, causing them to ___: they become thin and weak.

NOTE: Now check your answers to these questions by turning to page 176. Going over the answers carefully will help you prepare for the next two practices, for which answers are not given.

➤ *Sentence Check 2*

Using the answer lines provided, complete each item below with **two** words from the box. Use each word once.

_____
_____ 1–2. "Hands Across America" was a fund-raising effort to help ___ hunger in regions where ___ was widespread.

_____
_____ 3–4. Many people are so opposed to change that they ___ as potentially harmful just about anything that is new and ___.

_____ 5–6. It's hard to know what treatment is optimum° for a sprained ankle.
_____   Walking on the ankle can ___ the injury, but if you don't walk on it for
                             a long time, the muscles will start to ___.

_____ 7–8. If you want to be ___, it is ___ that you put aside your emotions and
_____   prejudices.

_____ 9–10. In deciding which over-the-counter medicine to take, it's important to
_____   use a(n) ___ approach. Choose a drug for the specific purpose it serves,
                              and don't rely on any one drug as a ___.

➤ _Final Check:_ Thomas Dooley

Here is a final opportunity for you to strengthen your knowledge of the ten words. First read the following selection carefully. Then fill in each blank with a word from the box at the top of the previous page. (Context clues will help you figure out which word goes in which blank.) Use each word once.

In the 1950s, a young American doctor named Thomas Dooley arrived in Laos, in southeast Asia. He was shocked by the ubiquitous° sickness and poverty he found there. The people lived without plumbing or electricity, and they had no knowledge of health care or even of basic hygiene. For example, one boy with an infected leg had been told not to walk at all, which caused both of his legs to (1)_____. The people's lack of knowledge was (2)_____(e)d by superstitions and by a reliance on well-meaning traditional healers, who sometimes inadvertently° gave useless or harmful advice. They might, for example, advocate° pig grease for a burn or treat a fracture by chanting. Dooley (3)_____(e)d the terrible (4)_____ he saw. He felt that it was (5)_____ to help these communities learn about modern medicine—to help them apply (6)_____ scientific knowledge—and equally essential for them to relinquish° their harmful superstitions. Dooley did not believe that modern medicine would be a (7)_____ for every problem in Laos, but he firmly believed that he could at least (8)_____ the people's suffering.

Dooley's (9)_____ approach to health care, based specifically on practical instruction, was (10)_____: no one before him had tried to teach the communities how to care for themselves. Dooley believed that teaching was an integral° part of medical care, that it was useless to treat symptoms and allow the causes to continue. So, subsidized° by local governments, he set up hospitals and taught the rudimentary° principles of hygiene, nursing, and medical treatment.

Tom Dooley died at a tragically young age, but his work and the tenets° that guided it benefited countless people.

Scores	Sentence Check 2 _____%	Final Check _____%

Enter your scores above and in the vocabulary performance chart on the inside back cover of the book.

CHAPTER

21

decorum	facilitate
espouse	orthodox
exhilaration	rejuvenate
exorbitant	synchronize
extricate	tenuous

Ten Words in Context

In the space provided, write the letter of the meaning closest to that of each **boldfaced** word. Use the context of the sentences to help you figure out each word's meaning.

1 decorum
(dĭ-kô′rəm)
-noun

- **Decorum** demands that you send a thank-you note for all wedding gifts, even those you don't like or will never use.
- In her newspaper columns, Miss Manners gives advice on **decorum** in all kinds of situations. For example, she says that at a dinner party, you must be polite even if you find a bug crawling in your salad.

__ *Decorum* means   a. a difficult situation.   b. beauty.   c. proper conduct.

2 espouse
(ĕ-spouz′)
-verb

- Some politicians **espouse** whatever ideas they think will win them votes.
- People who **espouse** animals' rights often find themselves in conflict with scientists who argue for the use of animals in medical experiments.

__ *Espouse* means   a. to speak for.   b. to argue against.   c. to study.

3 exhilaration
(ĕg-zĭl′ə-rā′shən)
-noun

- After the last exam of the year, Jan and I were so filled with **exhilaration** that we skipped all the way to the car.
- A marching band gives most people a feeling of **exhilaration**. The lively music makes them feel excited.

__ *Exhilaration* means   a. appropriateness.   b. liveliness.   c. commitment.

4 exorbitant
(ĕg-zôr′bĭ-tənt)
-adjective

- Even if I were rich, I wouldn't pay three hundred dollars for those shoes. That's an **exorbitant** price.
- The armed forces often spend **exorbitant** amounts on minor items, including an eight-hundred-dollar ashtray and a toilet seat that cost thousands of dollars.

__ *Exorbitant* means   a. estimated.   b. inconvenient.   c. extremely high.

5 extricate
(ĕks′trĭ-kāt′)
-verb

- The fly struggled and struggled but was unable to **extricate** itself from the spider's web.
- The young couple ran up so many debts that they finally needed a counselor to help them **extricate** themselves from their financial mess.

__ *Extricate* means   a. to untangle.   b. to distinguish.   c. to excuse.

6 facilitate
(fə-sĭl′ə-tāt′)
-verb

- Automatic doors in supermarkets **facilitate** the entry and exit of customers with bags or shopping carts.
- For those with poor eyesight, large print **facilitates** reading.

__ *Facilitate* means   a. to decrease.   b. to cause.   c. to assist.

7 orthodox
(ôr′thə-dŏks′)
-*adjective*

- When Father McKenzie brought drums and electric guitars into church, he shocked the more **orthodox** members of his congregation.
- The **orthodox** footwear for a sprint or distance race is some kind of running shoes, but a champion Ethiopian runner competed in the Olympics barefoot.

___ *Orthodox* means   a. revolutionary.   b. traditional.   c. important.

8 rejuvenate
(rĭ-jo͞o′və-nāt′)
-*verb*

- The Fountain of Youth was a legendary spring whose water could **rejuvenate** people.
- The grass had become brown and matted, but a warm spring rain **rejuvenated** it, perking it up and turning it green again.

___ *Rejuvenate* means   a. to set free.   b. to excite.   c. to give new life to.

9 synchronize
(sĭng′krə-nīz′)
-*verb*

- The secret agents **synchronized** their watches so that they could cross the border at exactly the same minute.
- We need to **synchronize** the clocks in our house: the kitchen clock is ten minutes slower than the alarm clock in the bedroom.

___ *Synchronize* means   a. to coordinate.   b. to repair.   c. to find.

10 tenuous
(tĕn′yo͞o-əs)
-*adjective*

- It doesn't take much to destroy an already **tenuous** relationship. Something as slight as forgetting to telephone can cause an unstable relationship to collapse.
- Del was opposed to the Equal Rights Amendment, but his position seemed **tenuous**. He couldn't support it with any facts, and his logic was weak.

___ *Tenuous* means   a. shaky.   b. easy.   c. established.

Matching Words with Definitions

Following are definitions of the ten words. Clearly write or print each word next to its definition. The sentences above and on the previous page will help you decide on the meaning of each word.

1. _____ Cheerfulness; high spirits
2. _____ To free from a tangled situation or a difficulty
3. _____ Having little substance or basis; weak; poorly supported
4. _____ Correctness in behavior and manners; standards or conventions of socially acceptable behavior
5. _____ To make (someone) feel or seem young again; to make (something) seem fresh or new again
6. _____ To support, argue for, or adopt (an idea or cause)
7. _____ To cause to occur at exactly the same time; to cause (clocks and watches) to agree in time
8. _____ To make easier to do or to get
9. _____ Following established, traditional rules or beliefs, especially in religion; following what is customary or commonly accepted
10. _____ Excessive, especially in amount, cost, or price; beyond what is reasonable or appropriate

CAUTION: Do not go any further until you are sure the above answers are correct. Then you can use the definitions to help you in the following practices. Your goal is eventually to know the words well enough so that you don't need to check the definitions at all.

➤ *Sentence Check 1*

Using the answer line provided, complete each item below with the correct word from the box. Use each word once.

a. **decorum**	b. **espouse**	c. **exhilaration**	d. **exorbitant**	e. **extricate**
f. **facilitate**	g. **orthodox**	h. **rejuvenate**	i. **synchronize**	j. **tenuous**

_____ 1. Ignoring all standards of cafeteria ___, students sat on the tables and threw french fries at each other.

_____ 2. Some premature babies are so tiny and weak that their hold on life is very ___.

_____ 3. The ads for the anti-wrinkle cream claim that it will ___ aging skin.

_____ 4. The new restaurant went out of business because of its ___ prices.

_____ 5. The children's ___ at the amusement park was contagious—their parents soon felt excited too.

_____ 6. If you're giving a dinner party, preparing some food platters ahead of time will ___ your work when the guests arrive.

_____ 7. At age two, Patrick got his head stuck between the bars of an iron railing. His parents had to call the fire department to come and ___ him.

_____ 8. During the 1960s and 1970s, there were bitter clashes between those who ___(e)d the United States' involvement in Vietnam and those who were opposed to it.

_____ 9. New members of the water ballet club have trouble coordinating their swimming, but with practice, the group is able to ___ its movements.

_____ 10. "The ___ treatment in this kind of case," the doctor said, "is surgery followed by chemotherapy. But some specialists are exploring the possibility of using surgery alone."

NOTE: Now check your answers to these questions by turning to page 177. Going over the answers carefully will help you prepare for the next two practices, for which answers are not given.

➤ *Sentence Check 2*

Using the answer lines provided, complete each item below with **two** words from the box. Use each word once.

_____
_____ 1–2. It filled the audience with ___ to see the dancers in the chorus line ___ their turns and kicks so perfectly.

_____
_____ 3–4. In any religion, ___ practices are slow to change. New ones are always in a(n) ___ position at first and require time to become widely accepted.

_____
_____ 5–6. Although it seems ___, an expensive vacation may be worth the money, as it can often ___ one's mind and body.

_____   7–8. Foreign Service officers must observe strict rules of conduct. If their behavior violates ___, their government may have to ___ itself from a diplomatic mess.

_____

_____   9–10. My grandmother ___(e)d garlic as a treatment for chest colds, in the belief that it ___(e)d breathing. Sometimes she made us eat it, and sometimes she rubbed it on our chests. As a result, we were often ostracized° by our friends, who found the smell of garlic repugnant°.

_____

➤ *Final Check:* Twelve Grown Men in a Bug

Here is a final opportunity for you to strengthen your knowledge of the ten words. First read the following selection carefully. Then fill in each blank with a word from the box at the top of the previous page. (Context clues will help you figure out which word goes in which blank.) Use each word once.

My college reunions are very traditional occasions, but there is usually very little that's (1)_____ about my husband's.

Take, for example, one of the final events of his reunion last year. It all began when a big, bearded man stood up to address the raucous° crowd. Over the noise, the man yelled, "You are about to see an amazing sight. The twelve large, robust° hunks of manhood you see up here, none with a waistline smaller than forty-two inches, are about to squeeze into this Volkswagen Beetle. We're not here to (2)_____ the use of economy cars, and we're not masochists° trying to torture ourselves. It's just that we all fit into the Beetle twenty years ago, and we aim to do it again today. Unless we occasionally (3)_____ ourselves by letting go of our serious side and doing something inane°, how can we stay young?

"Now, I know that some of you have (4)_____ bets in the amount of two whole bucks riding on this," he joked. "We won't fail those who believe in us. And those of you who consider our claim (5)_____, just watch."

Then the bear of a man turned to the eleven others. "Okay, heroes," he exhorted° them, "this is no time for (6)_____. Forget your manners, and do anything you can to (7)_____ this mighty task. Now, let's (8)_____ our start—all together: ready, set, go!"

Shoving, yelling, and cursing, the twelve men tried to squeeze into the car. "If they do get in," I said to my husband, "how will they ever (9)_____ themselves?"

Moments later, however, everyone was cheering vociferously°. All twelve men were inside the car. After a few seconds, they exploded out of it, wild with (10)_____. Sweaty but triumphant, they jumped up and down and hugged one another.

Scores	Sentence Check 2 _____%	Final Check _____%

Enter your scores above and in the vocabulary performance chart on the inside back cover of the book.

assimilate	indolent
belligerent	inherent
demeanor	nonchalant
denunciation	unassuming
dissipate	unilateral

Ten Words in Context

In the space provided, write the letter of the meaning closest to that of each **boldfaced** word. Use the context of the sentences to help you figure out each word's meaning.

1 **assimilate**
(ə-sĭm′ə-lāt′)
-verb

- To **assimilate** into the culture of a new country, it's essential to learn the language.
- The United States has often been called a "melting pot"—meaning that people of many cultures have **assimilated**, or blended together, within it.

__ *Assimilate* means   a. to be absorbed.   b. to spread thin.   c. to remain.

2 **belligerent**
(bə-lĭj′ə-rənt)
-adjective

- When Bruce drinks, he becomes **belligerent**. He has often started barroom fights and brawls.
- Angie was suspended for her **belligerent** behavior during an argument with one of her teachers. She actually shook her fist at him and threatened to hit him.

__ *Belligerent* means   a. overly casual.   b. quarrelsome.   c. confused.

3 **demeanor**
(dĭ-mēn′ər)
-noun

- Troy's **demeanor** was quiet and controlled, but inside he was boiling with anger.
- Proper **demeanor** during a lecture or religious service is obviously quite different from acceptable conduct at a ball game or rock concert.

__ *Demeanor* means   a. behavior.   b. feelings.   c. expectation.

4 **denunciation**
(dĭ-nŭn′sē-ā′shən)
-noun

- In an unusual **denunciation** of parents, the community leader said, "Parents have not been taking enough responsibility for their children."
- The mayor's public **denunciation** of the police chief angered many officers; local citizens, however, applauded the mayor's public statement of disapproval.

__ *Denunciation* means   a. appreciation.   b. ignoring.   c. criticism.

5 **dissipate**
(dĭs′ə-pāt′)
-verb

- After twenty minutes of meditation, I find that the stresses of my day have **dissipated**, and I'm relaxed enough to enjoy the evening.
- Teddy hates catching a cold. When anyone is sneezing and coughing in his presence, he opens a window and fans the air to **dissipate** the cold germs.

__ *Dissipate* means   a. to blend.   b. to scatter.   c. to assemble.

6 **indolent**
(ĭn′də-lənt)
-adjective

- My **indolent** sister says that the most work she ever wants to do is clicking the remote control to switch TV channels.
- My uncle has been fired from three jobs for being **indolent**. He shows up on time, but he does little work and leaves early.

__ *Indolent* means   a. destructive.   b. shy.   c. unwilling to work.

7 **inherent**
(ĭn-hîr′ənt)
-*adjective*

• An **inherent** danger of life in San Francisco is the possibility of earthquakes.
• Marco believes that kindness is **inherent** in human nature, but I think people are born selfish. Maybe we're both right.

___ *Inherent* means   a. shrinking.   b. humble.   c. natural.

8 **nonchalant**
(nŏn′shə-lŏnt′)
-*adjective*

• Because air travel is so commonplace today, many people have become **nonchalant** about flying. In the early days of flight, however, people saw it as an exciting and risky adventure.
• My friend was very **nonchalant** about giving her oral report in class, but I was a nervous wreck about giving mine.

___ *Nonchalant* means   a. coolly unconcerned.   b. anxious.   c. angry.

9 **unassuming**
(ŭn′ə-sōō′mĭng)
-*adjective*

• In the business world, you shouldn't be too **unassuming**. If you're overly modest about your skills and achievements, for example, you might not get a promotion you deserve.
• As **unassuming** as ever, Alice accepted the award in a quiet, modest way.

___ *Unassuming* means   a. argumentative.   b. lazy.   c. humble.

10 **unilateral**
(yōōn′ə-lăt′ər-əl)
-*adjective*

• Many people believe in **unilateral** disarmament; that is, they think their own nation should give up all weapons of war even if no other country will do so.
• Lonette's **unilateral** decisions are hurting her marriage. For instance, she recently bought nonrefundable tickets to Florida without consulting her husband.

___ *Unilateral* means   a. gradual.   b. one-sided.   c. group.

Matching Words with Definitions

Following are definitions of the ten words. Clearly write or print each word next to its definition. The sentences above and on the previous page will help you decide on the meaning of each word.

1. _____   Conduct; outward behavior; manner

2. _____   Lazy; avoiding or disliking work

3. _____   Modest; not boastful or arrogant

4. _____   To thin out or scatter and gradually vanish; drive away

5. _____   Calm, carefree, and casually unconcerned

6. _____   To become more similar to a larger whole; especially, to blend into or adjust to a main culture

7. _____   Involving or done by only one side

8. _____   Existing as a natural or essential quality of a person or thing; built-in

9. _____   Quick or eager to argue or fight; hostile; aggressive

10. _____   A strong expression of disapproval; an act of condemning, especially publicly

CAUTION: Do not go any further until you are sure the above answers are correct. Then you can use the definitions to help you in the following practices. Your goal is eventually to know the words well enough so that you don't need to check the definitions at all.

➣ *Sentence Check 1*

Using the answer line provided, complete each item below with the correct word from the box. Use each word once.

a. **assimilate**	b. **belligerent**	c. **demeanor**	d. **denunciation**	e. **dissipate**
f. **indolent**	g. **inherent**	h. **nonchalant**	i. **unassuming**	j. **unilateral**

_____ 1. The eye is not necessarily a(n) ___ part of the reading processs. Blind people can read Braille—a system of raised dots—with their fingertips.

_____ 2. Anger builds up if you hold it in. But expressing anger can help it to ___, leaving you much calmer.

_____ 3. Jerry is a(n) ___ child who frequently pushes and hits other children.

_____ 4. In a ___ of the union, the company president said that its members were "selfish and narrow-minded."

_____ 5. It's amazing how ___ kids can be about computers; they'll work at the keyboard as casually as if it were a coloring book.

_____ 6. Because she herself is a workaholic, my boss thinks that anyone who works less than ten hours a day is ___.

_____ 7. Airport security guards are trained to observe people's ___ so that they can notice and respond to any suspicious behavior.

_____ 8. Even though Marsha was the star of the team, she was always ___ and quick to give credit to the whole team for its successes.

_____ 9. Many Americans who live and work abroad make no attempt to ___ to foreign countries; they continue to eat only American food, speak only English, and see things only from an American perspective.

_____ 10. Governments are usually reluctant to take ___ action in international disputes. They want other countries to join them in their efforts.

NOTE: Now check your answers to these questions by turning to page 177. Going over the answers carefully will help you prepare for the next two practices, for which answers are not given.

➣ *Sentence Check 2*

Using the answer lines provided, complete each item below with **two** words from the box. Use each word once.

_____ 1–2. Esteban's ___ is consistently gentle and peaceful. By contrast, his
_____ brother Luis usually behaves in a rough and ___ way.

_____ 3–4. Tension was building between two gangs in the park when suddenly the
_____ leader of one gang made a brave ___ gesture: he held out his hand to the other leader. As they shook hands, the strain between the groups began to ___, and a fight was avoided.

_____ 5–6. Cara's calm, casual style seems to be a(n) ___ part of her personality. She

_____ remains ___ in tense situations that would make most people distraught°.

_____ 7–8. My mother, a zealot° for exercise, is loud in her ___ of my ___ ways.

_____ "Must you be so sedentary°?" she says. "Don't just sit around all the time like a lump of mashed potatoes!"

_____ 9–10. Because Wes is so quiet and ___, he found it difficult to ___ into a

_____ company in which people were very aggressive and competitive.

➤ *Final Check:* Adjusting to a Group Home

Here is a final opportunity for you to strengthen your knowledge of the ten words. First read the following selection carefully. Then fill in each blank with a word from the box at the top of the previous page. (Context clues will help you figure out which word goes in which blank.) Use each word once.

As Ken went up the path to the children's home, he dragged his feet, clenched his fists, and glared. His whole (1)_____ announced, "You can make me come here, but you can't make me like it." Ken was 11, and he had been sent to the group home by the court because there seemed to be no other recourse°—his mother was an alcoholic and his father had abandoned him.

Ken reacted angrily. His attitude toward the other children was (2)_____; he started fights over the smallest matters. His attitude toward the home was no better. When he was asked, "How are you getting on?" he would respond with a terse° (3)_____: "This place stinks." And his attitude toward his schoolwork and his assigned chores was (4)_____; he was so casual about his responsibilities that he was often scolded for being (5)_____.

One day, though, something happened that bolstered° Ken's spirits. A small, quiet boy was being teased by some older kids while others stood by watching, doing nothing to help. Risking a(n) (6)_____ action, Ken stood up for the child. When the younger boy thanked him, Ken was (7)_____, saying, "It's okay. It was nothing." After that incident, Ken started to (8)_____ more and more into the life of the home. As his anger (9)_____(e)d, his (10)_____ friendliness began to appear, and he became more gregarious°.

Naturally, Ken did not go through a complete metamorphosis°. He still fought now and then. But he had changed enough to become a happy and popular member of the group home.

Scores	Sentence Check 2 _____%	Final Check _____%	

Enter your scores above and in the vocabulary performance chart on the inside back cover of the book.

analogy	placebo
annihilate	proficient
criterion	staunch
emanate	subversive
holistic	vindicate

Ten Words in Context

In the space provided, write the letter of the meaning closest to that of each **boldfaced** word. Use the context of the sentences to help you figure out each word's meaning.

1 analogy
(ə-năl′ə-jē)
-noun

- To help students understand vision, instructors often draw an **analogy** between the eye and a camera.
- The commencement address, titled "You Are the Captain of Your Ship," used the **analogy** of life as an ocean-going vessel that the captain must steer between rocks.

__ *Analogy* means   a. picture.   b. comparison.   c. standard.

2 annihilate
(ə-nī′ə-lāt′)
-verb

- The movie was about a plot to **annihilate** whole cities by poisoning their water supply.
- "Universal Destroyer" is a warlike video game in which the aim is to **annihilate** the opponents.

__ *Annihilate* means   a. to escape from.   b. to seize.   c. to wipe out.

3 criterion
(krī-tēr′ē-ən)
-noun

- One **criterion** by which instructors judge a paper is clear organization.
- Some advertisers aren't concerned about telling the truth. Their only **criterion** for a good commercial is selling the product.

__ *Criterion* means   a. standard.   b. beginning.   c. answer.

4 emanate
(ĕm′ə-nāt′)
-verb

- As the cinnamon bread baked, a wonderful smell **emanated** from the kitchen.
- The screeching and scraping **emanating** from Keisha's bedroom tell me that she is practicing her violin.

__ *Emanate* means   a. to disappear.   b. to come out.   c. to expand.

5 holistic
(hō-lĭs′tĭk)
-adjective

- A good drug center takes a **holistic** approach to treatment, seeing each client not just as "an addict" but as a whole person. Along with medical aid, it provides emotional support, individual and family counseling, and follow-up services.
- Eastern cultures tend to take a more **holistic** view of learning than Western societies, focusing on the whole rather than analyzing parts.

__ *Holistic* means   a. easygoing.   b. concerned with the whole.   c. nonfinancial.

6 placebo
(plă-sē′bō)
-noun

- When my young son had a headache and I was out of aspirin, I gave him a **placebo**: a small candy that I told him was a "pain pill." It seemed to work—his headache went away.
- The doctor lost his license when it was found that the "nerve pills" he had been giving to many of his patients were actually a **placebo**—just sugar pills.

__ *Placebo* means   a. a fake medication.   b. a natural remedy.   c. an expensive cure.

7 proficient
(prə-fĭsh′ənt)
-adjective

- It's not all that hard to become **proficient** on a word processor. Be patient, and you'll develop the necessary skill.
- Wayne is a **proficient** woodworker. He is able to make professional-quality desks, bookshelves, and cabinets.

___ *Proficient* means   a. highly competent.   b. hard-working.   c. enthusiastic.

8 staunch
(stônch)
-adjective

- Although the mayor had been accused of taking bribes, he still had some **staunch** supporters.
- The newspaper's astrological predictions are often way off the mark, yet Tala remains a **staunch** believer in astrology and checks her horoscope every day.

___ *Staunch* means   a. busy.   b. unsteady.   c. faithful.

9 subversive
(səb-vûr′sĭv)
-adjective

- To some people, burning the American flag is a **subversive** act, aimed at destroying the nation. To others, it is simply an example of freedom of speech.
- The so-called "consulting company" was a cover for **subversive** activities; it was actually a ring of antigovernment agents.

___ *Subversive* means   a. having faith.   b. intended to overthrow.   c. blameless.

10 vindicate
(vĭn′də-kāt′)
-verb

- When Kai was accused of cheating on a geometry test, he **vindicated** himself by reciting several theorems from memory, proving that he knew the material.
- In our society, people falsely accused of crimes often must spend a great deal of money on legal fees in order to **vindicate** themselves.

___ *Vindicate* means   a. to prove innocent.   b. to make a commitment.   c. to weaken.

Matching Words with Definitions

Following are definitions of the ten words. Clearly write or print each word next to its definition. The sentences above and on the previous page will help you decide on the meaning of each word.

1. _____   To clear from blame or suspicion; justify or prove right

2. _____   A substance which contains no medicine, but which the receiver believes is a medicine

3. _____   To flow or come out from a source; come forth

4. _____   A comparison between two things in order to clarify or dramatize a point

5. _____   To destroy completely; reduce to nothingness

6. _____   A standard by which something is or can be judged

7. _____   Acting or intended to overthrow or destroy something established

8. _____   Firm; loyal; strong in support

9. _____   Emphasizing the whole and the interdependence of its parts, rather than the parts separately

10. _____   Skilled; expert

CAUTION: Do not go any further until you are sure the above answers are correct. Then you can use the definitions to help you in the following practices. Your goal is eventually to know the words well enough so that you don't need to check the definitions at all.

➤ *Sentence Check 1*

Using the answer line provided, complete each item below with the correct word from the box. Use each word once.

a. **analogy**	b. **annihilate**	c. **criterion**	d. **emanate**	e. **holistic**
f. **placebo**	g. **proficient**	h. **staunch**	i. **subversive**	j. **vindicate**

_____ 1. During the Vietnam War, some protesters poured blood over draft records. Supporters of the war considered this a ___ act.

_____ 2. Passenger pigeons no longer exist. They were ___(e)d by hunters.

_____ 3. I'm a ___ fan of Whitney Houston. I have all her recordings.

_____ 4. One ___ used to judge the children's artwork was their use of vivid colors.

_____ 5. Although I'm quite a good cook, I'm not very ___ at baking. My pies tend to be runny, and my bread won't rise.

_____ 6. A ___ view of business would take into account not just profits but also such things as the work environment and employees' job satisfaction.

_____ 7. The fortuneteller claims that a halo of colored light ___s from each client and that its color reveals the person's character and future.

_____ 8. To stress the importance of a rich vocabulary, the instructor used a(n) ___. "Writing with a poor vocabulary," she said, "is like trying to paint a circus scene using only two colors."

_____ 9. Accused of shoplifting, the customer insisted that she had already paid for the items. She was ___(e)d when she pulled the receipt out of her purse.

_____ 10. To test a new painkiller, researchers gave it to one group of volunteers, while a second group got a(n) ___, identical in appearance to the new medicine but with no built-in power to relieve pain.

NOTE: Now check your answers to these questions by turning to page 177. Going over the answers carefully will help you prepare for the next two practices, for which answers are not given.

➤ *Sentence Check 2*

Using the answer lines provided, complete each item below with **two** words from the box. Use each word once.

_____
_____ 1–2. So much charm ___(e)d from the evil cult leader that he was able to persuade his followers to ___ an entire community.

_____
_____ 3–4. "One ___ by which I'll judge your papers," the professor said, "is whether you are ___ at connecting your ideas into a cohesive° whole."

_____
_____ 5–6. The agent was accused of selling government secrets, but he was able to ___ himself by proving that it was his boss who was the ___ one.

_____ 7–8. To explain why she supported ___ medicine, the doctor used a(n) ___. She said that taking a narrow view of a health problem is like treating a dying tree's leaves but ignoring its roots, where the real problem lies.

_____ 9–10. Anton is a(n) ___ believer in the power of a ___. When his small daughter started having nightmares about monsters, he sprayed the room with water and told her it was "anti-monster medicine."

➤ *Final Check:* **A Different Kind of Doctor**

Here is a final opportunity for you to strengthen your knowledge of the ten words. First read the following selection carefully. Then fill in each blank with a word from the box at the top of the previous page. (Context clues will help you figure out which word goes in which blank.) Use each word once.

Dr. Wilson considers (1)_____ medicine the optimum° approach to health care. He believes that to facilitate° healing and well-being, it is imperative° to consider a patient's entire lifestyle, not just specific aches and pains. To explain to patients how to keep well, he uses the (2)_____ of a garden. "If a garden gets too much or too little rain, sun, or fertilizer, it won't do well," he says. "But a proper balance keeps the body healthy. In the same way, the body needs proper amounts of good food, exercise, work, and relaxation."

Dr. Wilson often treats patients without giving them drugs. Many of his patients have begun to feel healthier since they started taking his advice. They've adopted such new habits as eating more vegetables and taking a brisk walk every day. As a result, a new liveliness and an increased sense of pleasure and exhilaration° seem to (3)_____ from them; many say they feel rejuvenated°.

Despite Dr. Wilson's successes, many orthodox° physicians do not sanction° his methods, and some even deplore° them. They see him as dangerously (4)_____, a threat to the medical establishment, and they scoff° at his drug-free "prescriptions," calling them powerless (5)_____s. They fear he wants to (6)_____ medical progress.

Dr. Wilson, however, has no wish to destroy medical progress. To the contrary, he believes that his methods represent such progress and that they are (7)_____(e)d by the improved health of his patients. There are other doctors worldwide who agree and who believe he is so (8)_____ at medicine that they often invite him to speak at professional conferences.

Dr. Wilson's patients also believe he is highly skilled, and they are the ones who are his most (9)_____ supporters. They judge him by a different (10)_____ from those who think medical progress lies only in finding new ways to treat disease. They judge him by the extent to which he helps his patients stay well.

| *Scores* | Sentence Check 2 _____% | Final Check _____% |

Enter your scores above and in the vocabulary performance chart on the inside back cover of the book.

-cian, -ian	oct-, octo-
dec-	-ous
duc, duct	phil, -phile
-en	sur-
homo-	vol

Ten Word Parts in Context

Figure out the meanings of the following ten word parts by looking *closely* and *carefully* at the context in which they appear. Then, in the space provided, write the letter of the meaning closest to that of each word part.

1 -cian, -ian

__ The word part *-cian* or *-ian* means

- A **politician** must be a specialist both in getting elected and in governing.
- To become a **librarian**, Liana had to complete the course work in library science and also be an intern in a library during the summer.

   a. a similarity.   b. a person with expertise.   c. made of.

2 dec-

__ The word part *dec-* means

- Another name for the Ten Commandments is the **Decalogue**.
- Around 800 A.D., the Hindus invented the modern **decimal** system, a number system based on 10.

   a. eight.   b. having a certain knowledge.   c. ten.

3 duc, duct

__ The word part *duc* or *duct* means

- The **ducal** palace was the residence of the duke—the leader of his subjects.
- When my father listens to classical music on the radio, he often swings his arms as if he's **conducting** the orchestra.

   a. to lead.   b. to be marked by.   c. to be above.

4 -en

__ The word part *-en* means

- Hong can't wear a **woolen** sweater over bare skin. The scratchy wool drives him crazy.
- When the archaeologists opened the tomb of the ancient Egyptian king, they found dozens of **golden** bowls, necklaces, and bracelets.

   a. same as.   b. attracted to.   c. made of.

5 homo-

__ The word part *homo-* means

- The people working at the store are a fairly **homogeneous** group. They're all in their early 20s, they've all had a year or two of college, and they're all single.
- It's no secret that David is **homosexual**. He's always been open about preferring same-sex relationships.

   a. different.   b. alike.   c. loving.

6 oct-, octo-

__ The word part *oct-* or *octo-* means

- An **octagon** is a geometrical figure with eight sides and eight angles.
- An **octopus** has eight arms; that may seem like a lot, but a squid has ten.

   a. eight.   b. ten.   c. above.

7 -ous

- Marla dreams of having great fame, but she has no idea what she wants to be **famous** for.

- Rashid is very **serious** lately. He seems to be full of deep thoughts.

___ The word part *-ous* means   a. characterized by.   b. loving.   c. beyond.

8 phil, -phile

- **Philadelphia** is often called the "city of brotherly love."

- Martin is a complete **Anglophile**. He adores English accents, clothes, music, manners, and cars, saying they're superior to anything on this side of the ocean.

___ The word part *phil* or *-phile* means   a. above.   b. love.   c. before.

9 sur-

- Siri polished the **surface** of the table until it shone like glass.

- Once our chickens started laying eggs, we had such a **surplus** that we were giving away dozens of extra eggs to our neighbors.

___ The word part *sur-* means   a. choose.   b. support.   c. over.

10 vol

- Many retirees offer their talents as **volunteers** in their communities, nationwide, and even throughout the world.

- According to the defense attorney, the defendant's confession was made under force, but the police and the prosecutor said that it had been **voluntary**.

___ The word part *vol* means   a. by choice.   b. without payment.   c. with skill.

Matching Word Parts with Definitions

Following are definitions of the ten word parts. Clearly write or print each word part next to its definition. The sentences above and on the previous page will help you decide on the meaning of each word part.

1. _____   Ten

2. _____   Having; full of; characterized by

3. _____   Over; above; additional

4. _____   To lead; guide; draw off

5. _____   Loving; lover; friend

6. _____   Made of

7. _____   Eight

8. _____   To will; choose

9. _____   A person with a certain ability or a certain kind of knowledge

10. _____   Same; similar

CAUTION: Do not go any further until you are sure the above answers are correct. Then you can use the definitions to help you in the following practices. Your goal is eventually to know the word parts well enough so that you don't need to check the definitions at all.

➤ *Sentence Check 1*

Using the answer line provided, complete each *italicized* word in the sentences below with the correct word part from the box. Use each word part once.

a. -cian, -ian	b. dec-	c. duc, duct	d. -en	e. homo-
f. oct-, octo-	g. -ous	h. phil, -phile	i. sur-	j. vol

_____ 1. Doing something on one's own (. . . *ition*) ___ means doing it by choice, of one's own free will.

_____ 2. Ralph sprayed a protective coating over the (*wood* . . .) ___ fence so that it wouldn't be eaten by termites.

_____ 3. If Ana's pain isn't better by tomorrow, she really should see a (*physic* . . .) ___.

_____ 4. The (. . . *athlon*) is an athletic competition made up of ten events.

_____ 5. Since there were only eight people in my high school choral class, we had a(n) (. . . *tet*) ___ instead of a choir.

_____ 6. A(n) (. . . *phone*) ___ is a word that's pronounced the same as another word. Examples are the word *write* and the family surname Wright.

_____ 7. An (*aque* . . .) ___ is a channel for bringing water from one place to another. The water is usually drawn along by gravity.

_____ 8. The wealthy woman was a true (. . . *anthropist*) ___; out of love for her fellow humans, she made generous donations to many causes.

_____ 9. If the theater department wants this semester's play to (. . . *pass*) ___ last semester's in attendance, it will have to run an extra night, since both nights were sold out last semester.

_____ 10. The disappearance of twenty dollars from my wallet is (*mysteri* . . .) ___. I'm sure the wallet was in my pocket all day.

NOTE: Now check your answers to these questions by turning to page 177. Going over the answers carefully will help you prepare for the next two practices, for which answers are not given.

➤ *Sentence Check 2*

Using the answer lines provided, complete each *italicized* word in the sentences below with the correct word part from the box. Use each word part once.

_____ 1–2. The (*magic* . . .) ___ called for someone from the audience to come up
_____ on the stage and be sawed in half. My impetuous° sister was the first to (. . . *unteer*) ___.

_____ 3–4. If peanut butter is not (. . . *genized*) ___, making it the same
_____ throughout, the oil separates and rises to the (. . . *face*) ___.

_____   5–6. Thomas is such a staunch° (*Franco . . .*) ___ that he thinks everything French is (*marvel . . .*) ___. If he ever moves to France, he should find it easy to assimilate° there.
_____

_____   7–8. My neighbor is a(n) (*. . . genarian*) ___, but he's so robust° you'd never guess he's lived eight (*. . . ades*) ___ just by looking at him.
_____

_____   9–10. Superman has x-ray vision but still can't see through lead—so one criminal decided to (*con . . .*) ___ his illicit° business in a room with (*lead . . .*) ___ walls.
_____

➤*Final Check:* Grandpa and Music

Here is a final opportunity for you to strengthen your knowledge of the ten word parts. First read the following selection carefully. Then complete each *italicized* word in the parentheses below with a word from the box at the top of the previous page. (Context clues will help you figure out which word part goes in which blank.) Use each word part once.

My grandfather had a beautiful singing voice as a younger man, and he loved to talk about his three (*. . . ades*) (1)_____ (from age 20 until 50) as a member of a group called the (*Gold . . .*) (2) "_____ Voices."

When the original seven members of the group heard him sing solos in his church, they invited him to join them, not realizing that he couldn't read music. He was determined not to let this be a liability°, and he worked hard to (*e . . . ate*) (3)_____ himself about music and become a proficient° (*music . . .*) (4)_____. He wanted to join the group for two reasons: he loved singing, and he had a crush on its lively young pianist.

After Grandfather became a member, the (*. . . et's*) (5)_____ success began to (*. . . pass*) (6)_____ all expectations. Their voices, he used to say, were so (*. . . geneous*) (7)_____ and so cohesive° that they sometimes sounded like a single voice singing all eight parts. Eventually, the group became so popular that the singers performed for pay, rather than just (*. . . unteering*) (8)_____ their services. The zenith° of their musical careers, said Grandpa, came when the group was invited to perform with the (*. . . harmonic*) (9)_____ Society; the opportunity to collaborate° with this famous orchestra made all eight singers euphoric°.

In retrospect°, though, Grandpa would always say that his own greatest success was marrying that (*vivaci . . .*) (10)_____ young pianist. It's probably superfluous° to add that they made beautiful music together.

| *Scores* | Sentence Check 2 _____% | Final Check _____% |

Enter your scores above and in the vocabulary performance chart on the inside back cover of the book.

UNIT FOUR: Review

The box at the right lists twenty-five words from Unit Four. Using the clues at the bottom of the page, fill in these words to complete the puzzle that follows.

annihilate
atrophy
belligerent
chide
decorum
deprivation
diabolic
dissipate
emanate
espouse
extricate
holistic
indolent
inherent
integral
mitigate
nonchalant
noxious
panacea
placebo
rejuvenate
staunch
tenuous
utilitarian
yen

ACROSS

1. Made or intended for practical use
4. To free from a tangled situation or a difficulty
5. To support, argue for, or adopt (an idea or cause)
7. Correctness in behavior and manners
8. To thin out or scatter and gradually vanish; drive away
9. To destroy completely; to reduce to nothingness
11. A substance containing no medicine, which the receiver believes is a medicine
14. Quick or eager to argue or fight; hostile; aggressive
19. Lazy; avoiding work
20. To wear down, lose strength, or become weak
21. To scold mildly
22. Firm; loyal; strong in support
23. Calm, carefree, and casually unconcerned

DOWN

2. Necessary to the whole; belonging to the whole
3. To make (someone) feel or seem young again
6. To flow out; come forth
7. Lack or shortage of one or more basic necessities
10. Emphasizing the whole and the interdependence of its parts
11. Something supposed to cure all diseases or evils
12. Very cruel; wicked; demonic
13. A strong desire; craving
15. Harmful to life or health
16. To make less severe; relieve
17. Having little substance or basis; weak; poorly supported
18. Existing as a natural or essential quality of a person or thing; built-in

UNIT FOUR: Test 1

PART A
Choose the word that best completes each item and write it in the space provided.

_____ 1. Fairy tales, such as "Hansel and Gretel" and "Cinderella," have given stepmothers a reputation for being ___.
   a. holistic   b. diabolic   c. unprecedented   d. unassuming

_____ 2. Hang-gliding produces a feeling of ___ that few other activities can match.
   a. exhilaration   b. decorum   c. connotation   d. atrophy

_____ 3. Superstitious people believe that a cold, clammy wind ___ from the "haunted" house on Elm Street.
   a. synchronizes   b. vindicates   c. emanates   d. mitigates

_____ 4. To ___ their movements so well, the dancers must practice doing the steps together for hours.
   a. chide   b. extricate   c. mitigate   d. synchronize

_____ 5. Because of her sense of ___, Aunt Ethel was outraged when she found her nieces skinny-dipping in the river.
   a. analogy   b. decorum   c. panacea   d. placebo

_____ 6. I had to ___ my little daughter for picking our neighbors' flowers, but she was so excited about giving me a bouquet that I couldn't really be angry.
   a. facilitate   b. chide   c. assimilate   d. espouse

_____ 7. When my sister's new boyfriend came chugging up in a(n) ___ van with no windows, my father offered to pay for a taxi.
   a. exorbitant   b. objective   c. dilapidated   d. unprecedented

_____ 8. The severe whipping his father gave him was hardly ___ with the little boy's misbehavior. All he did was eat a cookie before dinner.
   a. commensurate   b. proficient   c. tenuous   d. exorbitant

_____ 9. In order to find a ring of spies trying to learn military secrets, the government agent pretended to be involved in ___ activities.
   a. indolent   b. unilateral   c. holistic   d. subversive

_____ 10. When my boyfriend wants to hide something, he tries so hard to keep up his normal ___ that he begins to behave strangely.
   a. demeanor   b. coalition   c. yen   d. placebo

_____ 11. After keeping her angry feelings about her brother bottled up for months, Lani finally exploded with a ___ of his irresponsible ways.
   a. yen   b. criterion   c. panacea   d. denunciation

(Continues on next page)

_____ 12. It's amazing how I can ___ a thousand mosquitoes with bug spray, and an hour later another thousand appear.

      a. espouse   b. annihilate   c. facilitate   d. vindicate

_____ 13. Neighbors of the chemical company became suspicious that ___ fumes were coming from the plant when several of them became mysteriously ill.

      a. utilitarian   b. unassuming   c. noxious   d. imperative

PART B

Write **C** if the italicized word is used **correctly**. Write **I** if the word is used **incorrectly**.

_____ 14. It takes a *tenuous* arm to pitch a no-hitter.

_____ 15. In an *orthodox* classroom, students' desks are lined up in rows.

_____ 16. The cat is a naturally *indolent* creature who will happily doze in the sun all day.

_____ 17. The load of oil dumped on the highway *facilitated* the flow of traffic for more than three hours.

_____ 18. A genuine affection for young people is an *integral* part of being a successful teacher.

_____ 19. Since my old sneakers had fallen apart, I was pleased to find a new pair at an *exorbitant* price.

_____ 20. Rather than *assimilate* into his new school, Brian picked fights and stole money from the other students.

_____ 21. Off-screen, the movie star's manner is so *unassuming* that he is often unrecognized even by his fans.

_____ 22. Several neighborhood families formed a *coalition* to assist another family who'd lost their home in a fire.

_____ 23. I have such a *yen* for meatloaf that whenever it's served, I leave the table immediately.

_____ 24. I learned that my neighbors *espouse* recycling when I read their letter to the editor encouraging others to recycle.

_____ 25. Although Sid had been calm throughout the trial, he grew *nonchalant* when he heard the prosecutor call him a liar and a thief.

Score   (Number correct) _____ x 4 = _____ %

Enter your score above and in the vocabulary performance chart on the inside back cover of the book.

UNIT FOUR: Test 2

PART A
Complete each item with a word from the box. Use each word once.

a. **atrophy**	b. **belligerent**	c. **connotation**	d. **criterion**	e. **deplore**
f. **deprivation**	g. **extricate**	h. **inherent**	i. **objective**	j. **placebo**
k. **rejuvenate**	l. **scenario**	m. **unilateral**		

_____ 1. Danger is a(n) ___ part of police work.

_____ 2. Judging people by their appearance makes it difficult to be ___ about their personalities.

_____ 3. One ___ I use in selecting clothing is that an item be made out of a comfortable fabric.

_____ 4. After Chrissy stayed awake studying for seventy-two hours, sleep ___ caused her to start having double vision and to hear voices that weren't there.

_____ 5. The little boy's foot was so firmly caught in the folding chair that it took three adults to ___ him.

_____ 6. My mother was feeling twice her age before her trip to Arizona, but the relaxing vacation really ___(e)d her.

_____ 7. Although I ___ the conditions that face children born to drug addicts, I don't know what to do to help.

_____ 8. The day after surgery, the nurses got Alonso out of bed and walking, so that his muscles would not begin to ___.

_____ 9. To make his case to the jury, the lawyer went through a possible ___ of the events leading up to the murder.

_____ 10. Neither Jessie nor Mel would make a(n) ___ move to end their feud, so the silence between them continued.

_____ 11. When I bumped the car in front of me as I was parking, the other driver emerged and stormed toward me in a most ___ manner.

_____ 12. The dictionary definition of _home_ is "a place in which one lives," but for many people the word has ___s of comfort and family.

_____ 13. When little Sarah couldn't sleep, her mother gave her a ___ and called it a "magic sleeping potion." It was a glass of milk tinted red with food coloring.

(Continues on next page)

PART B
Write **C** if the italicized word is used **correctly**. Write **I** if the word is used **incorrectly**.

_____ 14. The nursery school teacher used the *analogy* of a flower garden to describe her class, saying that just as each flower has its own special beauty, so does each child.

_____ 15. My doctor certainly takes a *holistic* approach to my health. He says he's here to prescribe medication, not to talk to patients.

_____ 16. I didn't know that Jerry was so *proficient* in geography until I saw that F on his report card.

_____ 17. It is *imperative* that my sister get her cholesterol level down, as she is now at high risk of a heart attack.

_____ 18. A *staunch* fan of mysteries, Fred rarely reads them. He much prefers science fiction and nonfiction.

_____ 19. The defendant, accused of murder, proclaimed his innocence and was *vindicated* when a man who looked just like him confessed.

_____ 20. Luz, saying she wants her works of art to be *utilitarian*, makes ceramic bowls and teapots.

_____ 21. During the convention, all the delegates *dissipated* into the auditorium to hear the keynote speech.

_____ 22. We've had snow in April for the last three years, so you see that this year's April snow is altogether *unprecedented*.

_____ 23. It was bad enough being grounded, but my father is going to *mitigate* my punishment by stopping my allowance.

_____ 24. My mother regards peppermint tea as a *panacea* and offers it as a cure for all kinds of ills: colds, flu, and broken hearts.

_____ 25. Lily's ankle injury is severe, but the doctor told her a couple of days of bed rest will *exacerbate* the sprain enough so that she can walk again.

Score (Number correct) _____ x 4 = _____ %

Enter your score above and in the vocabulary performance chart on the inside back cover of the book.

UNIT FOUR: Test 3

PART A
Complete each sentence in a way that clearly shows you understand the meaning of the **boldfaced** word. Take a minute to plan your answer before you write.

Example: Because Joanne had a sudden **yen** for M&Ms, she <u>*ran to the convenience store to buy some*</u>.

1. Two **utilitarian** objects are _____

   _____.

2. In a **belligerent** mood, my brother said, " _____

   _____."

3. I realized just how **indolent** Teri is when she _____

   _____.

4. To me, some **connotations** of the word *summer* are _____

   _____.

5. An **integral** part of school is _____

   _____.

6. A good way to **exacerbate** your sore throat is to _____

   _____.

7. I **deplore** _____ because _____

   _____.

8. Flo's boss **chided** her when _____

   _____.

9. I am quite **proficient** at _____. For example, _____

   _____.

10. **Emanating** from the kitchen was _____

    _____.

(Continues on next page)

PART B
After each **boldfaced** word are a *synonym* (a word that means the same as the boldfaced word), an *antonym* (a word that means the opposite of the boldfaced word), and a word that is neither. On the answer line, write the letter of the word that is the antonym.

          Example: __a__ **utilitarian**   a. useless   b. practical   c. late

____ 11. **chide**   a. avoid   b. praise   c. scold

____ 12. **unassuming**   a. humble   b. boastful   c. curious

____ 13. **diabolic**   a. good   b. effective   c. wicked

____ 14. **noxious**   a. harmful   b. accurate   c. beneficial

____ 15. **annihilate**   a. create   b. destroy   c. justify

PART C
Use five of the following ten words in sentences. Make it clear that you know the meaning of each word you use. Feel free to use the past tense or plural form of a word.

a. **analogy**	b. **assimilate**	c. **denunciation**	d. **dilapidated**	e. **exorbitant**
f. **imperative**	g. **nonchalant**	h. **panacea**	i. **rejuvenate**	j. **yen**

16. _____

_____

17. _____

_____

18. _____

_____

19. _____

_____

20. _____

_____

Score   (Number correct) _____ x 5 = _____ %

Enter your score above and in the vocabulary performance chart on the inside back cover of the book.

UNIT FOUR: *Test 4 (Word Parts)*

PART A
Listed in the left-hand column below are ten common word parts, along with words in which the parts are used. In each blank, write in the letter of the correct definition on the right.

Word Parts	Examples	Definitions
____ 1. **-cian, -ian**	politician, librarian	a. Loving; lover; friend
____ 2. **dec-**	decathlon, decimal	b. Eight
____ 3. **duc, duct**	ducal, conduct	c. Having; full of; characterized by
____ 4. **-en**	woolen, golden	d. A person with a certain ability or a certain kind of knowledge
____ 5. **homo-**	homogeneous, homosexual	e. To lead; guide; draw off
____ 6. **oct-, octo-**	octagon, octopus	f. Over; above; additional
____ 7. **-ous**	famous, serious	g. To will; choose
____ 8. **phil, -phile**	Philadelphia, Anglophile	h. Same; similar
____ 9. **sur-**	surface, surplus	i. Ten
____ 10. **vol**	volunteer, voluntary	j. Made of

PART B
Using the answer line provided, complete each *italicized* word in the sentences below with the correct word part from the box. Not every word part will be used.

a. **-cian**	b. **dec-**	c. **duct**	d. **-en**	e. **homo-**
f. **octo-**	g. **-ous**	h. **-phile**	i. **sur-**	j. **vol**

_____ 11. It's interesting that the (. . . *nyms*) ___ *boar* (a male pig) and *bore* both apply to Donald.

_____ 12. In the ancient Roman calendar, (. . . *ember*) ___ was the tenth month.

_____ 13. The (*con . . . or*) ___ led the orchestra in a lively encore.

_____ 14. In addition to technical knowledge, (*morti . . . s*) ___ must know how to be sympathetic and comforting.

_____ 15. When a new calendar system was adopted in England in 1752, many people felt it was (*ridicul . . .*) ___ that the day after September 2 was suddenly September 14.

(Continues on next page)

PART C

Use your knowledge of word parts to determine the meaning of the **boldfaced** words. On the answer line, write the letter of each meaning.

_____ 16. My brilliant two-year-old just played a scale, a straight **octave**, on the piano.

     a. an eight-note scale   b. a three-note scale   c. a ten-note scale

_____ 17. We all ate a **surfeit** of food at Thanksgiving dinner.

     a. what we chose   b. an excess   c. less than usual

_____ 18. Jose carried the water in an old **oaken** bucket.

     a. made of oak   b. broken   c. large

_____ 19. Ever since visiting Germany, Carl has been a real **Germanophile**.

     a. a student of Germany   b. an expert on Germany   c. an admirer of Germany

_____ 20. Pauline cleaned the entire apartment yesterday. She did it **of her own volition**.

     a. with her own supplies   b. by choice   c. on her day off

---

Score   (Number correct) _____   x 5 = _____ %

Enter your score above and in the vocabulary performance chart on the inside back cover of the book.

Unit Five

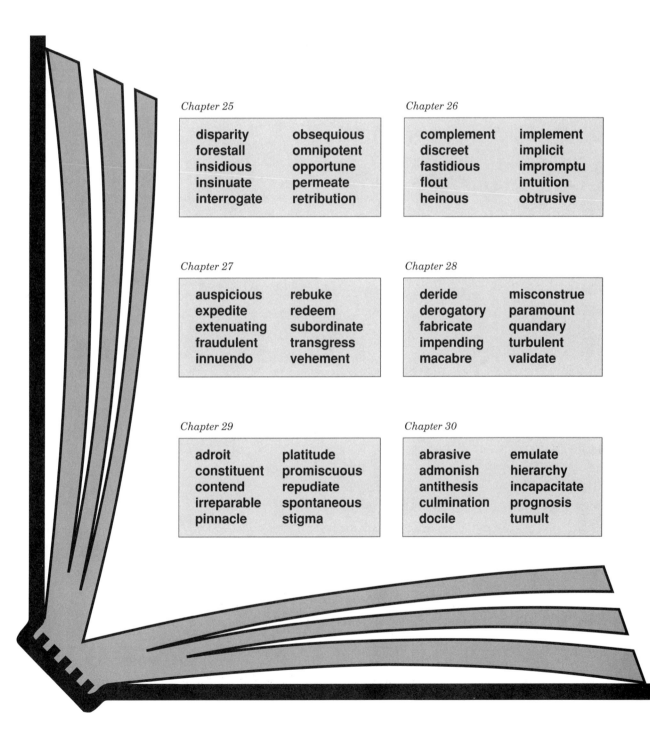

Chapter 25

disparity	obsequious
forestall	omnipotent
insidious	opportune
insinuate	permeate
interrogate	retribution

Chapter 26

complement	implement
discreet	implicit
fastidious	impromptu
flout	intuition
heinous	obtrusive

Chapter 27

auspicious	rebuke
expedite	redeem
extenuating	subordinate
fraudulent	transgress
innuendo	vehement

Chapter 28

deride	misconstrue
derogatory	paramount
fabricate	quandary
impending	turbulent
macabre	validate

Chapter 29

adroit	platitude
constituent	promiscuous
contend	repudiate
irreparable	spontaneous
pinnacle	stigma

Chapter 30

abrasive	emulate
admonish	hierarchy
antithesis	incapacitate
culmination	prognosis
docile	tumult

CHAPTER

25

disparity	obsequious
forestall	omnipotent
insidious	opportune
insinuate	permeate
interrogate	retribution

Ten Words in Context

In the space provided, write the letter of the meaning closest to that of each **boldfaced** word. Use the context of the sentences to help you figure out each word's meaning.

1 **disparity**
(dĭ-spăr′ə-tē)
-*noun*

- There's an enormous **disparity** between the million-dollar incomes of top executives and the modest paychecks most of us earn.
- Shirley and Jason don't let the **disparity** in their ages weaken their marriage, but Jason's mother isn't happy with a daughter-in-law her own age.

___ *Disparity* means   a. a combination.   b. a gap.   c. a closeness.

2 **forestall**
(fôr-stôl′)
-*verb*

- The owners of the failing store hoped that the huge sale would bring in enough cash to **forestall** bankruptcy.
- When the environmentalists were unable to **forestall** the destruction of the forest by legal means, they lay down in front of the developer's bulldozers.

___ *Forestall* means   a. to keep from happening.   b. to predict.   c. to pay for.

3 **insidious**
(ĭn-sĭd′ē-əs)
-*adjective*

- Lyme disease is **insidious** because although it is very serious, it starts with a nearly invisible tick bite, and its early symptoms are mild.
- Many people fear that farm chemicals have **insidious** effects. The chemicals don't seem harmful, but cancer rates have started to increase.

___ *Insidious* means   a. badly timed.   b. subtly harmful.   c. all-powerful.

4 **insinuate**
(ĭn-sĭn′yōō-āt′)
-*verb*

- He didn't come right out and say it, but Professor Shriber **insinuated** that someone in the class had gotten hold of the test ahead of time.
- "Paul's been seeing a lot of Lynn lately," Alan said, as if to **insinuate** that Paul was being unfaithful to his wife, Joanne.

___ *Insinuate* means   a. to hint.   b. to wish.   c. to state directly.

5 **interrogate**
(ĭn-tĕr′ə-gāt′)
-*verb*

- Before the police **interrogated** the suspect, they informed him of his right not to answer their questions.
- "You never just ask me if I had a nice time with my date," Leonard complained to his parents. "Instead, you sit me down at the kitchen table and **interrogate** me."

___ *Interrogate* means   a. to ask questions.   b. to delay.   c. to abuse.

6 **obsequious**
(ŏb-sē′kwē-əs)
-*adjective*

- Each of the queen's advisers tried to be more **obsequious** than the other, bowing as low as possible and uttering flowery compliments.
- Marge constantly flatters the boss, calls him "sir," and agrees loudly with everything he says. However, her **obsequious** behavior only annoys him.

___ *Obsequious* means   a. unequal in rank.   b. overly eager to please.   c. methodical.

144

7 omnipotent
(ŏm-nĭp′ə-tənt)
-adjective

- Small children think of their parents as **omnipotent**—able to do anything, control everything, and grant whatever a child might wish for.
- The American government is designed so that no one branch can be **omnipotent**. Congress, the President, and the Supreme Court share power and hold each other in check.

___ *Omnipotent* means   a. totally good.   b. willing to serve.   c. all-powerful.

8 opportune
(ŏp′ər-tōōn′)
-adjective

- Renee thought that her parents' anniversary would be an **opportune** time to announce her own engagement. They could have a double celebration.
- The job offer came at an especially **opportune** time. I had just decided that I might like to work for a year or so before returning to college.

___ *Opportune* means   a. appropriate.   b. difficult.   c. early.

9 permeate
(pûr′mē-āt′)
-verb

- The strong scent of Kate's perfume soon **permeated** the entire room.
- The weather was so rainy and damp that moisture seemed to **permeate** everything: curtains hung limp, towels wouldn't dry, and windows were fogged over.

___ *Permeate* means   a. to harm.   b. to penetrate.   c. to make unclear.

10 retribution
(rĕ′trə-byōō′shən)
-noun

- Some "sins" in life have their own built-in **retribution**. For example, if you get drunk, you'll have a hangover; if you overeat, you'll gain weight.
- For much of human history, before science could explain diseases, many people believed that any illness was a **retribution** for immoral behavior.

___ *Retribution* means   a. an inequality.   b. an obstacle.   c. a penalty.

Matching Words with Definitions

Following are definitions of the ten words. Clearly write or print each word next to its definition. The sentences above and on the previous page will help you decide on the meaning of each word.

1. _____ Overly willing to serve, obey, or flatter in order to gain favor

2. _____ To suggest slyly

3. _____ Something given or done as repayment, reward, or (usually) punishment

4. _____ An inequality or difference, as in ages or amounts

5. _____ Working or spreading harmfully but in a manner hard to notice; more harmful than at first is evident

6. _____ To flow or spread throughout (something)

7. _____ Suitable (said of time); well-timed

8. _____ To prevent or hinder by taking action beforehand

9. _____ All-powerful; having unlimited power or authority

10. _____ To question formally and systematically

CAUTION: Do not go any further until you are sure the above answers are correct. Then you can use the definitions to help you in the following practices. Your goal is eventually to know the words well enough so that you don't need to check the definitions at all.

➤ *Sentence Check 1*

Using the answer line provided, complete each item below with the correct word from the box. Use each word once.

a. **disparity**	b. **forestall**	c. **insidious**	d. **insinuate**	e. **interrogate**
f. **obsequious**	g. **omnipotent**	h. **opportune**	i. **permeate**	j. **retribution**

_____ 1. When our dog was sprayed by a skunk, the smell soon ___(e)d the house.

_____ 2. To ___ complaints about unrepaired potholes, the township set up a "pothole hotline" and promised to fill in any reported hole within two days.

_____ 3. Because no one else's hand was raised, I considered it a(n) ___ moment to ask a question.

_____ 4. In many countries, political prisoners who are being ___(e)d by the secret police are likely to be tortured in an attempt to force answers from them.

_____ 5. When the Earl of Essex plotted against his queen, Elizabeth I of England, ___ was swift and harsh: she had him beheaded for treason.

_____ 6. "There seems to be quite a ___," Shannon objected to the car dealer, "between your cost and the sticker price."

_____ 7. The effects of certain prescription drugs, such as Valium, can be ___. People who take them may slip into addiction without being aware of it.

_____ 8. According to legend, King Canute—an ancient ruler of England, Denmark, and Norway—thought he was ___. He actually ordered the tide to stop rising.

_____ 9. Instead of directly saying "Buy our product," many ads use slick images to ___ that the product will give the buyer sex appeal, power, or prestige.

_____ 10. The headwaiter's manner toward customers who looked rich was ___. Ignoring the rest of us, he gave them the restaurant's best tables and hovered over them, all smiles.

NOTE: Now check your answers to these questions by turning to page 177. Going over the answers carefully will help you prepare for the next two practices, for which answers are not given.

➤ *Sentence Check 2*

Using the answer lines provided, complete each item below with **two** words from the box. Use each word once.

_____
_____ 1–2. The wide ___ between men's and women's pay in our company led to a protest by the women. The management tried to squelch° the protest and ___(e) that the women were subversive° and were trying to ruin company morale.

_____
_____ 3–4. The noxious° chemical spray used to eradicate° tentworms had ___ effects: after killing the worms, it gradually seeped down, ___(e)d the soil, and poisoned Duck Lake.

_____ 5–6. The ex-convict was filled with rancor°. As ___ for his years in prison, he planned to attack, at the first ___ moment, the judge who had sentenced him.

_____ 7–8. The remote control of my VCR makes me feel ___. I can ___ any imminent° disaster—a fire, a flood, an earthquake, a sordid° crime—by pressing a button and stopping the movie dead.

_____ 9–10. In a job interview, use discretion°. Don't react as though you were being ___(e)d by the police; but don't be ___ either, as if the interviewer were a king or queen and you were a humble servant.

➤ _Final Check:_ My Devilish Older Sister

Here is a final opportunity for you to strengthen your knowledge of the ten words. First read the following selection carefully. Then fill in each blank with a word from the box at the top of the previous page. (Context clues will help you figure out which word goes in which blank.) Use each word once.

Anyone who thinks older sisters protect younger ones has never heard me tell about my sister Pam. There's no great (1)_____ in our ages—Pam is only three years older—but throughout our childhood she was always able to beat me at cards, at jacks, at all board games. This seemingly unlimited power to win made me think of her as (2)_____. I obeyed all her orders ("Relinquish° that lollipop!") and accepted all her insults ("You're grotesque°!" "You're positively repugnant°!") in the most timid, (3)_____ manner. Privately, I longed for revenge.

When Pam made up her mind to tease or trick me, there was nothing I could do to (4)_____ her plans. And she never missed a(n) (5)_____ moment to terrorize me. When our old dog growled at the empty air, she would (6)_____ that evil spirits must have (7)_____(e)d the atmosphere, saying, "Dogs, you know, can sense the supernatural." Once I made the mistake of revealing that crabs terrified me. After that, I was inundated° with photos of crabs, drawings of crabs, even labels from cans of crabmeat. In retrospect°, though, her most diabolic° trick was giving me some "chocolate candy" that I impetuously° gobbled up. It turned out to be Ex-Lax. After that, if Pam offered me anything, no matter how innocuous° it looked, I always (8)_____(e)d her: "What is it really? Do you still have the wrapping? Will you take a bite first?" But this episode also had a more (9)_____ effect: for years, I was afraid of new foods.

Now that we're grown, Pam has greatly improved. She no longer likes to torment me, and she even seems contrite° about the past. However, I still sometimes think up various scenarios° of (10)_____ in which _I_ am the older sister, and at last I get my revenge.

Scores	Sentence Check 2 _____%	Final Check _____%

Enter your scores above and in the vocabulary performance chart on the inside back cover of the book.

CHAPTER

26

complement	implement
discreet	implicit
fastidious	impromptu
flout	intuition
heinous	obtrusive

Ten Words in Context

In the space provided, write the letter of the meaning closest to that of each **boldfaced** word. Use the context of the sentences to help you figure out each word's meaning.

1 complement
(kŏm'plə-mənt)
-verb

- The new singer's voice **complemented** the other voices, rounding out the group's sound.
- A red tie would **complement** Pedro's gray suit and white shirt, giving the outfit a needed touch of color.

__ *Complement* means   a. to go perfectly with.   b. to reach out for.   c. to overpower.

2 discreet
(dĭ-skrēt')
-adjective

- The mayor's affair with one of her aides was **discreet**—they were very quiet and careful about it—but the truth eventually came out anyway.
- "Be **discreet** about these drawings, Wilson," the boss said. "Don't show them to just anyone. We don't want another company stealing our designs."

__ *Discreet* means   a. honest.   b. cautious.   c. obvious.

3 fastidious
(făs-tĭd'ē-əs)
-adjective

- Tilly was a **fastidious** housekeeper who vacuumed every day, dusted twice a day, and never allowed so much as a pencil or safety pin to be out of place.
- A **fastidious** dresser, Mr. Lapp never leaves his home without looking as if he had just stepped out of a fashion magazine.

__ *Fastidious* means   a. working quickly.   b. having insight.   c. very particular.

4 flout
(flout)
-verb

- My neighbors were evicted from their apartment because they **flouted** the building's rules. They threw trash in the hallway, had loud all-night parties, and just laughed at anyone who complained.
- The men in the warehouse **flouted** the company's new regulations about sexual harassment: they covered the walls with pinups.

__ *Flout* means   a. to mock and defy.   b. to put into effect.   c. to show off.

5 heinous
(hā'nəs)
-adjective

- The decision to drop the atomic bomb on Hiroshima and Nagasaki has been debated for half a century: was it a **heinous** crime on the part of the United States, or was it a necessary action to win the war?
- Millions of people were shocked recently by news reports of a **heinous** act: a woman had starved her little daughter to death.

__ *Heinous* means   a. wicked.   b. unplanned.   c. detailed.

6 implement
(ĭm'plə-mĕnt')
-verb

- NASA expects to **implement** its plan for a mission to Mars in 2015.
- Brett is full of ideas about starting his own business, but he never follows through and **implements** them.

__ *Implement* means   a. to recall.   b. to put into effect.   c. to criticize.

7 **implicit**
(ĭm-plĭs′ĭt)
-*adjective*

• In our society, a wedding invitation is also an **implicit** request for a gift.
• A threat was **implicit** in the gambler's angry statement: "I don't like being cheated."

__ *Implicit* means   a. unusual.   b. unstated.   c. unintended.

8 **impromptu**
(ĭm-prŏmp′tōō′)
-*adjective*

• My speech at my cousin's birthday dinner was **impromptu**; I hadn't expected to be called on to say anything.
• When Kianna discovered that she and Barry had both brought guitars to the party, she suggested an **impromptu** duet.

__ *Impromptu* means   a. not rehearsed.   b. not very good.   c. very quiet.

9 **intuition**
(ĭn′tōō-ĭsh′ən)
-*noun*

• "I paint by **intuition**," the artist said. "In a flash, I see how a work should look. I don't really think it out."
• "The minute I met your mother," my father said, "my **intuition** told me that we'd get married someday."

__ *Intuition* means   a. careful study.   b. memory.   c. instinct.

10 **obtrusive**
(ŏb-trōō′sĭv)
-*adjective*

• The huge, sprawling new mall seemed **obtrusive** in the quiet little country town.
• My brother's stutter is often hardly noticeable, but when he is nervous or in a hurry, it can become **obtrusive**.

__ *Obtrusive* means   a. overly obvious.   b. unplanned.   c. greatly improved.

Matching Words with Definitions

Following are definitions of the ten words. Clearly write or print each word next to its definition. The sentences above and on the previous page will help you decide on the meaning of each word.

1. _____   To treat with scorn or contempt; defy insultingly

2. _____   The ability to know something without the conscious use of reasoning

3. _____   To carry out; put into practice

4. _____   Undesirably noticeable

5. _____   Wise in keeping silent about secrets and other information of a delicate nature; prudent; tactful

6. _____   Performed or spoken without practice or preparation

7. _____   Extremely evil; outrageous

8. _____   Suggested or understood, but not directly stated; implied

9. _____   To add (to something or someone) what is lacking or needed; round out; bring to perfection

10. _____   Extremely attentive to details; fussy

CAUTION: Do not go any further until you are sure the above answers are correct. Then you can use the definitions to help you in the following practices. Your goal is eventually to know the words well enough so that you don't need to check the definitions at all.

➤ *Sentence Check 1*

Using the answer line provided, complete each item below with the correct word from the box. Use each word once.

a. **complement**	b. **discreet**	c. **fastidious**	d. **flout**	e. **heinous**
f. **implement**	g. **implicit**	h. **impromptu**	i. **intuition**	j. **obtrusive**

_____ 1. Rachel's ___ told her not to date a man who kept tropical fish in his bathtub.

_____ 2. To outsiders, a nudist colony seems to ___ all standards of modesty. The nudists—who prefer the term *naturists*—say they are just living naturally.

_____ 3. In the American system of justice, anyone charged with a crime, no matter how ___ the offense, is entitled to be defended by a lawyer.

_____ 4. The ___ press conference turned out to be a bad idea. The senator should have planned his remarks beforehand.

_____ 5. "Loose lips sink ships" was a famous World War II slogan. It warned Americans to be ___ and not say anything that might reveal military plans.

_____ 6. To ___ their plan for a surprise attack on the girls' club, the boys needed squirt guns and a gallon of grape juice.

_____ 7. The writer Ernest Hemingway had a "tough guy" image but was ___ about using words; he rewrote the ending of one novel forty-four times.

_____ 8. White wine is said to ___ some meals and red wine to add the finishing touch to others, but I can't tell the difference.

_____ 9. Alicia signed her card to Mario "Warm regards." Mario thought that the ___ meaning was "I feel *only* warm regards, not love."

_____ 10. The new partition between the restaurant's smoking and nonsmoking sections looks ___. Some plants or flowers might help it blend in better.

NOTE: Now check your answers to these questions by turning to page 177. Going over the answers carefully will help you prepare for the next two practices, for which answers are not given.

➤ *Sentence Check 2*

Using the answer lines provided, complete each item below with **two** words from the box. Use each word once.

_____
_____ 1–2. My ___ told me that a man who ironed his bed sheets was too ___ for a slob like me. I'm notorious° for cleaning my apartment only once a year.

_____
_____ 3–4. The dark, rumbling voice of the bass ___(e)d the high, sweet tones of the soprano as they sang a(n) ___ but flawless duet. Having just met, they were surprised and delighted at how good they sounded together.

_____
_____ 5–6. Kay said only, "It would be ___ not to discuss the missing funds in front of Debra." But her ___ meaning was "I think she stole them."

_____ 7–8. Connoisseurs° of science fiction love one movie in which evil alien
_____ invaders decide to destroy all life on Earth. The aliens ___ this ___ plan
by constructing a "space shield" that cuts off all sunlight.

_____ 9–10. The rule was "No sidewalk vendors on campus," but the venders seem
_____ to have made a conspiracy° to ___ it. They have set up their tables and
stands in a spot university administrators consider ___—right in front
of the Administration Building.

➤ *Final Check:* Harriet Tubman

Here is a final opportunity for you to strengthen your knowledge of the ten words. First read the following
selection carefully. Then fill in each blank with a word from the box at the top of the previous page.
(Context clues will help you figure out which word goes in which blank.) Use each word once.

In 1849 Harriet Tubman—then in her late twenties—fled from the (1)_____

brutality she had endured as a slave. Aware that a lone black woman would be a(n)

(2)_____ figure among ordinary travelers, she traveled on foot and only

at night, over hundreds of miles, to reach Pennsylvania. There, for the first time in her life, she was

free, but her parents, brothers, and sisters remained behind in Maryland, still slaves. Harriet

decided to go back for them—and, over the next ten years, for many more.

Harriet had several qualities that (3)_____(e)d each other and facilitated°

her mission. First, because she was knowledgeable and had good (4)_____,

she could always sense when the time for an escape had arrived, and who could and couldn't be

trusted. Second, she was (5)_____ about planning; she always worked out

a plan to the last detail before she (6)_____(e)d it. Third, she was

flexible, capable of taking (7)_____ actions if an unexpected problem

arose. Time and again, when a disaster seemed imminent°, she was able to forestall° it. For

instance, when she learned that slave-hunters had posted a description of a runaway man, she

disguised him as a woman. When the slave-hunters turned up at a railroad station, she fooled them

by having the runaways board a southbound train instead of a northbound one. Fourth, she was

(8)_____ about her plans. She knew how important it was to be reticent°,

since anyone might be a spy. Often, her instructions about where and when to meet were not

actually stated, but were (9)_____ in references to songs and Bible

stories familiar to those waiting to escape. Fifth, she was physically strong, able to endure

extended periods of deprivation°; she could go for a long time without food, shelter, or rest.

Harriet Tubman (10)_____(e)d the unjust laws of an evil system,

but she was never captured, and she never lost a single runaway. She led more slaves to freedom

than any other individual—over three hundred—and her name is venerated° to this day.

Scores	Sentence Check 2 _____%	Final Check _____%

Enter your scores above and in the vocabulary performance chart on the inside back cover of the book.

auspicious	rebuke
expedite	redeem
extenuating	subordinate
fraudulent	transgress
innuendo	vehement

Ten Words in Context

In the space provided, write the letter of the meaning closest to that of each **boldfaced** word. Use the context of the sentences to help you figure out each word's meaning.

1 **auspicious**
(ô-spĭsh′əs)
-adjective

• The beginning of the semester was **auspicious** for Liza; she got an A on the first quiz and saw this as a promise of more good grades to come.

• Jen and Robert's marriage did not get off to an **auspicious** start. They couldn't agree on what kind of ceremony they wanted or which guests to invite.

__ *Auspicious* means   a. deceptive.   b. indirect.   c. favorable.

2 **expedite**
(ĕks′pə-dīt′)
-verb

• Express lanes in supermarkets **expedite** the checkout process for shoppers who buy only a few items.

• To **expedite** payment on an insurance claim, be sure to include all the necessary information on the form before mailing it in.

__ *Expedite* means   a. to hasten.   b. to reduce the cost of.   c. to delay.

3 **extenuating**
(ĕk-stĕn′yōō-ā′tĭng)
-adjective

• I know I promised to come to the party, but there were **extenuating** circumstances: my car broke down.

• When my father had a heart attack, I missed a final exam. Due to the **extenuating** circumstances, the professor agreed to let me take a makeup exam.

__ *Extenuating* means   a. providing a good excuse.   b. assigning blame.   c. encouraging.

4 **fraudulent**
(frô′jə-lənt)
-adjective

• Leroy was jailed for filing **fraudulent** income tax returns. He had been cheating the government for years.

• The art dealer was involved in a **fraudulent** scheme to pass off worthless forgeries as valuable old paintings.

__ *Fraudulent* means   a. inferior.   b. deceitful.   c. careless.

5 **innuendo**
(ĭn′yōō-ĕn′dō)
-noun

• People weren't willing to say directly that the mayor had taken a bribe, but there were many **innuendos** such as "Someone must have gotten to him."

• When Neil said, "Emily's home sick. Again," he was using an **innuendo**. He really meant that she was just taking another day off.

__ *Innuendo* means   a. a sharp scolding.   b. an obvious lie.   c. a suggestion.

6 **rebuke**
(rĭ-byōōk′)
-verb

• When the puppy chews the furniture, don't hit him; instead, **rebuke** him in a harsh voice.

• Although my father scolded me many times in private, I'm grateful that he never **rebuked** me in public.

__ *Rebuke* means   a. to criticize.   b. to make excuses for.   c. to hit.

7 **redeem**
(rĭ-dēm')
-*verb*

• Ricardo's parents were angry with him for neglecting his chores, but he **redeemed** himself by washing and waxing their car.

• Cal was suspended from the basketball team because of his low grades, but he **redeemed** himself the next semester by earning a B average.

___ *Redeem* means   a. to reveal.   b. to make up for past errors.   c. to punish.

8 **subordinate**
(sə-bôr'də-nĭt)
-*adjective*

• As a waiter, I take orders from the headwaiter, and he's **subordinate** to the manager of the restaurant.

• The federal District Courts are lower than the United States Court of Appeals, which in turn is **subordinate** to the Supreme Court.

___ *Subordinate to* means   a. lower than.   b. a substitute for.   c. superior to.

9 **transgress**
(trăns-grĕs')
-*verb*

• Adam **transgressed** by eating an apple Eve gave him; God punished them both.

• Traci knew she had **transgressed** against family wishes when she sold the ring her grandmother had given her.

___ *Transgress* means   a. to benefit.   b. to tell a lie.   c. to commit an offense.

10 **vehement**
(vē-ə'mənt)
-*adjective*

• I knew my parents would not be happy about my plan to live with my girlfriend, but I didn't expect their objections to be so **vehement**.

• When Nell's boyfriend slapped her, she responded with **vehement** anger. Yelling "That's the last time you'll ever touch me!" she walked out on him.

___ *Vehement* means   a. strong.   b. secret.   c. unjustified.

Matching Words with Definitions

Following are definitions of the ten words. Clearly write or print each word next to its definition. The sentences above and on the previous page will help you decide on the meaning of each word.

1. _____   An indirect remark or gesture, usually suggesting something belittling; an insinuation; a hint

2. _____   To speed up or ease the progress of

3. _____   To scold sharply; express blame or disapproval

4. _____   Intense; forceful

5. _____   Characterized by trickery, cheating, or lies

6. _____   Being a good sign; favorable; encouraging

7. _____   Serving to make (a fault, an offense, or guilt) less serious or seem less serious through some excuse

8. _____   To sin or commit an offense; break a law or command

9. _____   Under the authority or power of another; inferior or below another in rank, power, or importance

10. _____   To restore (oneself) to favor by making up for offensive conduct; make amends

CAUTION: Do not go any further until you are sure the above answers are correct. Then you can use the definitions to help you in the following practices. Your goal is eventually to know the words well enough so that you don't need to check the definitions at all.

➤ Sentence Check 1

Using the answer line provided, complete each item below with the correct word from the box. Use each word once.

a. **auspicious**	b. **expedite**	c. **extenuating**	d. **fraudulent**	e. **innuendo**
f. **rebuke**	g. **redeem**	h. **subordinate**	i. **transgress**	j. **vehement**

_____ 1. The company president is ___ only to the board of directors. She takes orders from the board, and only the board can fire her.

_____ 2. When young children ___, they may lie to cover up their misdeeds.

_____ 3. If you get a letter announcing that you've won a free car or free trip in some contest you've never heard of, watch out. It's probably ___.

_____ 4. To ___ the registration process, fill out all the forms before you get in line.

_____ 5. After showing up late for the fund-raising dinner and then falling asleep during the speeches, the politician tried to ___ himself with a public apology.

_____ 6. According to tradition, it's ___ if March "comes in like a lion" with stormy weather, because it will then "go out like a lamb."

_____ 7. Edna was ___ in her opposition to the proposed budget cuts. She let everyone in the department know just how strongly she felt.

_____ 8. Later, Edna's supervisor ___(e)d her, saying "No one asked for your opinion about the budget, so just get on with your work."

_____ 9. In court, defense attorneys often subject a rape victim to ___s about her morals, appearance, and behavior—to suggest that she led her attacker on.

_____ 10. "Yes, my client robbed the bank," the lawyer said, "but there were ___ circumstances. She didn't have time to wait in line to make a withdrawal."

NOTE: Now check your answers to these questions by turning to page 177. Going over the answers carefully will help you prepare for the next two practices, for which answers are not given.

➤ Sentence Check 2

Using the answer lines provided, complete each item below with **two** words from the box. Use each word once.

_____
_____ 1–2. Rudy certainly ___(e)d against decorum° when he showed up at his sister's wedding in jeans. Later, he tried to ___ himself by giving the newlyweds an ostentatious° present.

_____
_____ 3–4. First the judge ___(e)d the charlatans° for "violating the public trust." Then he fined them thousands of dollars for engaging in ___ advertising.

_____
_____ 5–6. The tour did not get off to a(n) ___ start—the singer missed the first concert. But there was a(n) ___ reason: he had developed bronchitis, and trying to sing would have exacerbated° the infection.

_____   7–8. The owner of our company is ___ in his insistence that managers
_____   implement° a plan to communicate better with workers in ___ positions.

_____   9–10. The restaurant critic wrote, "Those customers who are oblivious° to the
_____   headwaiter's outstretched hand will have an overly long wait to be
seated." Her ___ implied that customers could ___ getting a table only
by slipping the headwaiter some money.

➤ *Final Check:* **Tony's Rehabilitation**

Here is a final opportunity for you to strengthen your knowledge of the ten words. First read the following
selection carefully. Then fill in each blank with a word from the box at the top of the previous page.
(Context clues will help you figure out which word goes in which blank.) Use each word once.

When he was 18, Tony was arrested for possessing a small amount of cocaine. Instead of
panicking, he was nonchalant°. He didn't think of himself as having (1)_____(e)d;
the cocaine was just for fun, not some heinous° offense. On the way to the police station, he
wasn't worried about being interrogated°. He figured he could claim that there were
(2)_____ circumstances. He'd say he was just holding the stuff for a friend—
maybe he'd even insinuate° that the "friend" was making him the victim of some
(3)_____ scheme—and then he'd be released right away.

But things didn't work out according to Tony's scenario°. When he told his story to the police
captain, the captain's response was hardly (4)_____: "Tell it to the judge,
kid. I've heard it all before." Then, turning to a(n) (5)_____ officer, the
captain said, "Book him." Tony still wasn't distraught°. He just thought, "Well, my father will
extricate° me from this mess. First he'll (6)_____ me, of course, but after
he's through yelling at me, he'll pay my bail. And he knows plenty of influential people who can
(6)_____ the legal process so my case will be dismissed quickly." So
Tony wasn't prepared for his father's (8)_____ anger, or for his parting
words: "You got yourself into this. Now you'll take the consequences."

With no bail, Tony had to wait for his hearing in jail. He was terrified, especially by the other
inmates. Some were belligerent°, trying to start fights; others used (9)_____s,
such as calling him "the millionaire"—with an implicit° threat of retribution° for his easy life. He
got through his nine-day stay without being attacked, though, and the experience woke up his
dormant° good sense. He realized that fooling around with drugs is insidious°—his involvement
would get worse and worse unless he turned his life around.

Therefore, at his court hearing, Tony asked to be sent to a drug treatment center, and as a first-
time offender, he got his wish. Today, six years later, Tony is still "clean." And he still wonders
what would have become of him if he hadn't managed to (10)_____ himself in
his family's eyes—and in his own.

Scores	Sentence Check 2 _____%	Final Check _____%

Enter your scores above and in the vocabulary performance chart on the inside back cover of the book.

deride	misconstrue
derogatory	paramount
fabricate	quandary
impending	turbulent
macabre	validate

Ten Words in Context

In the space provided, write the letter of the meaning closest to that of each **boldfaced** word. Use the context of the sentences to help you figure out each word's meaning.

1 deride
(dĭ-rīd′)
-verb

- One nightclub comedian **derides** members of the audience, poking fun at their looks, clothing, and mannerisms. He says they know it's just part of the act.
- Walter went on a diet after several classmates **derided** him by calling him "Lardo" and "Blimpy."

__ *Deride* means   a. to misunderstand.   b. to mock.   c. to argue with.

2 derogatory
(dĭ-rŏg′ə-tôr′ē)
-adjective

- Lorenzo's **derogatory** remark about his boss—he called her an airhead—caused him to get fired.
- Charisse makes **derogatory** comments about Kareem behind his back, saying that he's vain, sloppy, and lazy. But she never says such things to his face.

__ *Derogatory* means   a. uncomplimentary.   b. mistaken.   c. provable.

3 fabricate
(făb′rĭ-kāt′)
-verb

- Supermarket tabloids often **fabricate** ridiculous stories, such as "Boy Is Born Wearing Green Sneakers."
- When she handed in her term paper late, Diane **fabricated** a story that her computer had crashed. The truth is that she doesn't even work on a computer.

__ *Fabricate* means   a. to avoid.   b. to prove.   c. to invent.

4 impending
(ĭm-pĕnd′ĭng)
-adjective

- Gary never studies until an exam is **impending**. If he'd start sooner, he wouldn't have to cram so hard.
- "Because of the company's **impending** move," the office manager said, "I'm not ordering any supplies until next month, when we'll be in the new office."

__ *Impending* means   a. approaching.   b. apparent.   c. important.

5 macabre
(mə-kŏb′rə)
-adjective

- Edgar Allan Poe's story "The Fall of the House of Usher" is a **macabre** tale in which someone is buried alive.
- The movie opened with a **macabre** scene: a row of bodies lying in drawers in the city morgue.

__ *Macabre* means   a. confusing.   b. mocking.   c. gruesome.

6 misconstrue
(mĭs′kən-strōō′)
-verb

- Conchita would like to date Matt, but when she told him she was busy last weekend, he **misconstrued** her meaning, thinking she wasn't interested in him.
- Many readers **misconstrue** Robert Frost's well-known line "Good fences make good neighbors." They think it's Frost's own opinion, but the line is spoken by an unneighborly character.

__ *Misconstrue* means   a. to misunderstand.   b. to understand.   c. to ignore.

7 **paramount**
(păr′ə-mount′)
-adjective

- When you are driving on rain-slick, icy, or curvy roads, good traction is of **paramount** importance, so always be sure your tires are in top condition.
- **Paramount** Pictures must have chosen its name to suggest that its movies were superior to all others.

___ *Paramount* means   a. supreme.   b. growing.   c. successful.

8 **quandary**
(kwŏn′də-rē)
-noun

- Bonita was in a **quandary**—she couldn't decide whether to return to school, take a job she had just been offered, or move to Alaska with her boyfriend.
- My son is in a **quandary** over financial matters: he is baffled by the problems of making a budget, handling credit, and paying taxes.

___ *Quandary* means   a. a state of confusion.   b. a state of anger.   c. a state of confidence.

9 **turbulent**
(tûr′byoo-lənt)
-adjective

- The **turbulent** air made the plane rock so wildly that passengers felt as if they were on a roller coaster.
- The Warreners' household tends to be **turbulent**. Whenever Mr. Warrener gets drunk, he yells and throws things.

___ *Turbulent* means   a. violent.   b. distant.   c. unusual.

10 **validate**
(văl′ə-dāt′)
-verb

- Many people believe Columbus sailed west to **validate** the theory that the world is round. But in 1492, the fact that the world is round was already well known.
- There is no real doubt about the dangers of smoking; the claim that smoking is a serious health risk has been **validated** by many studies.

___ *Validate* means   a. to misinterpret.   b. to confirm.   c. to invent.

Matching Words with Definitions

Following are definitions of the ten words. Clearly write or print each word next to its definition. The sentences above and on the previous page will help you decide on the meaning of each word.

1. _____   Full of wild disorder or wildly irregular motion; violently disturbed

2. _____   Suggestive of death and decay; frightful; causing horror and disgust

3. _____   A state of uncertainty or confusion about what to do; predicament

4. _____   Expressing a low opinion; belittling

5. _____   To show to be true; prove

6. _____   To misinterpret; misunderstand the meaning or significance of

7. _____   To make fun of; ridicule

8. _____   To make up (a story, information) in order to deceive; invent (a lie)

9. _____   About to happen; imminent

10. _____   Of greatest concern or importance; foremost; chief in rank or authority

CAUTION: Do not go any further until you are sure the above answers are correct. Then you can use the definitions to help you in the following practices. Your goal is eventually to know the words well enough so that you don't need to check the definitions at all.

➤ *Sentence Check 1*

Using the answer line provided, complete each item below with the correct word from the box. Use each word once.

a. **deride**	b. **derogatory**	c. **fabricate**	d. **impending**	e. **macabre**
f. **misconstrue**	g. **paramount**	h. **quandary**	i. **turbulent**	j. **validate**

_____ 1. Mel has a(n) ___ hobby—he visits places where murders were committed.

_____ 2. We had skipped dinner in order to get to the play on time, so throughout the performance, food—not the drama—was ___ in our thoughts.

_____ 3. Just before I was fired, I had a sense of ___ disaster; I could tell that something bad was about to happen.

_____ 4. Delia ___(e)d Miguel's friendliness as romantic interest. She didn't realize that he already had a girlfriend.

_____ 5. When my daughter said her teacher was "different," I wasn't sure if she meant the description to be complimentary or ___.

_____ 6. Dwane didn't show up for the final exam because he hadn't studied, but he ___(e)d a story about having a flat tire.

_____ 7. In our psychology class, we had an interesting team assignment. We had to make some statement about human nature and then ___ it by finding supporting evidence.

_____ 8. Ivan is in a ___ over his car. He doesn't know whether to get his old car the major repairs it desperately needs, take out a loan and buy his dream car, or spend the money he has on another used car he doesn't like.

_____ 9. The sun may seem to be shining calmly and steadily, but in fact, nuclear reactions inside the sun are causing a seething mass of ___ flames.

_____ 10. A critic once ___(e)d a book he disliked by saying, "This is not a novel to be tossed aside lightly. It should be thrown with great force."

NOTE: Now check your answers to these questions by turning to page 177. Going over the answers carefully will help you prepare for the next two practices, for which answers are not given.

➤ *Sentence Check 2*

Using the answer lines provided, complete each item below with **two** words from the box. Use each word once.

_____
_____ 1–2. Many surfers prefer ___ water to more uniform waves. Their ___ goal is excitement, and they get a feeling of exhilaration° from confronting a dangerous situation.

_____
_____ 3–4. I was in a ___ over whether to study, practice the piano, or go to a movie with my friend Sal. To complicate things further, Sal wanted to see a(n) ___ horror film, and I dislike anything gruesome.

_____ 5–6. When the evidence does not ___ their theories, scrupulous° researchers
_____   will report this honestly. But less conscientious researchers will flout°
                               scientific ethics and ___ fake "results" to appear to prove their theories.

_____ 7–8. With the trial ___, the defense lawyer tried to forestall° negative news
_____   stories by asking for a "gag" order. The lawyer argued that if ___
                               stories about his client's character were published, the trial would be a
                               travesty° of justice.

_____ 9–10. When Craig called Peggy "the perfect secretary," she was offended. He
_____   was complimenting her, but she ___(e)d his comment, thinking he had
                               ___(e)d her by saying she belonged in a subordinate° position.

➤ *Final Check:* Rumors

Here is a final opportunity for you to strengthen your knowledge of the ten words. First read the following
selection carefully. Then fill in each blank with a word from the box at the top of the previous page.
(Context clues will help you figure out which word goes in which blank.) Use each word once.

Did you hear that K-Mart sold sweaters with baby snakes inside? The story, of course, was
untrue, but it was not easy to squelch°.

How do such rumors get started? Sometimes they are (1)_____(e)d. In the
case of the K-Mart rumor, the story was actually fraudulent°; someone had deliberately made it up
and disseminated° it to discredit the store. Often, though, a rumor starts with an innocent misinter-
pretation. For instance, when a magazine article drew an analogy° between a worm farm turning out
bait and McDonald's turning out hamburgers, some readers (2)_____(e)d this to
mean that McDonald's was grinding up worms in its burgers—and the preposterous° story spread.

Rumors about individuals can start when someone makes a(n) (3)_____
statement or (4)_____(s) someone else, out of rancor° or jealousy: "Josie got an
A because she's dating Professor X," or "Al isn't in class today— he left town because he knew his
arrest for being a Peeping Tom was (5)_____." Even an innuendo°—something
that's merely hinted at—can start a rumor: "Josie and Professor X are really quite discreet°, aren't
they?" No story is too gruesome to make the rounds, not even the (6)_____ tale of
"devil worshippers" who cut children to pieces and hung their heads in trees.

Once a rumor gets started, people who hear it are sometimes in a (7)_____.
Even if there's nothing to corroborate° the rumor, they may be afraid to ignore it. And so there is a
proliferation° of rumors, spreading fear, damaging reputations, and turning calm situations into
(8)_____ ones. To stop or forestall° rumors, one thing is probably of
(9)_____ importance: before accepting any story, be sure the facts
(10)_____ it.

| *Scores* | Sentence Check 2 _____% | Final Check _____% |

Enter your scores above and in the vocabulary performance chart on the inside back cover of the book.

29

adroit	platitude
constituent	promiscuous
contend	repudiate
irreparable	spontaneous
pinnacle	stigma

Ten Words in Context

In the space provided, write the letter of the meaning closest to that of each **boldfaced** word. Use the context of the sentences to help you figure out each word's meaning.

1 adroit
(ə-droit′)
-adjective

- Doris is **adroit** in any kind of discussion or debate. She's very skillful at getting others to see things her way.
- **Adroit** chess players can make it seem as if the opponent is winning, when in fact he or she is about to lose in another move or two.

__ *Adroit* means   a. impulsive.   b. expert.   c. unselective.

2 constituent
(kən-stĭch′o͞o-ənt)
-noun

- Our senator genuinely wants to represent the citizens, so she makes serious efforts to find out how her **constituents** feel about important issues.
- Many of Councilman Hall's **constituents** live in poverty, so one way he helps those he represents is by working for programs to assist the poor.

__ *Constituent* means   a. someone represented.   b. someone who speaks well.   c. an officeholder.

3 contend
(kən-tĕnd′)
-verb

- The artist **contends** that he was born in Paris, but actually he was born in a small town in Missouri.
- John **contended** that smoking hadn't hurt his health, but right after making that claim, he had a fit of coughing that lasted ten minutes.

__ *Contend* means   a. to conceal.   b. to realize.   c. to declare.

4 irreparable
(ĭr-rĕp′ə-rə-bəl)
-adjective

- The damage to the vase is **irreparable**. It broke into so many pieces that it cannot possibly be put together again.
- Connie apologized to Fred for her angry words, but I'm afraid the harm to their friendship is **irreparable**.

__ *Irreparable* means   a. untrue.   b. not able to be fixed.   c. unnatural.

5 pinnacle
(pĭn′ə-kəl)
-noun

- The rock singer seems to have reached the **pinnacle** of her career: she's at the height of her popularity, and her recordings are selling more than ever before.
- Robin felt that being elected class president was the **pinnacle** of her college years. Her parents, though, wish that she had thought of her "personal best" more in terms of academic achievement.

__ *Pinnacle* means   a. topmost point.   b. starting point.   c. end.

6 platitude
(plăt′ə-to͞od′)
-noun

- Some conversations are made up entirely of **platitudes**: "Good to see you." "We've got to get together sometime." "Well, take care."
- I made no response to the clerk's "Have a nice day." He meant well, but I'm tired of **platitudes** like that.

__ *Platitude* means   a. good advice.   b. an unoriginal comment.   c. a lie.

160

7 promiscuous
(prə-mĭs′kyoō-əs)
-*adjective*

- In this age of HIV and AIDS, it's more important than ever for people to be choosy about sexual partners. Being **promiscuous** can have deadly consequences.
- When it comes to women, Erik and Harry are opposites. Erik dates one woman at a time and is serious about commitment, but Harry is totally **promiscuous**.

___ *Promiscuous* means   a. faithful.   b. unselective.   c. rude.

8 repudiate
(rĭ-pyoō′dē-āt′)
-*verb*

- The actor **repudiated** his biography, saying it had been written without his consent or cooperation and that it was filled with lies.
- After the millionaire died, several people showed up claiming to be his children and demanding a share of his estate, but his real family **repudiated** their claims.

___ *Repudiate* means   a. to accept.   b. to discuss.   c. to reject.

9 spontaneous
(spŏn-tā′nē-əs)
-*adjective*

- The key to good acting is to be so well prepared that all words and actions seem natural and **spontaneous**, not rehearsed.
- When I asked Shan to the movies, I tried to make the invitation sound **spontaneous**, as if I'd just thought of it. I didn't want him to know that I'd been planning it, nervously, for days.

___ *Spontaneous* means   a. unplanned.   b. clever.   c. irresistable.

10 stigma
(stĭg′mə)
-*noun*

- In the past, seeing a psychiatrist might harm a person's reputation, but now there's little or no **stigma** attached to seeking help for psychological problems.
- For a long time, there was a **stigma** associated with divorce. Today, of course, divorce is so common that it's no longer considered a disgrace.

___ *Stigma* means   a. dishonor.   b. insight.   c. argument.

Matching Words with Definitions

Following are definitions of the ten words. Clearly write or print each word next to its definition. The sentences above and on the previous page will help you decide on the meaning of each word.

1. _____   Not able to be repaired or remedied

2. _____   Skillful and clever under challenging conditions

3. _____   A mark of shame or disgrace; blemish on character or reputation

4. _____   To deny the truth, validity, or authority of

5. _____   Occurring or done as a result of a natural feeling or impulse; not forced or planned

6. _____   Lacking standards of selection, especially in sexual relations

7. _____   A peak of achievement

8. _____   A member of a group represented by an elected official

9. _____   A remark that is commonplace or has become uninteresting through repeated use

10. _____   To claim to be true

CAUTION: Do not go any further until you are sure the above answers are correct. Then you can use the definitions to help you in the following practices. Your goal is eventually to know the words well enough so that you don't need to check the definitions at all.

➤ *Sentence Check 1*

Using the answer line provided, complete each item below with the correct word from the box. Use each word once.

a. **adroit**	b. **constituent**	c. **contend**	d. **irreparable**	e. **pinnacle**
f. **platitude**	g. **promiscuous**	h. **repudiate**	i. **spontaneous**	j. **stigma**

_____ 1. Some animals are ___ in their breeding habits, mating freely with no apparent effort at selection.

_____ 2. The painting was being auctioned off as an early work of a well-known artist—until the artist ___(e)d it, saying that she had never painted it at all.

_____ 3. There is still some ___ attached to being an unmarried parent, but it has certainly weakened in recent years.

_____ 4. After the earthquake, some houses that were still standing nevertheless had to be completely destroyed; the damage to them was ___.

_____ 5. Trina is a(n) ___ sales representative; she can convince anyone on the phone, and she can get her foot in any door.

_____ 6. Many people say that the plays of William Shakespeare represent the ___ of English drama.

_____ 7. Our football game was ___; we had no plans to play, but then we found an old football as we walked across the field.

_____ 8. When Galileo ___(e)d that the sun, not the Earth, is the center of our planetary system, the Catholic Church forced him to deny what he knew to be true.

_____ 9. Some elected representatives vote as the majority of their ___s wish, but others follow their own choice, even if it represents a minority opinion.

_____ 10. When Jimmy tells me about his problems, I don't know what to say. I just mumble ___s like "That's too bad" or "Oh well, I'm sure you'll work it out."

NOTE: Now check your answers to these questions by turning to page 177. Going over the answers carefully will help you prepare for the next two practices, for which answers are not given.

➤ *Sentence Check 2*

Using the answer lines provided, complete each item below with **two** words from the box. Use each word once.

_____
_____ 1–2. Serving time in prison leaves a ___ that can do ___ harm to someone's ability to find a job. Ex-convicts who try to redeem° themselves may find that any attempt to get honest work is impeded° by their record.

_____
_____ 3–4. "No matter how often Kevin ___s that he loves me," Tammy said, "it always sounds perfunctory° and insincere because he uses ___s."

_____ 5–6. Greta was so ___ at mechanical drawing in high school that I wasn't
_____ surprised to hear she'd reached the ___ of success as an architect.

_____ 7–8. Senator Harper's warm welcome to any of his ___s isn't just a sham°,
_____ meant to get votes; it's a(n) ___ expression of his genuine interest and
inherent° good will.

_____ 9–10. I am proud of my good reputation, so when I heard that a rumor was
_____ going around that I was sexually ___, I called all my friends and
acquaintances to ___ it.

➤ _Final Check:_ The End of a Political Career

Here is a final opportunity for you to strengthen your knowledge of the ten words. First read the following selection carefully. Then fill in each blank with a word from the box at the top of the previous page. (Context clues will help you figure out which word goes in which blank.) Use each word once.

Our mayor was not only a proficient° politician but also a very (1)_____

speechmaker. Warmth and charm emanated° from him. Whenever he addressed an audience of his

(2)_____s, potential voters always came away thinking, "He's one of us."

His speeches always sounded (3)_____, never rehearsed. When he

made his way through a crowd, even (4)_____s like "Great to see you!"

and "What a beautiful baby!" sounded original and sincere. He was reelected several times.

But at the (5)_____ of the mayor's career, rumors and innuendos°

about his sex life began to circulate. He had been considered a model of decorum°, but now it was

insinuated° that this image was fraudulent°, that in fact he was (6)_____.

People said that he was paying hush money to former lovers and was visiting prostitutes on a

regular basis. Then one newspaper published an interview with a call girl who

(7)_____(e)d that the mayor was her client. Although he tried hard to

(8)_____ her story, she produced photographs to prove it. The mayor could

not escape the (9)_____ of this sordid° scandal. His reputation as a man of

impeccable° character was destroyed, and the damage was (10)_____. He

lost the support of his party and even his staunch° friends, and he soon retired from politics.

Scores	Sentence Check 2 _____%	Final Check _____%

Enter your scores above and in the vocabulary performance chart on the inside back cover of the book.

abrasive	emulate
admonish	hierarchy
antithesis	incapacitate
culmination	prognosis
docile	tumult

Ten Words in Context

In the space provided, write the letter of the meaning closest to that of each **boldfaced** word. Use the context of the sentences to help you figure out each word's meaning.

1 abrasive
(ə-brā′sĭv)
-adjective

- Pumice stone, a naturally **abrasive** substance, can be used for rubbing away rough spots on the feet.
- Roz has an **abrasive** personality—critical and negative. She always seems to rub people the wrong way.

___ *Abrasive* means   a. simple.   b. harsh.   c. common.

2 admonish
(ăd-mŏn′ĭsh)
-verb

- When the guide found the hikers deep in the woods but unhurt, he **admonished** them for straying off the trail.
- Because the little girl had spent her entire allowance on candy, her parents **admonished** her for wasting her money.

___ *Admonish* means   a. to lead.   b. to criticize.   c. to irritate.

3 antithesis
(ăn-tĭth′ə-sĭs)
-noun

- My taste in music is the **antithesis** of my brother's. I like heavy metal, played loud; he likes soft, low classical music.
- Pauline's free-spirited second husband is the **antithesis** of her first, who was a very timid and cautious man.

___ *Antithesis* means   a. the reverse.   b. something superior.   c. an imitation.

4 culmination
(kŭl′mə-nā′shən)
-noun

- For an actor or actress, receiving an Academy Award is often the **culmination** of many years of effort, progressing from drama school to bit parts to major roles.
- The Super Bowl is the **culmination** of the entire professional football season. All the rivalries, victories, and defeats lead up to this final contest.

___ *Culmination* means   a. a series.   b. a cause.   c. a final high point.

5 docile
(dŏs′ĭl)
-adjective

- After only a month of obedience training, our uncontrollable puppy calmed down, learned to pay attention to us, and became far more **docile**.
- Drugs and even surgery have been used in mental hospitals to make violent patients **docile**, so that they could be managed more easily.

___ *Docile* means   a. obedient.   b. strong.   c. curable.

6 emulate
(ĕm′yōō-lāt′)
-verb

- Jessie has always tried to **emulate** her older sister; she tries hard to do just as well as her sister—if not better—in school, at sports, and in popularity.
- Youngsters often want to **emulate** famous athletes. They train almost as hard as the champions do, with dreams of someday being as skilled as their heroes.

___ *Emulate* means   a. to admire.   b. to imitate.   c. to submit to.

7 hierarchy
(hī′ər-är′kē)
-noun

- The armed forces are a clear example of a strict **hierarchy**. Everyone has a specific rank and must follow the orders of those whose rank is higher.
- Pam soon learned that all requests and suggestions had to be passed up through the levels of the company **hierarchy**. She could communicate directly with her own boss, but not with the boss's boss—let alone the company president.

__ *Hierarchy* means   a. a ranked system.   b. a training system.   c. a large system.

8 incapacitate
(ĭn′kə-pǎs′ə-tāt′)
-verb

- The lecture was canceled because the speaker was **incapacitated** by the flu.
- My mother can't tolerate alcohol. Even half a glass of wine **incapacitates** her; all she can do is giggle for a while and then go to sleep.

__ *Incapacitate* means   a. to irritate.   b. to be concerned with.   c. to disable.

9 prognosis
(prŏg-nō′sĭs)
-noun

- Nathan's operation went well. The surgeon's **prognosis** is that Nathan will fully recover.
- Unless strict legislation is passed to reduce acid rain, the **prognosis** for the world's forests will remain poor.

__ *Prognosis* means   a. a forecast.   b. an illness.   c. an organization.

10 tumult
(too′mŭlt′)
-noun

- Spectators at a hockey match are often wild and noisy, and the **tumult** becomes even greater during a "sudden-death" overtime.
- On New Year's Eve, the **tumult** in Times Square reached such proportions that the crowd could be heard a mile away.

__ *Tumult* means   a. damage.   b. uproar.   c. friction.

Matching Words with Definitions

Following are definitions of the ten words. Clearly write or print each word next to its definition. The sentences above and on the previous page will help you decide on the meaning of each word.

1. _____   The noisy disorder of a crowd; a commotion

2. _____   To make unable or unfit, especially for normal activities; disable

3. _____   Tending to give in to the control or power of others without resisting; easy to handle or discipline; willingly led

4. _____   Able to cause a wearing away by rubbing or scraping; rough; irritating

5. _____   A prediction of the course, outcome, or fate of something, especially a disease or injury

6. _____   To scold gently but seriously

7. _____   The exact opposite

8. _____   The highest point or degree or a series of actions or events; the climax

9. _____   To try to equal or surpass, especially by imitation; imitate

10. _____   Organization of people in a series of levels, according to importance or authority

CAUTION: Do not go any further until you are sure the above answers are correct. Then you can use the definitions to help you in the following practices. Your goal is eventually to know the words well enough so that you don't need to check the definitions at all.

➤ *Sentence Check 1*

Using the answer line provided, complete each item below with the correct word from the box. Use each word once.

a. **abrasive**	b. **admonish**	c. **antithesis**	d. **culmination**	e. **docile**
f. **emulate**	g. **hierarchy**	h. **incapacitate**	i. **prognosis**	j. **tumult**

_____ 1. At the rock concert, the audience grew more and more excited and out of control. There was such ___ that no one could hear the music.

_____ 2. I ruined my nonstick frying pan by using a(n) ___ cleanser on it—the surface rubbed right off.

_____ 3. The runner was ___(e)d by a sprained ankle and had to miss the big race.

_____ 4. Wendell's ideas about furniture are the ___ of mine. He likes colonial maple, but I like ultramodern tubular steel.

_____ 5. The ___ of the Roman Catholic Church goes from the parish priest up through bishops, archbishops, and cardinals, to the Pope at the head.

_____ 6. Mother ___(e)d us for spending too much money on her birthday gift, but we could see that she was pleased.

_____ 7. The company is financially sick, and unless some changes are made in top management, the ___ is poor—it could go out of business.

_____ 8. In the prison movie, the convicts acted very ___ while planning a riot. The guards—who weren't too bright—kept congratulating the inmates on being so well-behaved.

_____ 9. In colonial America, many people believed in and feared witches. Hysteria over "witch-hunting" reached its ___ in Salem, Massachusetts, where nineteen supposed witches were put to death.

_____ 10. "If you want to ___ Elvis Presley, fine," my mother said. "But try to match his energy and warmth onstage—not his self-destructiveness."

NOTE: Now check your answers to these questions by turning to page 177. Going over the answers carefully will help you prepare for the next two practices, for which answers are not given.

➤ *Sentence Check 2*

Using the answer lines provided, complete each item below with **two** words from the box. Use each word once.

_____
_____ 1–2. The rebellious little girl, always demanding more and more autonomy°, was the ___ of her obedient, ___ sister. They were an incongruous° pair of siblings.

_____
_____ 3–4. The ___ for Dale's arthritis is not encouraging. Her doctor didn't equivocate° but told her frankly that in time it may ___ her completely.

_____ 5–6. Beth moved steadily up the company ___ until she was named president. This appointment, the ___ of twenty years of hard work and dedication, put her at the pinnacle° of her career.

_____ 7–8. Cory has many good qualities that I would like to ___. But his ___ manner is a handicap; he estranges° people because he rejects any ideas that diverge° from his own.

_____ 9–10. I didn't expect the children's behavior in the car to be impeccable°, but the ___ in the back seat finally reached such a level that I had to ___ them.

➤ *Final Check:* Firing Our Boss

Here is a final opportunity for you to strengthen your knowledge of the ten words. First read the following selection carefully. Then fill in each blank with a word from the box at the top of the previous page. (Context clues will help you figure out which word goes in which blank.) Use each word once.

My stint° in the bookkeeping department had lasted for three years when Jay Keller was brought in as department head. I don't expect supervisors to be pals with their subordinates°, and I don't object to being (1)_____(e)d when I've done something wrong. Keller's criticism, however, was constant and harsh, and the office atmosphere seemed permeated° by his antipathy° toward us. His (2)_____ style made everyone in the department miserable. Keller was the complete (3)_____ of Chandra Borden, our previous boss, who had been so thoughtful that we all tried to (4)_____ her. In contrast, Keller's mere presence could (5)_____ us to a point where we could hardly add two and two.

Within a few weeks, even the most (6)_____ employees were getting rebellious and starting to have subversive° thoughts. Our frustration and anger finally reached a (7)_____ when Keller loudly belittled a new worker in front of everyone else, using such derogatory° terms ("Stupid! Airhead!") that he made her cry. Furious, we suddenly decided that our only recourse° was to go over Keller's head—to ignore the company (8)_____ and present our denunciation° of Keller directly to *his* boss.

Our meeting in her office began in (9)_____, but then we settled down and told our story, trying to be as lucid° as possible so she could understand exactly what had been going on. We concluded by contending° that ours was a deeply troubled department and that if Keller stayed, the (10)_____ for it was not good: everyone else would quit. That was Friday afternoon. On Monday morning, our spontaneous° action proved to be successful: we had a new boss.

Scores   Sentence Check 2 _____%   Final Check _____%

Enter your scores above and in the vocabulary performance chart on the inside back cover of the book.

UNIT FIVE: Review

The box at the right lists twenty-five words from Unit Five. Using the clues at the bottom of the page, fill in these words to complete the puzzle that follows.

adroit
auspicious
contend
deride
discreet
disparity
docile
emulate
expedite
flout
forestall
heinous
impending
implicit
impromptu
macabre
opportune
permeate
pinnacle
platitude
stigma
transgress
tumult
validate
vehement

ACROSS

1. About to happen; imminent
3. To make fun of; ridicule
6. Skillful and clever under challenging conditions
7. A peak of achievement
8. To treat with scorn or contempt; defy insultingly
9. To prevent or hinder by taking action beforehand
11. To claim to be true
15. Favorable; encouraging
18. To show to be true; prove
21. To try to equal or surpass, especially by imitation
22. Extremely evil; outrageous
23. Performed or spoken without practice or preparation
24. To sin or commit an offense; break a law or a command

DOWN

2. To flow or spread throughout
3. Easy to handle or discipline; willingly led
4. Wise in keeping silent about secrets and other information of a delicate nature; tactful
5. Suitable (said of time); well-timed
10. To speed up or ease the progress of
12. An inequality or difference, as in ages or amounts
13. A remark that is commonplace or has become uninteresting through repeated use
14. Suggestive of death and decay; frightful; causing horror and disgust
16. Suggested or understood but not directly stated; implied
17. Intense; forceful
19. The noisy disorder of a crowd; a commotion
20. A mark of shame or disgrace; a blemish on character or reputation

168

UNIT FIVE: Test 1

PART A
Choose the word that best completes each item and write it in the space provided.

_____ 1. When my foot falls asleep, it ___ me for several minutes.
    a. interrogates   b. incapacitates   c. misconstrues   d. insinuates

_____ 2. The fear of AIDS has discouraged some people from being ___.
    a. fastidious   b. auspicious   c. impending   d. promiscuous

_____ 3. The man's ___ maltreatment of his horses left them crippled and starving.
    a. docile   b. obsequious   c. heinous   d. paramount

_____ 4. Since my uncle was made vice president of his company, he's ___ only to the president.
    a. subordinate   b. adroit   c. vehement   d. omnipotent

_____ 5. The mayor ___ citizens for their lack of cooperation in keeping the parks and streets clean.
    a. emulated   b. rebuked   c. fabricated   d. validated

_____ 6. Harsh rules ___ life in Puritan New England, where people were forbidden even to celebrate Christmas.
    a. emulated   b. permeated   c. contended   d. repudiated

_____ 7. When the public learned that the senator had accepted bribes, many of his ___ regretted having voted for him.
    a. constituents   b. pinnacles   c. intuitions   d. tumults

_____ 8. Since I needed the tax forms as soon as possible, I requested them by phone rather than mail, to ___ matters.
    a. insinuate   b. forestall   c. expedite   d. deride

_____ 9. The length of an Academy Award acceptance speech may depend on the number of ___ uttered.
    a. platitudes   b. stigmas   c. hierarchies   d. pinnacles

_____ 10. A novelist once commented on how wonderfully ___ a writer feels when creating "an entire universe."
    a. derogatory   b. omnipotent   c. extenuating   d. irreparable

_____ 11. Since petting an animal appears to lower a person's blood pressure, the ___ for survival after a heart attack is probably better for people with pets.
    a. prognosis   b. constituent   c. innuendo   d. quandary

(Continues on next page)

_____ 12. Victor and Diane ___ each other, making a perfect couple. He's rich but doesn't care about money; she's poor and cares about it a lot.

    a. complement   b. fabricate   c. contend   d. validate

_____ 13. The comedian Henny Youngman ___ his wife in many of his jokes. He would say, for example, "My wife is a light eater. As soon as it's light, she starts to eat."

    a. implemented   b. redeemed   c. derided   d. interrogated

PART B
Write **C** if the italicized word is used **correctly**. Write **I** if the word is used **incorrectly**.

_____ 14. Lightning and thunder are signs of an *impending* storm.

_____ 15. My trip began with an *auspicious* event: my luggage got lost between airports.

_____ 16. Those who view the world as a *hierarchy* usually assume that they should be at the top of it.

_____ 17. To *forestall* completion of his college credits, Jim will continue his course work right through the summer.

_____ 18. A snake's digestive juices are so *docile* that they quickly turn bone into powder.

_____ 19. A baseball injury caused *irreparable* damage to Howard's left eye, which was left sightless.

_____ 20. The play's opening-night performance was the *spontaneous* result of months of rehearsing.

_____ 21. Margery's remark about my new beard was certainly *derogatory*. She said, "You look like an armpit."

_____ 22. There's a large *disparity* in ages between Arlene's two daughters. The elder one is more like a mother to the younger one than a sister.

_____ 23. Because my friend phoned at an *opportune* time—just before the end of a suspenseful mystery—I hurriedly asked, "Can I call you back?"

_____ 24. The scientist had the courage and honesty to *repudiate* his earlier theory when he discovered new evidence that contradicted it.

_____ 25. Just as humans often *admonish* each other by shaking hands, elephants often greet each other by intertwining their trunks.

Score   (Number correct) _____ x 4 = _____ %

Enter your score above and in the vocabulary performance chart on the inside back cover of the book.

UNIT FIVE: Test 2

Complete each item with a word from the box. Use each word once.

a. **abrasive**	b. **adroit**	c. **antithesis**	d. **contend**	e. **emulate**
f. **extenuating**	g. **implicit**	h. **impromptu**	i. **intuition**	j. **pinnacle**
k. **quandary**	l. **stigma**	m. **validate**		

_____ 1. The cockroach is ___ at squeezing into cracks because it can flatten its skeleton, which is on the outside of its body.

_____ 2. Hal's anger was ___ in his failure to kiss his wife goodbye.

_____ 3. Don't use a(n) ___ cleanser on your car. It will rub the paint off.

_____ 4. As if being poor isn't bad enough, there is often a social ___ attached to poverty.

_____ 5. Last year, the town experienced a sizzling summer that was the ___ of its frigid winters.

_____ 6. My ___ told me to stay away from anyone who called me "darling" after only five minutes of acquaintance.

_____ 7. I tried to ___ my sister's ability to make money, but I ended up imitating only her readiness to spend it.

_____ 8. Mitch ___s that he deserved a higher grade in history, but I think the instructor was generous in giving him a C.

_____ 9. From the mountain's snowy ___, the climbers looked down on a layer of clouds that hid the valley below.

_____ 10. Toshiko is in a(n) ___ as to whether she should start college now part-time or wait until she can go full-time.

_____ 11. The police officer didn't consider my being late for a party a(n) ___ circumstance, so he went ahead and wrote the ticket for speeding.

_____ 12. Acting students often perform ___ scenes. Without a script, they must fully imagine how a particular character might speak and behave.

_____ 13. The study ___(e)d claims that drinking is strongly related to violence, providing evidence that alcohol is involved in about half of all murders in the United States.

(Continues on next page)

PART B
Write **C** if the italicized word is used **correctly**. Write **I** if the word is used **incorrectly**.

_____ 14. City streets with names like Oak, Pine, and Elm seem *fraudulent* when there aren't any trees on the streets.

_____ 15. Bonnie is so *discreet* that the minute someone tells her a secret, she gets on the phone to pass it along.

_____ 16. Some people feel that we *transgress* against nature when we try to create life in a test tube.

_____ 17. It's more difficult to deal with *innuendos* against oneself than to fight out-and-out accusations.

_____ 18. As *obsequious* as ever, Daniel refused to get in line for the fire drill.

_____ 19. The circus clown's beaming smile and *insidious* makeup made all the children at the party laugh.

_____ 20. The book's number-one place on the best-seller list was the *culmination* of months of advertising efforts.

_____ 21. People usually walk past the *obtrusive* statue without noticing it.

_____ 22. The elderly man was *vehement* in his refusal to move out of the condemned building. "I don't care if the bulldozers come," he said. "I'm staying!"

_____ 23. We had a *turbulent* day at the park, just relaxing on the grass, snoozing, and enjoying the picnic we had packed.

_____ 24. It would be fitting *retribution* if my brother, who stays on the phone for hours at a time, had to live in some country with a twenty-year waiting period for phone service.

_____ 25. Even the most *paramount* worker at the very bottom of the ladder gets as much vacation time as anyone else who has been with our company for the same length of time.

Score	(Number correct) _____	x 4 = _____	%

Enter your score above and in the vocabulary performance chart on the inside back cover of the book.

UNIT FIVE: Test 3

PART A
Complete each sentence in a way that clearly shows you understand the meaning of the **boldfaced** word. Take a minute to plan your answer before you write.

Example: Jeff should be **discreet** about the party because _____*it's meant to be a surprise*_____.

1. One extremely **macabre** movie is _____

   _____.

2. Ted **flouted** the traffic laws by _____

   _____.

3. There was a huge **tumult** when _____

   _____.

4. After the date, my parents **interrogated** me by _____

   _____.

5. Charles **misconstrued** my dinner invitation to be _____

   _____.

6. Maureen obviously had **fabricated** her excuse. She told the instructor, "_____

   _____."

7. To **implement** her vacation plans, Ruth started to _____

   _____.

8. After getting a D in psychology, I tried to **redeem** myself by _____

   _____.

9. You can tell that my sister is **fastidious** by looking at her bedroom, where _____

   _____.

10. When Len said that his brother wouldn't even give him the time of day, he meant to **insinuate** that

    _____

    _____.

(Continues on next page)

PART B

After each **boldfaced** word are a *synonym* (a word that means the same as the boldfaced word), an *antonym* (a word that means the opposite of the boldfaced word), and a word that is neither. On the answer line, write the letter of the word that is the antonym.

Example: __b__ **fraudulent**   a. weak   b. honest   c. dishonest

____ 11. **adroit**   a. clumsy   b. skillful   c. loud

____ 12. **disparity**   a. equality   b. difference   c. sadness

____ 13. **heinous**   a. hidden   b. noble   c. wicked

____ 14. **deride**   a. mock   b. explore   c. praise

____ 15. **expedite**   a. ease   b. interfere with   c. remove

PART C

Use five of the following ten words in sentences. Make it clear that you know the meaning of each word you use. Feel free to use the past tense or plural form of a word.

a. **antithesis**	b. **complement**	c. **contend**	d. **emulate**	e. **intuition**
f. **irreparable**	g. **paramount**	h. **quandary**	i. **rebuke**	j. **spontaneous**

16. _____

_____

17. _____

_____

18. _____

_____

19. _____

_____

20. _____

_____

Score   (Number correct) _____ x 5 = _____%

Enter your score above and in the vocabulary performance chart on the inside back cover of the book.

A. Limited Answer Key

Important Note: Be sure to use this answer key as a learning tool only. You should not turn to this key until you have considered carefully the sentence in which a given word appears.

Used properly, the key will help you to learn words and to prepare for the activities and tests for which answers are not given. For ease of reference, the title of the "Final Check" passage in each chapter appears in parentheses.

Chapter 1 (Apartment Problems)

Sentence Check 1

1. discretion
2. detriment
3. dexterous
4. gregarious
5. scrupulous
6. ostentatious
7. vicarious
8. optimum
9. sensory
10. facetious

Chapter 2 (Hardly a Loser)

Sentence Check 1

1. rudimentary
2. despondent
3. instigate
4. zealot
5. venerate
6. scoff
7. collaborate
8. squelch
9. retrospect
10. resilient

Chapter 3 (Grandfather at the Art Museum)

Sentence Check 1

1. lethargy
2. sporadic
3. subsidize
4. inadvertent
5. squander
6. embellish
7. juxtapose
8. dissident
9. ambiguous
10. inane

Chapter 4 (My Brother's Mental Illness)

Sentence Check 1

1. regress
2. zenith
3. euphoric
4. relinquish
5. estrange
6. infallible
7. berate
8. ubiquitous
9. maudlin
10. impetuous

Chapter 5 (A Get-Rich-Quick Scam)

Sentence Check 1

1. diverge
2. charlatan
3. irrevocable
4. dormant
5. precipitate
6. illicit
7. hoist
8. disseminate
9. corroborate
10. proliferation

Chapter 6 (Holiday Blues)

Sentence Check 1

1. antipasto
2. revived
3. injection
4. defrosting
5. dormitories
6. extraordinary
7. liberated
8. Regicide
9. vocabulary
10. anachronism

Chapter 7 (A Phony Friend)

Sentence Check 1

1. solace
2. impeccable
3. predisposed
4. solicitous
5. reprehensible
6. sham
7. propensity
8. fortuitous
9. liaison
10. equivocate

Chapter 8 (Coco the Gorilla)

Sentence Check 1

1. oblivious
2. vociferous
3. sanction
4. robust
5. circumvent
6. cohesive
7. grievous
8. inundate
9. attrition
10. reticent

Chapter 9 (Our Annual Garage Sale)

Sentence Check 1

1. terse	6. replete
2. indiscriminate	7. relegate
3. bolster	8. nebulous
4. depreciate	9. sedentary
5. tenet	10. inquisitive

Chapter 10 (A Debate on School Uniforms)

Sentence Check 1

1. autonomy	6. tenacious
2. ostracize	7. utopia
3. reiterate	8. bureaucratic
4. tantamount	9. mandate
5. raucous	10. recourse

Chapter 11 (My Large Family)

Sentence Check 1

1. incongruous	6. exonerate
2. reinstate	7. prolific
3. liability	8. clandestine
4. indigenous	9. superfluous
5. contingency	10. egocentric

Chapter 12 (Alex's Search)

Sentence Check 1

1. confident	6. bibliotherapy
2. very	7. Synonyms
3. panorama	8. Hinduism
4. primary	9. anonymous
5. direct	10. renovate

Chapter 13 (Ann's Love of Animals)

Sentence Check 1

1. precarious	6. emancipate
2. advocate	7. jurisdiction
3. inclusive	8. antipathy
4. imminent	9. preposterous
5. impede	10. idiosyncrasy

Chapter 14 (A Costume Party)

Sentence Check 1

1. travesty	6. esoteric
2. notorious	7. mesmerize
3. provocative	8. perfunctory
4. grotesque	9. austere
5. facsimile	10. Metamorphosis

Chapter 15 (The Missing Painting)

Sentence Check 1

1. contrite	6. conspiracy
2. plight	7. germane
3. symmetrical	8. distraught
4. connoisseur	9. lucid
5. verbose	10. cursory

Chapter 16 (An Ohio Girl in New York)

Sentence Check 1

1. presumptuous	6. homogeneous
2. adept	7. encompass
3. sordid	8. stringent
4. stint	9. entrepreneur
5. eradicate	10. standardize

Chapter 17 (How Neat Is Neat Enough?)

Sentence Check 1

1. repugnant	6. innocuous
2. magnanimous	7. rancor
3. masochist	8. recrimination
4. foible	9. meticulous
5. exhort	10. flamboyant

Chapter 18 (A Cult Community)

Sentence Check 1

1. archangel	6. dismissed
2. benefactor	7. postmortem
3. mortality	8. polygraph
4. travelogues	9. animation
5. tenets	10. nominees

Chapter 19 (Halloween Troubles)

Sentence Check 1

1. chide	6. commensurate
2. diabolic	7. connotation
3. integral	8. dilapidated
4. coalition	9. noxious
5. yen	10. scenario

Chapter 20 (Thomas Dooley)

Sentence Check 1

1. deprivation	6. utilitarian
2. mitigate	7. objective
3. exacerbate	8. panacea
4. unprecedented	9. imperative
5. deplore	10. atrophy

Chapter 21 (Twelve Grown Men in a Bug)

Sentence Check 1

1. decorum
2. tenuous
3. rejuvenate
4. exorbitant
5. exhilaration
6. facilitate
7. extricate
8. espouse
9. synchronize
10. orthodox

Chapter 22 (Adjusting to a Group Home)

Sentence Check 1

1. integral
2. dissipate
3. belligerent
4. denunciation
5. nonchalant
6. indolent
7. demeanor
8. unassuming
9. assimilate
10. unilateral

Chapter 23 (A Different Kind of Doctor)

Sentence Check 1

1. subversive
2. annihilate
3. staunch
4. criterion
5. proficient
6. holistic
7. emanate
8. analogy
9. vindicate
10. placebo

Chapter 24 (Grandpa and Music)

Sentence Check 1

1. volition
2. wooden
3. physician
4. decathlon
5. octet
6. homophone
7. aqueduct
8. philanthropist
9. surpass
10. mysterious

Chapter 25 (My Devilish Older Sister)

Sentence Check 1

1. permeate
2. forestall
3. opportune
4. interrogate
5. retribution
6. disparity
7. insidious
8. omnipotent
9. insinuate
10. obsequious

Chapter 26 (Harriet Tubman)

Sentence Check 1

1. intuition
2. flout
3. heinous
4. impromptu
5. discreet
6. implement
7. fastidious
8. complement
9. implicit
10. obtrusive

Chapter 27 (Tony's Rehabilitation)

Sentence Check 1

1. subordinate
2. transgress
3. fraudulent
4. expedite
5. redeem
6. auspicious
7. vehement
8. rebuke
9. innuendo
10. extenuating

Chapter 28 (Rumors)

Sentence Check 1

1. macabre
2. paramount
3. impending
4. misconstrue
5. derogatory
6. fabricate
7. validate
8. quandary
9. turbulent
10. deride

Chapter 29 (The End of a Political Career)

Sentence Check 1

1. promiscuous
2. repudiate
3. stigma
4. irreparable
5. adroit
6. pinnacle
7. spontaneous
8. contend
9. constituent
10. platitude

Chapter 30 (Firing Our Boss)

Sentence Check 1

1. tumult
2. abrasive
3. incapacitate
4. antithesis
5. hierarchy
6. admonish
7. prognosis
8. docile
9. culmination
10. emulate

B. Dictionary Use

It isn't always possible to figure out the meaning of a word from its context, and that's where a dictionary comes in. Following is some basic information to help you use a dictionary.

HOW TO FIND A WORD

A dictionary contains so many words that it can take a while to find the one you're looking for. But if you know how to use guide words, you can find a word rather quickly. *Guide words* are the two words at the top of each dictionary page. The first guide word tells what the first word is on the page. The second guide word tells what the last word is on that page. The other words on a page fall alphabetically between the two guide words. So when you look up a word, find the two guide words that alphabetically surround the word you're looking for.

• Which of the following pair of guide words would be on a page with the word *skirmish*?

   skimp / skyscraper   **skyward / slave**   **sixty / skimming**

The answer to this question and the questions that follow are given on the next page.

HOW TO USE A DICTIONARY LISTING

A dictionary listing includes many pieces of information. For example, here is a typical listing. Note that it includes much more than just a definition.

> **driz•zle** (drĭz′əl), *v.*, **-zled, -zling,** *n.* — *v.* To rain gently and steadily in fine drops. — *n.* A very light rain. —**driz′zly,** *adj.*

Key parts of a dictionary entry are listed and explained below.

Syllables. Dots separate dictionary entry words into syllables. Note that *drizzle* has one dot, which breaks the word into two syllables.

• To practice seeing the syllable breakdown in a dictionary entry, write the number of syllables in each word below.

   gla•mour _____   **mic•ro•wave** _____   **in•de•scrib•a•ble** _____

Pronunciation guide. The information within parentheses after the entry word shows how to pronounce the entry word. This pronunciation guide includes two types of symbols: pronunciation symbols and accent marks.

Pronunciation symbols represent the consonant sounds and vowel sounds in a word. The consonant sounds are probably very familiar to you, but you may find it helpful to review some of the sounds of the vowels—*a, e, i, o,* and *u.* Every dictionary has a key explaining the sounds of its pronunciation symbols, including the long and short sounds of vowels.

Long vowels have the sound of their own names. For example, the *a* in *pay* and the *o* in *no* both have long vowel sounds. Long vowel sounds are shown by a straight line above the vowel.

In many dictionaries, the *short vowels* are shown by a curved line above the vowel. Thus the *i* in the first syllable of *drizzle* is a short *i*. The pronunciation chart on the inside front cover of this book indicates that the short *i* has the sound of *i* in *sit*. It also indicates that the short *a* has the sound of *a* in *hat*, that the short *e* has the sound of *e* in *ten*, and so on.

• Which of the words below have a short vowel sound? Which has a long vowel sound?

   drug _____   **night** _____   **sand** _____

Another pronunciation symbol is the *schwa* (ə), which looks like an upside-down *e*. It stands for certain rapidly spoken, unaccented vowel sounds, such as the *a* in *above*, the *e* in *item*, the *i* in *easily*, the *o* in *gallop*, and the *u* in *circus*. More generally, it has an "uh" sound, like the "uh" a speaker makes when hesitating. Here are three words that include the schwa sound:

in·fant (ĭn′fənt)   **bum·ble** (bŭm′bəl)   **de·liv·er** (dĭ-lĭv′ər)

• Which syllable in *drizzle* contains the schwa sound, the first or the second? _____

Accent marks are small black marks that tell you which syllable to emphasize, or stress, as you say a word. An accent mark follows *driz* in the pronunciation guide for *drizzle,* which tells you to stress the first syllable of *drizzle.* Syllables with no accent mark are not stressed. Some syllables are in between, and they are marked with a lighter accent mark.

• Which syllable has the stronger accent in *sentimental*? _____

sen·ti·men·tal (sĕn′tə-mĕn′tl)

Parts of speech. After the pronunciation key and before each set of definitions, the entry word's parts of speech are given. The parts of speech are abbreviated as follows:

noun—*n.*   pronoun—*pron.*   adjective—*adj.*   adverb—*adv.*   verb—*v.*

• The listing for *drizzle* shows that it can be two parts of speech. Write them below:

_____   _____

Definitions. Words often have more than one meaning. When they do, each meaning is usually numbered in the dictionary. You can tell which definition of a word fits a given sentence by the meaning of the sentence. For example, the word *charge* has several definitions, including these two: **1.** To ask as a price. **2.** To accuse or blame.

• Show with a check which definition (1 or 2) applies in each sentence below:

The store charged me less for the blouse because it was missing a button.   1 ___   2 ___

My neighbor has been charged with shoplifting.   1 ___   2 ___

Other information. After the definitions in a listing in a hardbound dictionary, you may get information about the *origin* of a word. Such information about origins, also known as *etymology,* is usually given in brackets. And you may sometimes be given one or more synonyms or antonyms for the entry word. *Synonyms* are words that are similar in meaning to the entry word; *antonyms* are words that are opposite in meaning.

WHICH DICTIONARIES TO OWN

You will find it useful to own two recent dictionaries: a small paperback dictionary to carry to class and a hardbound dictionary, which contains more information than a small paperback version. Among the good dictionaries strongly recommended are both the paperback and the hardcover editions of the following:

The American Heritage Dictionary
The Random House College Dictionary
Webster's New World Dictionary

ANSWERS TO THE DICTIONARY QUESTIONS
Guide words: *skimp/skyscraper*
Number of syllables: 2, 3, 5
Vowels: *drug, sand* (short); *night* (long)
Schwa: second syllable of *drizzle*

Accent: stronger accent on third syllable *(men)*
Parts of speech: noun and verb
Definitions: 1; 2

C. List of Words and Word Parts

Note: Word parts are in *italics*.

abrasive, 164
adept, 88
admonish, 164
adroit, 160
advocate, 76
ambiguous, 16
a-, an-, 62
analogy, 126
anima, 96
annihilate, 126
ante-, anti-, 28
antipathy, 76
antithesis, 164
arch, -archy, 96
assimilate, 122
attrition, 46
atrophy, 114
auspicious, 152
austere, 80
autonomy, 54
belligerent, 122
ben-, bene-, 96
berate, 20
bibl-, biblio-, 62
bolster, 50
bureaucratic, 54
charlatan, 24
chide, 110
chron, chrono-, 28
-cian, -ian, 130
-cide, 28
circumvent, 46
clandestine, 58
coalition, 110
cohesive, 46
collaborate, 12
commensurate, 110
complement, 148
connoisseur, 84
connotation, 110
conspiracy, 84
constituent, 160
contend, 160
contingency, 58

contrite, 84
corroborate, 24
criterion, 126
culmination, 164
cursory, 84
de-, 28
dec-, 130
decorum, 118
demeanor, 122
denunciation, 122
deplore, 114
depreciate, 50
deprivation, 114
deride, 156
derogatory, 156
despondent, 12
detriment, 8
dexterous, 8
diabolic, 110
dilapidated, 110
discreet, 148
discretion, 8
disparity, 144
disseminate, 24
dissident, 16
dissipate, 122
distraught, 84
diverge, 24
docile, 164
dorm, 28
dormant, 24
duc, duct, 130
-ee, 96
egocentric, 58
emanate, 126
emancipate, 76
embellish, 16
emulate, 164
-en, 130
encompass, 88
entrepreneur, 88
equivocate, 42
eradicate, 88
esoteric, 80

espouse, 118
estrange, 20
euphoric, 20
exacerbate, 114
exhilaration, 118
exhort, 92
exonerate, 58
exorbitant, 118
expedite, 152
extenuating, 152
extra-, 28
extricate, 118
fabricate, 156
facetious, 8
facilitate, 118
facsimile, 80
fastidious, 148
fid, 62
flamboyant, 92
flout, 148
foible, 92
forestall, 144
fortuitous, 42
fraudulent, 152
germane, 84
gregarious, 8
grievous, 46
grotesque, 80
heinous, 148
hierarchy, 164
hoist, 24
holistic, 126
homo-, 130
homogeneous, 88
idiosyncrasy, 76
illicit, 24
imminent, 76
impeccable, 42
impede, 76
impending, 156
imperative, 114
impetuous, 20
implement, 148
implicit, 148